Communicating
Social Support

Communicating
Social Support

Terrance L. Albrecht
Mara B. Adelman
and Associates

SAGE PUBLICATIONS
The Publishers of Professional Social Science
Newbury Park   Beverly Hills   London   New Delhi

For information address:

SAGE Publications, Inc.
2111 West Hillcrest Drive
Newbury Park, California 91320

SAGE Publications Inc.
275 South Beverly Drive
Beverly Hills
California 90212

SAGE Publications Ltd.
28 Banner Street
London EC1Y 8QE
England

SAGE PUBLICATIONS India Pvt. Ltd.
M-32 Market
Greater Kailash I
New Delhi 110 048 India

Printed in the United States of America

Library of Congress Cataloging-in-Publication Data

Albrecht, Terrance L.
  Communicating social support.

  1. Interpersonal relations. 2. Interpersonal
communication. I. Adelman, Mara B. II. Title.
HM132.A353 1987   302   87-4962
ISBN 0-8039-2679-0

Contents

Foreword

As an occasional contributor to the study of social support, and as a chronicler of the progress of inquiry on this topic, I heartily welcome this addition to the multidisciplinary library devoted to research on the character and effects of supportive social relations. In several ways it is a particularly significant contribution to the study of the supportive dimension of human interaction. First, the contributors call on their own special disciplinary perspective to illuminate facets of human interaction that communicate social support and functions served by the expression of support that have been overlooked. Second, they treat the subject of human interaction directly, examining the impact of supportive transactions on the conduct and course of relationships and, reciprocally, the impact of the broader social field on the incidence and character of supportive transactions. In doing so, the contributors have effectively linked the study of social support to the broader study of personal relationships, enriching our understanding of both fields of inquiry.

Third, the volume brings a persuasive, unifying theoretical framework to bear on its study of the process whereby supportive communications foster both improved coping *and* relationship development. This framework is buttressed by the new empirical evidence presented in the volume, and by reinterpretations of the findings of many other studies of social support. Fourth, out of an interest in verifying this theory, the authors present examples of apparently different and incomparable transactions but show that they are governed by the actors' common need to reduce their uncertainty about themselves, their plight, and their relationships. Despite differences in the circumstances calling for supportive interaction, in the settings where the actors find themselves, and in

9

the nature of the relationship between the actors, there exists a fundamental need for control, a need that can be satisfied through the special information conveyed in supportive human dialogue. In short, the volume's theme centers on the manner in which human interdependence, especially during times of adversity, paradoxically fosters or augments independence, mastery, and a sense of personal agency.

The scholarship that forcefully commends this book to the reader reflects the authors' careful examination of the nuances and the tensions surrounding the communication of support. They give equal attention to the exchange of verbal and nonverbal messages between the parties to the helping transaction, concentrating not only on these observable dynamics but also on the equally impactful symbolic codes and shared meanings that arise in the process. Further, they offer incisive analyses of the motives driving these overt and covert communications, highlighting the ways they enhance the support recipient's sense of control and both parties' sense of reliable alliance. At the same time, the authors fully realize that the social world that people inhabit extends beyond their intimate ties. It encompasses second-order relationships with neighbors, familiar strangers, and other acquaintances whose structural position in the social network and less intense affective involvement with the help-seeker yield access to unique though less diverse supportive provisions than those rendered by close ties. Indeed, one of the most striking features of the volume is the authors' penetrating analyses of the many intersecting avenues to support that are afforded by the social ecology in which people are embedded. Equally important, they show that the specialized support rendered by weak ties is predicated as much on their pattern of linkage to other actors inside and outside the help-seeker's social network as it is on their relationship to the help-seeker.

Although this volume concentrates on the mutual interplay between the signals and messages sent by the provider and the recipient of support, between the expression of support and relationship development, and between behavior and cognition, it does not attend only to the level of dyadic communication, nor does it ignore supportive messages that are broadcast by the public media and by health and human service organizations. There is a finely crafted chapter by Arntson and Droge (Chapter 7) that carefully analyzes the form and latent functions of the personal testimonies offered by members of a mutual-aid group for epileptics, revealing how "story-telling" contributes to both the narrator's and the listeners' sense of control over their medical and social conditions. There is also a chapter on the design of interventions aimed to optimize supportive communications, containing important ideas about the impact of the language used by social agencies to label their services and market them. This language can powerfully influence the public's use of services by inadvertently stigmatizing prospective users, by inducing a more threatening appraisal of their circumstances and personal attributes, and by emphasizing pejorative causal and control attributions. In a companion chapter, Albrecht and Adelman address the tensions and dilemmas faced by the would-be provider and recipient of support, showing how social psychological barriers and mismanaged communications can lead to miscarried support or, worse, its nonmaterialization and relationship demise.

In its dual focus on the form and substance of supportive communications and on the personal and social functions they play, this volume offers instruction to students of social support and students of personal relationships alike. To the former, the contributors offer a deeper contextual understanding of the socially situated self in commerce with the personal community, while the latter can profit from the authors' explication of the ways in which the communication of support, or its miscommunication, can alter the trajectory of personal relationships. If this volume prompts collaborative research between students in both fields of investigation, spurring them to emulate the theoretical integration it has achieved, then it has performed a truly laudable service on their behalf.

—Benjamin H. Gottlieb
Guelph, Ontario, Canada

Acknowledgments

We would like to thank the contributors and coauthors who have joined us now and in the past in this research and writing endeavor. We thank them for their careful work and their friendship. We are grateful to Malcolm Parks for his reviews of the foundation chapters, our friend Charlotte Underwood for her tireless research and editorial assistance, and Mary Toepel for her patient word processing and proofing of our manuscript drafts. We also thank the Department of Speech Communication at the University of Washington for providing resources to complete this project and Sarah Miller McCune and Ann West of Sage Publications for their encouragement and sound advice.

The communication of support is a subject that we are learning about through research and, importantly, from the people who have touched our lives with love and hope. We are most indebted to our families, our friends, and our colleagues whose actions have inspired our inquiry by showing us what real support means for the quality of life itself.

—T.L.A.
M.B.A.

Rethinking the Relationship Between Communication and Social Support:
An Introduction

TERRANCE L. ALBRECHT
MARA B. ADELMAN

To think of life without any supportive relationships is to think of a profoundly isolated and difficult life indeed. We have known since Durkheim's work at the turn of the century that few individuals are able to lead healthy and contented lives without the sustenance of close personal ties (Brownell & Shumaker, 1984).

Certainly the hundreds of studies published just in the past five years across the social and health sciences have shown links between objective and subjective qualities of relationships and well-being. The ways social support affects physical and psychological health have been explored for the normal population as well as numerous special groups where stressful life events have made the necessity for support acute (i.e., single mothers, the elderly, stressed workers, adolescents with eating disorders, cancer patients, rape victims, stroke victims, epileptics, parents of handicapped and terminally ill children, and divorced persons). We have also learned from a narrower range of these studies that supportive ties can be at once helpful and harmful; people in supportive relationships can experience relational binds that place a high price on the support they so desperately need.

Our central thesis in this book is that social support is a process inextricably woven into communication behavior. The types of supportive communication that truly help distressed individuals are interactions that assist people through the anxiety and uncertainty of difficult life events. Such transactions enable people to cope independently with stress and perceive some personal control over their situations. Offering sympathy is not supportive communication unless relational and/or content messages (Watzlawick, Beavin, & Jackson, 1967) reduce the recipient's situational uncertainty to manage better the problems at hand.

Clearly the logical and empirical tie between social support and communication is overdue. And researchers have begun to consider explicitly supportive behavior in terms of the interactional influences occurring between providers and receivers (see Albrecht & Adelman, 1984; Gottlieb, 1985). But most empirical work to date has been geared toward the study of the range of effects apparent from presumed supportive ties (a reasonable research track given the quest to understand the uniqueness of these relationships as phenomena). Given the progress that has been made at the individual level, the mandate now is for research to move to the relational level to determine further what it is about the process, structure, and function of transactional communication behavior that has ramifications for the quality of individual life.

Forging the overlay of a communication perspective on support carries the added benefit of crisper conceptual distinctions and a broadening of inquiry in the topic to relational behavior. We argue in Chapter 1 that many of the functions of support identified across studies in the literature (e.g., tangible support, informational support, emotional support, and appraisal support; see, for example, House, 1981; Schaefer, Coyne, & Lazarus, 1981) are linked together at a deeper level to central notions of information, uncertainty reduction, and personal control. The idea of social support comes to lose value unless conceptual reins are placed on the plethora of functions found in numerous, unrelated studies. And the quest for theory building is hampered until general explanations can be drawn to connect these issues together.

Taking a communication perspective also expands the viability of support as an area for research. Supportive episodes are but moments in relationship life cycles; those interactions have consequences for the overall development and dissolution of such ties.

How supportive exchanges affect relational processes (and vice versa) widens the horizon of empirical inquiry. These are the themes that will be addressed in many ways in this volume. The work undertaken for this book was an effort to draw together the vast literatures on social support and communication and to begin to develop an interactional perspective on support. We hope this framework will be useful for generating sensible directions for future research and the application of research findings.

The book is organized into three sections. The basic theoretical frame and key methodological issues are presented in Part I. These chapters lay the foundation for later discussions of the contexts of social support presented in Part II. We discuss in Chapter 1 the functions of support and aspects of interactional processes. The structure of supportive communication is reviewed in Chapter 2 on communication networks. We describe support networks in terms of useful analytical properties and review bodies of research relevant to each of the prominent architectural features of those structures. In Chapter 3 we address central methodological issues in the empirical study of support as communication.

Supportive communication is a process that occurs in settings that shape the interactions that take place in overt and subtle ways. We and our contributors present a select review of significant contexts of supportive behavior in Part II, contexts that are explained within our initial framework of uncertainty and control. Chapters 4 and 5 are descriptions of supportive communication within the contexts of close personal relationships: family systems and friendship ties. In contrast to the support occurring in close ties is the support that occurs in weak ties (to acquaintances, secondary attachments, urban agents, and community gatekeepers) described in Chapter 6. The role of communication in promoting perceptions of control is explored in the discussion of support in self-help groups in Chapter 7. Beyond strong, weak, and self-help group ties we have chosen specialized contexts where supportive transactions are critical to societal functioning: the organization and the immigrant experience. The function of supportive communication for uncertainty reduction is emphasized in Chapter 8 on coping with occupational stress and Chapter 9 on adaptation during cross-cultural transitions. Finally, a distinct channel of support is presented in Chapter 10. A less explored but important source of assistance is the information provided from mass media channels that enhances the health coping processes of individuals, particularly those with life threatening illnesses.

Part III incorporates main avenues for future research and applied considerations. This begins with important caveats about the dilemmas of supportive transactions in Chapter 11. The implications of research findings for applied efforts are discussed in Chapter 12. And as our intention in this book is to generate future options for communication research, we suggest several directions in the Epilogue.

Research activity in this area has literally exploded across disciplines in just the past few years. Our knowledge and understanding of these complex phenomena are rapidly developing yet becoming more and more differentiated and cumbersome. However, it is our belief that viewing the support process as communication will be an important integrating vehicle for attaining considerable theoretical coherence and unity across this vast body of knowledge.

PART I

Theoretical and Methodological Foundations

1

Communicating Social Support:
A Theoretical Perspective

TERRANCE L. ALBRECHT
MARA B. ADELMAN

We are called not to own but to serve each other and to create the
space where that is possible [p. 69] . . . where strangers can reflect
on their pain and suffering without fear, and find the confidence
that makes them look for new ways right in the center of their confusion. (Nouwen, 1975, p. 68)

Social support is a topic with compelling appeal. To put the
issue simply: Studying the ways human relationships relate to physical and emotional health has real social and theoretical value. Certainly the complex findings in this area are creating ways we can all
live richer and longer lives (e.g., Berkman & Syme, 1979; Hammer, 1983; Henderson, 1984). Why do people seek support from
others to cope with life stress? And why do people give it? What
are the functional and dysfunctional effects on the interactants?
The answers to these questions have profound implications for the
quality of our everyday existence.

Among the most influential research has been the studies on
support relationships and the etiology of disease. Among the most
noteworthy findings have been that supportive relationships can
reduce pregnancy complications, aid recovery from illness, protect against clinical depression or deviant behavior, reduce the risk

of suicide, decrease psychological and physiological stress symptoms from work pressures and bereavement experiences, assist
in the adaptation to change, encourage behavioral commitment to
prescribed medical regimens, and promote the use of community
health services (see Hamburg & Killilea, 1979; Hammer, 1983;
Slater & Depue, 1981). Similarly, the loss of social support or disruption in social ties has been associated with such pathologies as
disease and depression, and deviant, abusive behavior to self
and others (see Goering, Wasylenki, Lancee, & Freeman, 1983;
Mitchell & Hodson, 1983; Rook, 1985; Salzinger, Kaplan, &
Artemyeff, 1983; Schaefer, Coyne, & Lazarus, 1981; Wortman,
1984). (The controversy over whether the perception of support
has direct or buffering effects on stress and illness is discussed in
Chapter 3.)

Coverage of the past twenty years of research on support has led
us to three fundamental conclusions. First, engaging in supportive
interactions is a search for human contact and at the same time a
search for meaning to interpret or make sense of one's circumstances of life events. Second, in successful interactions, support
occurs when meanings are obtained that reduce uncertainty, both
for one's situation as well as the relationship. Reducing uncertainty
provides a personal sense of control or mastery over immediate
stressors and creates closer bonding between interactants (Berger
& Calabrese, 1975; Parks & Adelman, 1983). Finally, the giving and receiving of support is a reciprocal process occurring in
socially constructed networks of both strong (or primary) ties
to family and friends, and weak ties to acquaintances, friends of
friends, coworkers, and general others in the community. (Given
the breadth of this last topic, we will address the subject of network
structures of supportive exchange in Chapter 2.)

Our analysis of social support as a communication phenomenon
framed from the above conclusions leads us to the following definition of the process:

Social support refers to verbal and nonverbal communication
between recipients and providers that reduces uncertainty about the
situation, the self, the other, or the relationship, and functions to
enhance a perception of personal control in one's life experience.

An Expanded Definition
of Supportive Communication

**A Communication Theory Perspective
on Social Support**

Our three-point framework described above is grounded in the understanding that social support is fundamentally a *communication* process. The communication of help is a symbolic activity embedded in personal relationships. Conceiving of social support from a communication perspective casts it as a transactional, symbolic process of mutual influence occurring between two or more individuals that alters their affective, cognitive, or behavioral states. (Our definition of supportive communication as a process of influence is consistent with other general definitions of communication including those by Burgoon & Ruffner, 1978; Cappella, 1981; Miller & Steinberg, 1975; Wilson, 1975.) This interaction occurs within a network structure of relationships that affects how the specific helping relationship operates, the ways helpers and recipients are linked together over time, and the extent to which individuals have access to pathways of help through other contacts.

Communication is a transactional influence process in that a change in any one aspect of the process can modify all other aspects (Burgoon & Ruffner, 1978). When one person communicates a supportive message to another, that behavior can affect both persons' feelings and cognitions, the state of the relationship and future message exchange sequences. As the receiver gives feedback to the source about the supportive message, both parties become sources and receivers caught up in a web that is ongoing and dynamic in character (see Burgoon & Ruffner, 1978, p. 9). If one is providing support to a friend, one may affect the way the receiver thinks about a situation and/or may alter the physical and environmental condition of the individual. The provider may also influence the way the receiver sees him or her, and the level of attachment felt to the relationship. In the same interaction, the person receiving support may gain emotional comfort, knowledge of a course of action to take, and/or tangible assistance to better cope with the particular life stress experienced. He or she may also be attempting to persuade the supporter to understand the need for help as legitimate, so as not to be judged negatively, and may reaffirm a level of indebtedness and commitment to the relationship.

Communication is also symbolic activity. Meaning does not reside in the messages exchanged but in the perceptual processes of each participant. Individuals attach referents to the symbols they exchange (e.g., the words they hear and the nonverbal behaviors they see) in order to create meaning. To the extent interactants have similar referents for the symbols they exchange, meaning is shared between relational participants. For example, it may be the intention of a provider to be supportive and his or her behavior is perceived that way by a receiver. It is also possible that one's supportive action could be interpreted as manipulative or condescending. There are also situations where although a source may not necessarily intend to be supportive, a remark or gesture may be interpreted in supportive ways by the receiver.

Included in our conceptualization of support as communication behavior is the understanding that supportive messages are mediated through various channels on different levels (see Cappella, 1981). Supportive messages are conveyed using verbal and nonverbal channels (i.e., a supporter may tell a recipient that she will do well on that major exam; a hug and a facial expression of encouragement may communicate a similar message). The extent to which the two channels convey consistent messages of support increases the likelihood that the recipient will perceive the exchange in positive terms. However, should the receiver perceive mixed messages from different channels (i.e., a supportive verbal message but offhanded disinterest from paralinguistic or kinesic cues) either confusion or negation of the supportive verbal message will likely result.

Supportive messages can be analyzed at content and relational levels (Cappella, 1981; Watzlawick, Beavin, & Jackson, 1967). The content level is the meaning attached to the message by the receiver and the source about the issue at hand (for example, I assist you in getting adjusted to your first day on the job by telling you I am glad you will be working with us, introducing you to others, and by cautioning you to watch out for the office gossip). But such supportive messages may also be interpreted as information about the state of the relationship between the source and receiver. In this case, my supportive messages and actions that help you become familiar with your new job situation also may be construed as early signs encouraging the development of mutual trust and liking between us. The distinctiveness of a communication perspective is that it enables us to describe supportive behavior as a dynamic interaction involving persons who mutually influence one another's attitudes, beliefs, emotions, and/or behaviors. Whether one's communication behavior is seen as supportive may or may not be shared (and this theoretic ground is useful for better understanding the dilemmas that do occur in supportive transactions—see Chapter 11). While we agree with other authors that support involves actions that function for the benefit of a receiver, this communication approach lodges those functions as outcomes of interactions occurring between sources and receivers; interactions that are tightly woven into the larger fabric of their relational dynamics.

**Uncertainty Reduction
and the Function of Support**

Nearly all definitions of support have included some type of functional effect of the process for the recipient and the provider. Individuals are generally motivated to seek support for a reason; supportive interactions generally *do something* for recipients and providers alike in ways that are meaningful and usually positive for them. This is a process with intended (and sometimes unintended) consequences.

Specific definitions and functions elaborated in the literature have focused mostly on the benefits for the recipient. Social support has been defined in numerous ways by researchers representing diverse fields across the social and health sciences. As shown in Table 1.1, some of the major definitions and functions of such relationships involve enhanced control, self-acceptance, and social interaction (see Thoits, 1983).

Most definitions and functions identified have been positive in nature (see Cobb, 1976; House, 1981; Moss, 1973; Tolsdorf, 1976). But it has been increasingly apparent that there are dilemmas in some supportive relationships that may diminish many positive effects that could be obtained (see Adelman, 1986; Chesler & Barbarin, 1984; McLeroy, DeVellis, DeVellis, Kaplan, & Toole, 1984; Rook, 1984; Shumaker & Brownell, 1984; Wortman & Lehman, 1985). Our increased understanding of the paradoxical aspects

TABLE 1.1
Selected Definitions and Functions of Social Support[a]

Control and Mastery	Self-Acceptance	Social Interaction
Representative definitions:	Representative definitions:	Representative definitions:
"any action or behavior that functions to assist the focal person in meeting his personal goals or in dealing with the demands of any particular situation" (Tolsdorf, 1976, p. 410)	"the subjective feeling of belonging, of being accepted, of being loved, of being needed all for oneself and not for what one can do" (Moss, 1973, p. 237)	"continuing social aggregates . . . that provide individuals with opportunities for feedback about themselves and for validation of their expectations about others, which may offset deficiencies in these communications within the larger community context" (Caplan, 1976, p. 19)
"information and resources from others in the environment that . . . minimize the perception of threat, maximize actual and perceived mastery, and facilitate direct action and anticipatory modes of coping" (Eyres & MacElveen-Hoehn, 1983, p. 3)	"information leading the subject to believe that he is cared for and loved . . . esteemed and valued . . . that he belongs to a network of communication and mutual obligation" (Cobb, 1976, p. 300)	"interpersonal transactions that include . . . affect, affirmation and aid" (Kahn & Antonucci, cited in House, 1981, p. 16)
	"expressive and affectual ties essential to maintaining the integrity of the self and the feelings of group solidarity" (Bharadwaj & Wilkening, 1980, p. 338)	"an evaluation or appraisal of whether and to what extent an interaction, pattern of interactions, or relationship is helpful" (Schaefer, Coyne, & Lazarus, 1981, p. 384)
(Functions)	(Functions)	(Functions)
facilitates personal goals aids in personal coping	enhances self-esteem confirms sense of belonging to a group	meets needs for intimacy and affection, and communication

a. See also Thoits (1985), whose functions of identity and belonging, reflected self-esteem (by taking the other's role), and comparative mastery fit with the above framework.

of communicating support will undoubtedly necessitate future revisions of some of the more simplified conceptual images (see Chapter 11).

Central to our conceptualization of support is the notion of uncertainty reduction and the occurrence of this process both within and between individuals. Uncertainty is essentially the lack of attributional confidence about causes and their effects (Berger & Calabrese, 1975). It is the cognitive response that occurs when one does not know how and why events are occurring. Such cognitive states make it less probable the individual will believe he or she can act in ways to produce positive outcomes for self and others (see Heider, 1958; Fiske & Taylor, 1984; Kelley, 1971). Supportive communication helps people when the process functions to decrease the anxiety and stress caused by the experience of the unknown.[1] Such transactions assist people in their attributional judgments by framing events in terms of causes and effects. This enables them to predict better the types of outcomes they can create and will experience—and reasons for those outcomes.

The significance of supportive communication that reduces one's perceptions of uncertainty is that it helps the receiver in developing a sense of perceived control over stressful circumstances. The state of unpredictability about one's circumstances has been linked to higher levels of distress in those who perceive they cannot control the events around them (McFarlane, Norman, Streiner, & Roy, 1983). As Eyres and MacElveen-Hoehn (1983, p. 3), drawing from Lazarus (1974, 1975), note, support occurs when "information and resources from others in the environment . . . minimize the perception of threat, maximize actual and perceived mastery and facilitate direct action and anticipatory modes of coping."

The specific notion of uncertainty has been explored in a few studies in the support literature. The idea has emerged as a generally undesirable state associated with a stressful experience. Defined as a lack of appropriate cues that produce confusion (Budner, 1962; Mishel, 1984b), Mishel (1985) based the experience of uncertainty during illness on four factors (which we have elaborated): *ambiguity* (multiple meanings for one's situation); *complexity* (in managing and coping with the stressors—producing confusion and overload); *lack of information* and *unpredictability* (concerning one's present and future situation). While not a mutually exclusive typology, these sources of uncertainty refer to differing types of information states that leave a person nervous for lacking a definition of the situation, and fearful of the future, regardless whether those feelings are valid (Mishel, 1984b). In each case, the individual experiences the lack of a dependable attributional framework that produces helplessness. One perceives he or she is without recourse or concrete options that can be fairly evaluated for action.

Satisfying the need for information early during a confused or troubled state orients the individual during succeeding stages of the stressful event. Mishel (1984a) and Mishel, Hostetter, King, and Graham (1984) found that when women received diagnosis of gynecological cancer, any information that initially clarified their personal crisis (e.g., about the nature and severity of the illness and its course and outcomes) moderated their feelings of threat later on. Women (n = 44) with more positive affirming support were able to form what she termed "cognitive schema" around the diagnosis and were more positive in their attitudes toward their health care plans. Mishel (1984a, p. 12) noted that "as time goes by, unpredictability seems to increase its impact on psychosocial adjustment. What is tolerated as unpredictable during diagnosis is not as easily tolerated during treatment."

The experience of a stressful event, then, often reflects the uncomfortable (sometimes painful) experience of uncertainty, produced by the stressor conditions. Knowledge and the power of explanation serve to help us perceive order in the world.[2] When we are struck by affliction (particularly if it strikes at random) we are left in a state of uncertainty or ambiguity over what will happen to us or a loved one (Comaroff & Maguire, 1981). We are then motivated to undertake an exhausting search for answers (Comaroff & Maguire, 1981) to impose meaning on otherwise inexplicable circumstances.

Comaroff and Maguire (1981) described a tragic irony encountered by parents of leukemic children when uncertainty was drawn out over time. Recent medical advances have improved the diagnostic and treatment methods for stricken children, but many cannot be cured. The stress is simply prolonged for the children and their families in not knowing when the final outcome of death will occur. Even the notion of "remission" carries profound ambiguity as to its meaning and duration. The authors argue:

Our own observations reinforced this view of the social and psychological effects of improved prognosis. For the most striking feature of the condition is now the *unpredictability* of its course and outcome, which turns upon the starkest of alternatives—life or death. In fact, overall improvement in the length of survival of victims dramatically heightens the perceptions of uncontrollable threat in particular cases. . . . The condition thus raises problems of meaning, management and communication, both in face-to-face and in less bounded social contexts. (pp. 116-117)

The experience of uncertainty and ambiguity is thus an impetus for communication as a way through the helplessness and hopelessness. Individuals who need to communicate during these situations are subject to influence by those who offer messages of clarity and explanation, affecting not only how those individuals assign meaning to their stressors, but also how they see themselves and interpret similar or pertinent future events (see Weick, 1979).

Personal Control: The Central Function

Decreased uncertainty usually carries a companion function of perceived mastery or control over the environment (Miller & Steinberg, 1975). Having options, a plan of action, or knowledge for anticipating how to cope with events can empower an individual. Having sufficient information for understanding a situation or for effectively evaluating alternatives in decision making moves one from a position of dependency on others to a point of independent resourcefulness and enhanced self-esteem (Parks, 1985; Rodin, Rennert, & Solomon, 1980).

Indeed, others have argued that a basic reason we communicate is to control the personal environments in which we live (Miller & Steinberg, 1975; Parks, 1985). Striving for personal control is a presumption in much of the psychosocial literature on human behavior and the inability to exert control or influence over one's surroundings is cause for feelings of personal inadequacy (deCharms, 1968; Parks, 1985). In our view, a major function of supportive interactions is to empower those in stressful experiences to have personal impact on their situations. In this way human contact can help provide beneficial outcomes in the face of life stress, given "the lack of communication may intensify feelings of victimization" (Silver & Wortman, 1980, p. 315).

The foundation of perceived control. The perception of "contingency" is at the heart of an individual's sense of mastery or control (Abramson & Alloy, 1980; Alloy & Abramson, 1982; Fisher, 1984). Knowledge based on contingency thinking results when one believes that acting in a certain manner will produce a causal effect on something in the environment (Fisher, 1984). Put another way, perceived control is essentially the belief that one's communication behavior has produced an effect (Parks, 1985). (Again, the notion of a communicative "effect" due to influence is central here as it was in our earlier description of supportive communication.) People communicate in ways that influence others. But it is the personal belief that one's communication behavior can be used to achieve a desired effect on another that is the basis for a perception of control. Mastery of one's goals, or at least the strong perception that certain goals are obtainable through one's efforts puts the individual on a track of progressive optimism and action.

Conversely, successive failures at controlling the course of physical or social circumstances increase the amount of self-blame that occurs, generally with a concomitant outcome of depression (Fisher, 1984). Indeed, stressful life events often *change* the level of control one has established over his or her environment (see also Caplan, 1981). Fisher (1984, p. xx) notes how this becomes a dual-level entrapment:

> Precisely because stressful conditions are undesirable, a person will seek to control them as part of homeostasis, in order to minimize unpleasantries experienced. Both behavior and physiological response form an integral part of the attempt to minimize the duration and intensity of stress. Failure of control maximizes the effects of these conditions and provides knowledge in which failure to cope is represented. Both aspects of control loss may influence subsequent reactions.

Dimensions of control. Control is a multidimensional concept with at least three continua relevant to our discussion of supportive communication: *locus, stability/instability,* and *generality/specificity* (see Abramson, Seligman, & Teasdale, 1978; Parks, 1985). In such studies where control and support have been empirically linked, most operationalizations of control have been limited to the locus dimension. That is, one's successful management of a stress event has been associated with the perception of an internal (personal) causal attribution rather than one of an external (environmental) origin.

In general, studies have shown that people who think they can intervene and ameliorate the negative side of a stressful experience have more positive emotional and behavior patterns than those who feel the control of circumstances is beyond them. The implications are important for how distressed individuals cope with their circumstances and whether they feel their supportive relationships are reinforcing or useful. Sullivan and Reardon (1986) found that breast cancer patients who felt personally helpless in affecting their illnesses (external locus) and who were dissatisfied with their support networks were most likely to use passive, dysfunctional behavior in coping with the stress of the disease. Similarly, Seeman and Seeman (1983) found that a sense of low control was associated with less self-directed preventive health care, less optimism regarding the effects of early treatment methods, self-perceptions of weaker health, more illness periods, and greater reliance on physicians. Sandler and Lakey (1982) found that supportive ties produced a buffering effect against stress only for those who perceived an internal locus of control. Consistent with these findings, Eckenrode (1983) found that those with an internal locus were most able to mobilize needed resources during times of stress. Lefcourt, Martin, and Saleh (1984) extended Sandler and Lakey's work to find that those with an internal locus of control obtained more benefit from social support than others; these were also people who were more autonomous and purposeful in their relationships. Finally, Turner and Noh (1983) found that social support and personal control were negatively related to the psychological distress of postpartum women.

Less tested but just as important are two additional dimensions: the stability/instability dimension and the global/specificity dimension (Abramson et al., 1978). Perceptions vary according to whether one's causal effects are enduring across situations, temporarily limited to present circumstances, or unpredictable as to future situations. Clearly the more traitlike the perception, the stronger the personal sense of mastery over immediate stressors as well as similar future ones. For example, a source who praises a student for studying hard and performing well on an exam is supporting the student for behaving in a way that should be stable for continued production of desired results. To the extent the student does study hard but performs inadequately, supporters can still help by focusing on temporary factors in the immediate situation that will be contributors to the problem. Finally, perceptions of control may be global or specific, depending on the degree to which one's behavior is focused. A person may perceive that his or her behavior will serve to direct a variety of experiences at a level of generality, or it could be limited to controlling for specific outcomes. The more global the perception, the wider the span of direction perceived for obtaining desirable outcomes. In the example of the student, should he or she perform well, supportive statements might reinforce more general attributions such as the student's abilities, study skills, and so on as reasons for the desirable outcomes. If the performance is poor, the supportive focus could be on specific details of the immediate test-taking situation. This reduces uncertainty and precludes negative self attributions of lack of intelligence or learning problems.

In short, support that functions to enhance control will assist the individual in making useful attributions about the origin or locus of the cause, the stability of the cause-effect pattern, and the degree of general versus specific reasons for occurrences.

Illusions of control. Just as the perception of inadequate control or loss of control is dysfunctional, so too are many inflated perceptions of personal influence or mastery. Individual biases or incentives can distort perceptions (Alloy & Abramson, 1979; Fisher, 1984) leading to an "illusion of control" or "invulnerability." Overconfident judgments of cause-effect contingencies may motivate people to persist at tasks despite obvious signs of failure, making uncontrollable outcomes even more difficult to handle (Wortman, 1976), perhaps causing manic behavior displays (Langer, 1975). Victims who have inflated perceptions of the level of power they have over their circumstances tend to engage in excessive self-blame. This can result in hopelessness and the loss of confidence and esteem (Wortman, 1976). Medea and Thompson (1974, also cited in Wortman, 1976) described why some rape victims blame themselves for "causing" their assaults. Although rape is a criminal act against a victim, many injured women assume responsibility as a way to gain control over the reasons for the occurrence. Believing she caused the act is preferable to the insecure feeling of thinking that such vicious crimes are perpetrated at random against guiltless, private citizens. Such randomness also implies the crime could happen again (Wortman, 1976).

Certainly not all illusions are dysfunctional. There are times when exaggerated positive perceptions of oneself and one's circumstances may be incentives for action and a preservation of one's self-esteem and outlook. Alloy and Abramson (1979) demonstrated that depressed students were most accurate in predicting their own effects on outcomes while nondepressed students tended to overestimate their abilities to bring out certain results. As Mechanic (1974) notes:

> A serious misconception that appears to run throughout the stress literature—the notion that successful adaptation requires an accurate perception of reality. There is perhaps no thought so stifling as to see ourselves in proper perspective. We all maintain our sense of self-respect and energy for action through perceptions that enhance our self-importance and self-esteem, and we maintain our sanity by suppressing the tremendous vulnerability we all experience in relation to the risks of the real world. (pp. 37-38)

Summary. However, even unfounded illusions may be put in balance through the crafted support of others. In this section we have conceptualized support as a communication process in which supporters and receivers influence one another by reducing uncertainty and increasing control over their environments. In the next section we discuss some specific characteristics of supportive messages exchanged in such interactions and describe types of supportive relationships.

The Nature of
Supportive Interactions

Functions and Types
of Supportive Messages

What makes a message supportive? What kinds of communication behaviors are interpreted as supportive by receivers? Several categories of message functions (which are clues for message design) are derived from our perspective on communication, uncertainty, and control. Many are also buttressed by research findings in the literature. Support providers directly reduce uncertainty and enhance control by reframing a recipient's cognitive perspective, improving the recipient's skill levels, offering tangible assistance, and expressing acceptance or reassurance. Providers also offer support when they act as catalysts by enabling recipients to ventilate about their stressors, thus offering indirect help with easing initial states of uncertainty.

Perspective shifts on cause-effect contingencies. Control-producing messages may be those that are geared to encouraging the individual to think in terms of realistic yet useful contingencies (see Abramson et al., 1978; Thoits, 1985). Specific communication strategies can be developed along the locus, stability, and specificity dimensions of control.[3] For example, others can help modify a distressed person's causal attributions for success and failure at a task. They can redirect the assigned causes for failure toward external, unstable, and specific sources (e.g., those that are outside, temporary, and highly specified).[4] Hence, one avoids taking personal responsibility for negative outcomes that will be debilitating for self-esteem (Rodin et al., 1980) (as in the case of the rape victims mentioned in the previous section). Conversely, causes for successful outcomes can be assigned to internal, stable, and global factors (such as the individual's personal, enduring, and general skills or abilities). Support providers can also assist the individual by *reducing the desirability* or significance of unattainable goals and *increasing the desirability* of achievable goals or objectives. Finally, they can help individuals change their personal expectations of control by direct assistance that will reinforce perceptions that certain outcomes are personally controllable. Aiding an individual by atomizing complex tasks into simpler, achievable units that can be accomplished in a shorter time may help manage an otherwise overwhelming situation (Parks, personal communication, March, 1986).

Enhanced control through skill acquisition. Interactions that increase the skills of a recipient function to decrease feelings of inadequacy by creating specific outcomes. These instructional messages of support reorient one's perspective to recognize internal, stable, and global causes for desired ends. Such supportive strategies include training recipients in problem-solving techniques (Gottlieb & Todd, 1979; see also Denoff, 1982; Schaefer et al., 1981) and communication skills (e.g., instruction in affinity-seeking behaviors, persuasive influence principles, or conflict management techniques). The process of providing information on problem solving and social skills gives the individual a way to define and reconcile a quagmire of stressors during times when one lacks confidence due to uncertainty over appropriate behavior. Disadvantaged teenaged mothers can be supported when given advice on communication strategies for handling domestic conflict (Colletta, Hadler, & Gregg, 1981). This aids the young mothers in gaining a degree of control over their often turbulent living situations and provides opportunities for them to see direct positive effects of their own strategic communication behaviors.

Enhanced control through tangible assistance. The exchange of time, resources, and labor also conveys an important type of support that has clear benefits for recipients. Supporters who intervene in stressful events and provide direct, positive outcomes or decrease the possibility of negative outcomes (with such assistance as medical care, money, or conflict mediation) create causal patterns that can improve the emotional, psychological, and physical welfare of recipients. Although the causal contingencies are shifted from the person in need to external sources, the helping acts may be framed as temporary, specific behaviors designed to assist the individual toward assuming independence. (Hence the label *instrumental support* is apt in discouraging learned dependencies on external aid.)

These supportive acts also carry important symbolic overlays. While such behaviors directly address the individual's specific needs, they also communicate a relational message from provider to recipient. The $1,000 loan for college accompanied by the note, "Love, Dad" has a significantly different meaning from an alternative situation of a signed contract for a loan with designated monthly payments. Tangible, instrumental support is rarely given by anonymous donors. Thus relational messages can greatly influence whether content messages are seen as supportive. These exchanges can either seed bonds of helpfulness and affection or incur feelings of deep indebtedness and anxiety.

Enhanced control through acceptance or assurance. Support is also communicated when recipients are personally validated or reassured about their relationships (see Finlayson, 1976; Litman, 1966). Giving emotional aid functions to reinforce one's capabilities and sense of belonging, reducing any insecure uncertainties experienced about one's self-worth and value in the eyes of others.

In the organization, communication of "appraisal support" in the workplace (House, 1981) could include messages that reduce uncertainty by giving personal affirmation of one's importance to the organization along with helpful feedback on job performance. Even the simple presence of another person during a stressful event (for example, bereavement) may not directly reduce one's anguish at a content level but does reinforce knowledge at the relational level that one is not alone. Barrera and Ainlay (1983) described this as "nondirective counseling," behaviors that included intimacy, unconditional availability, esteem, trust, affection, and listening to talk about private feelings (see also Young, Giles, & Plantz, 1982). They also noted the function of "positive social interaction" (joking, kidding, talk about diverse activity) to establish a firm knowledge of relational bonding despite a person's specific source of stress.

Enhanced control through ventilation. The process of venting is a way to relieve internalized pressures but also to create through talk imagery that crystallizes somewhat unknown cognitions into known and shared entities. Uncertainty over cause-effect patterns may be reduced and control increased by distressed individuals *themselves* if they interact with providers who are active listeners. The "sounding board" function enables receivers to articulate their uncertainties and problems in ways that help them to be more objective and perhaps even resolve the troubling issues that they face. Silver and Wortman (1980) argued that supportive exchanges are helpful when care givers encourage or prompt stressed persons to vent their frustrations openly about myriad topics. Gottlieb and Todd (1979) reported that listening and empathizing were emotionally sustaining and Carey (1974) said that when kin and friends were perceived to show personal "concern" and relational "closeness," patients with serious illnesses felt freer to disclose fears about impending death. As Wortman (1984) notes, "Verbalizing personal concerns during a time of stress can help clarify feelings, to develop strategies for managing them more effectively, and to begin active problem-solving" (p. 2343).

Supporters who are effective listeners provide more direct eye contact, are receptive to disclosures, and ask more follow-up questions (Miller, Berg, & Archer, 1983). These interactions relieve the individual of frustrations and despair, while providing confirmation, not rejection from others. Once again, this improves the recipient's perception of control; he or she has the opportunity to express an inner concern until a satisfying cause-effect pattern can be described and personal reinforcement given for the receiver's own attributions.

The Nature of Supportive Relationships

Central to any supportive interaction (regardless of the type of supporter) is the nature of the relationship between the provider and receiver. Both persons are engulfed in a relationship where a shared code system comes to tie them together.

Much work in the interpersonal communication literature on relationship development is relevant for an understanding of how supportive ties evolve (see also Chapter 5 for a further discussion of this literature). A prominent direction of the research has been the role of uncertainty in aspects of relationship development and dissolution (see Berger & Bradac, 1982; Berger & Calabrese, 1975; Parks & Adelman, 1983), where uncertainty toward others has been found to motivate communication. As information is exchanged bonds start to form. As greater amounts of mutual information are shared leading to increased uncertainty reduction (for example, reciprocal support is offered to help one another during the mutual disclosure of personal concerns), a relationship can develop and is more likely to endure over time (see Parks & Adelman, 1983). Conversely, if events occur that *increase* uncertainty toward the relational partner, several perceived aspects of the tie, particularly supportiveness, will be negatively affected (Planalp & Honeycutt, 1985).

Selection of sources as relational partners. It has been suggested from previous research that in times of stress, people are likely to seek support from those whom they know well (Clark, 1983). Some stressful contexts, such as undergoing exams with colleagues, is also likely to influence who people will seek for support. However, stress conditions that may be perceived as irreversible (such as announced job layoffs) may deter the selection of similarly stressed persons as supporters. Comparison with suffering others may exacerbate one's feeling of powerlessness (see Brickman & Bulman, 1977).

Personal credibility and higher status may also determine the selection of providers, since well-defined relational distinctions, the veracity of the person's explanations, and ability to help may be perceived as more supportive than sources with lower credibility and status (see Albrecht, 1982; Albrecht & Adelman, 1984; Albrecht, Irey, & Mundy, 1982; Chiriboga, Coho, Stein, & Roberts, 1979; House, 1981; Wortman & Dunkel-Schetter, 1979).

Types of relationships. While likely sources of support have been identified in research, these must be considered in tandem with the nature of relationships to those persons. These may be more or less supportive for an individual, depending on the nature of information exchanged. Again, the interpersonal research literature informs us for considering levels of supportive ties. Miller and Steinberg (1975) distinguished between interpersonal and noninterpersonal relationships based on three types of information: cultural, sociological, and psychological. They argued that each level of information affected how accurately interactants could predict the effects of their communication on the other.

Relationships at the cultural level are the most socially distant, relying on information about the other's native or regional background. For example, initial interactions with strangers are usually accompanied by highly general, scripted, predictable content and rules for speaking (for instance, brief exchanges about the weather or local surroundings). Relationships at the sociological level are based on knowledge about the other's various roles or position in reference groups. These relationships are somewhat closer than cultural level ties but the view of the partner is still limited because the individual is not seen as a unique individual apart from his or her role or group identification. Predictions about behavior are based on generalizations drawn from knowledge about the standard role or group behavior of others, not the individual's own idiosyncratic inclinations. For example, interactions with unfamiliar waitresses or secretaries are often structured by expectancies based on context and role relationships. Finally, relationships based on psychological-level information are distinctly interpersonal because partners in the relationship can predict one another's personal cognitive and behavioral patterns. Saying "He really knows me" is an acknowledgment of a partner's recognition of one's uniqueness apart from any role, group, or cultural involvement.

Miller and Steinberg (1975) essentially argued that relationships based on cultural- and sociological-level data are "noninterpersonal" and relationships based on psychological-level data are "interpersonal" in nature. Their categories are used to emphasize that in cultural- and sociological-level relationships, interactants are limited to *generalized* information about one another's backgrounds and social roles, but relationships based on psychological-level data are more interpersonal because partners are able to *discriminate* one another apart from cultural heritage, group membership, or role occupancy. The ability to discriminate a person from his or her role or cultural context improves one's accuracy in attributional judgments of that person's behavior (see Miller & Steinberg, 1975).

This category scheme is useful for classifying supportive communication relationships. Support from "weak ties" (see Chapter 6 in this volume) may be channeled from acquaintances, coworkers, or others in the community whom we may not know well but who are able to help because of some generalized cultural or role expectation. Support from those to whom we are closest (friends and family whom we know at a psychological level) helps because such persons are presumably in a better position to discriminate our distinctive needs and know the types of strategies that will and will not be effective with us.

Indeed, Young et al. (1982) and recent work by Burleson and Samter (1985) have shown that the ability to take a troubled person's perspective was effective in offering comfort. Burleson and Samter (1985) suggested that "person-centered" messages that legitimize and elaborate on the feelings of another are the most useful. Building on a constructivist framework, their hierarchical scheme for comforting strategies ranges from those that demonstrate an effort to take the perspective of the other to those of a confrontational and condemnation stance. Their results are further evidence that in some situations, those with whom one has the closest psychological-level relationships or who share a stressful context are perhaps in the best position to help (see Miller & Steinberg, 1975). They have the requisite knowledge for effectively understanding the individual's view and thus can more easily assist in encouraging ventilation of feelings, redirecting attributions, and so on.

Of the range of supporters available, it appears that those with whom we have the closest interpersonal ties are also those whom we depend on for the broadest scope of supportive interactions. Denoff (1982) found that the spouse and best friend were those who provided the widest spectrum of supportive behaviors, including opportunities to "be oneself"; share common interests, advice,

TABLE 1.2
Summary Table of Supportive Resources (Denoff, 1982)

Supportive Resource	Best Friend	Friend	Neighbor	Parent	Relative	Spouse	F	d
Cumulative support index	4.25	4.01	3.07	3.89	3.84	4.80	30.88*	.86[a]
Discuss problems or personal concerns	4.33	4.13	2.40	3.50	3.97	4.80	26.91	1.41
Share personal items	4.47	4.27	2.50	3.77	3.94	4.77	26.75*	1.35
Advice and guidance	4.20	4.07	2.77	4.04	3.77	4.67	20.93*	1.21
Borrowing items	3.90	3.07	4.27	3.10	3.20	4.77	7.10*	1.93
Accessibility	4.10	3.67	3.67	4.40	3.90	4.77	8.01*	1.35
Ability to be oneself	4.87	4.74	3.93	4.37	4.44	4.97	12.84*	.94
Dependability	4.73	4.07	4.04	4.43	4.49	4.97	4.78*	1.19
Common interests	4.17	4.07	2.73	3.37	3.40	4.20	13.96*	1.23
See socially	3.67	3.13	2.10	2.58	2.87	4.77	19.26*	1.87
Express interest in	4.37	4.27	3.37	4.77	4.24	4.84	24.72*	.93
Closeness	3.94	4.00	2.27	4.33	4.03	4.80	31.51*	1.34
Express feelings	4.27	4.17	2.87	4.07	3.93	4.73	17.41*	1.30

SOURCE: Reprinted from M. S. Denoff (1982). "The differentiation of supportive functions among networks: An empirical inquiry." *Journal of Social Science Research*, Vol. 5, Table 2. Reprinted with permission by the Haworth Press, Inc., 75 Griswold Street, Binghamton, NY 13904.
NOTE: Under pairwise deletion, 10 cases were dropped from ANOVA with absent members within groups (6 parents, 3 neighbors, and 1 relative). Degree range: 5 = a great deal, 3 = somewhat, 1 = not at all.
a. Dunn Paired Comparison range, n = 30.
*p = .001.

and guidance; and discuss personal problems. (See Table 1.2.)

While later chapters in this volume will further delineate the differences in supportive relationships between close and weak ties, it is worth noting here that Denoff's findings are useful evidence of the greater dependability and breadth of support perceived from psychological-level relationships, both at personal and instrumental levels. Conversely, support from such ties as neighbors are more restricted to instrumental help (e.g., for borrowing needed items) rather than emotional support, probably because such people have limited perspective-taking capabilities or are less able to communicate messages in ways that can be perceived as supportive.

Concluding Note

We conclude by returning to our initial three claims regarding the process of support. As we demonstrated, the search for meaning amidst uncertainty propels individuals to seek out others in verifying and constructing their personal interpretations. We posit that social support is a communication process where the recipient and the provider mutually influence each other to reduce uncertainty about the situation, themselves, each other, and the relationship. Accompanying uncertainty reduction is the recipient's increased sense of personal control over an otherwise unpredictable and confusing situation. In turn, the relational dynamics between recipient and provider influence who people will turn to for help. We propose that this process is moderated by the varying levels of familiarity between the recipient and provider based on noninterpersonal and interpersonal information. Familiarity enables both participants to construct messages and expectations that shape the breadth and depth of the social support exchanged. Moving from the processual and micro level of analysis, we devote Chapter 2 to the ways communication networks embed the helping relationship within a web of supportive ties.

NOTES

1. Thoits (1982) argues a similar point from the perspective of Durkheimian anomie theory. Drawing from the writings of Durkheim, she asserts that social

integration based on stable rules for conduct in a group are supportive for giving people "a sense of certainty and purpose in living" (p. 154). Hence social support is functional when people are imparted knowledge for conduct in their immediate environments, decreasing the anxiety of uncertain psychological states.

2. Indeed, in a study of functions of support and morale, Schaefer et al. (1981) found that of three functions of support identified (emotional, tangible, and informational) only informational support was positively associated with positive morale. Such a finding is an indicator of the tremendous need people have for knowledge of their environments and life events, and the impact on outlook.

3. In outlining models of coping and helping, Brickman, Rabinowitz, Karuza, Coates, Cohn, and Kidder (1982) proposed that recipients and providers can make different assumptions regarding internal or external responsibility for problems and solutions. Karuza, Zevon, Rabinowitz, and Brickman (1982) hypothesized that future coping is more likely to depend on the recipients' attributions about solutions than their responsibilities for the problem. These authors argue that internal attribution for solving a problem or improving a situation is more beneficial than external responsibility for the solution. The potential conflict between helpers and receivers based on incongruent assumptions about internal versus external responsibility for problems and solutions can be moderated by the relative power (status, prestige) between the helper and recipient (Karuza et al., 1982). Still, conflict may be inevitable if the receiver is not seeking uncertainty reduction but rather has a steadfast cognitive frame for the situation. As such, one may not be willing to listen to counter points of view offered by supporters.

4. However, any corrected attribution of this nature should be carefully applied. Coates, Renzaglia, and Embree (1983) caution that providing external explanations can subvert the individual's process of learning from mistakes, thus undermining his or her self-perceptions of control and further promoting helplessness. Clearly external attributions need to be clearly defined as specific and focused so as to encourage the individual's sense of responsibility for future events, yet not become burdened by feelings of failure.

2

Communication Networks as Structures of Social Support

TERRANCE L. ALBRECHT
MARA B. ADELMAN

> There is also a hidden benefit in using helping networks. Without reaching out to build such ties, an individual may develop a sense of isolation and alienation from life. . . . By becoming entwined in helping networks, the individuals may come to revitalize and reaffirm their sense of belonging—their attachment to community. This is one way to avoid the anomie so often described as a disease of urban life. (Warren, 1982, p. 20)

Supportive relationships do not exist in isolation from other relationships in people's lives (see Parks, Stan, & Eggert, 1983; Salinger, 1982). Ties to others are embedded in constellations of links that have the potential for enriching the quality of a person's life and diminishing the sense of loss, loneliness, and anomie noted above (e.g., Berkman, 1984; Parks, 1977a). Indeed, networks of relational patterns have been viewed as the "infrastructure" of social support (Badura & Waltz, 1982, p. 5).

While the focus of the previous chapter was on the process and function of support in micro-level relationships, we shift now to the macro network level of relationship analysis. The specific interest here is how the social architecture of an individual's environment augments areas of that person's life that are weakened by stressful experiences (Caplan, 1981). An individual's support network can be mapped as a traceable set of channels for help (Mitchell & Trickett, 1980). Such structures develop when recurring patterns of supportive message transactions are perceived or observed; these create overlapping linkages among multiple individuals (Farace, Monge, & Russell, 1977).

The process and function of support described in Chapter 1 occurs within these structures of communication. In this chapter we will describe the conceptual nature of support networks, review a representative sample of the research, and discuss operational strategies for the empirical study of such patterns.

Support Networks: An Overview

Networks are the outcomes of micro-level structuring (or interactive) behaviors. "Structuring" is the process of communication taking place in each relationship (Albrecht & Ropp, 1982; Mehan, 1978). A social support network is thus the manifestation over time of dyadic interactions.

We emphasize that networks are not merely the aggregation of a set of dyadic relationships. What makes them interesting is that relational linkages form a social web characterized not by aggregation but by *integration*. The network system that embeds the individual has numerous functional and dysfunctional potentialities because of the possibility of interconnectedness (or "density") among all contacts. Because of this property, the larger network can influence the nature of single relationships (Ridley & Avery, 1979).

For purposes of visually illustrating some preliminary themes, consider for a moment the network of a single mother, as a target individual. Let us assume that she has a family support structure similar to one depicted in Figure 2.1. Such visual representations as these are useful in identifying the strength of supportive ties at micro (relationship and group) and macro (whole network) levels.

As shown in the diagram, the parent has strong supportive ties to her sister and mother, a moderately supportive relationship with her brother, and only a weak tie to an uncle. She is likely to exchange the broadest range of help in her strongest relationships, such as financial aid, child care, and emotional reassurance (Denoff, 1982). But note that the family members also have ties to each

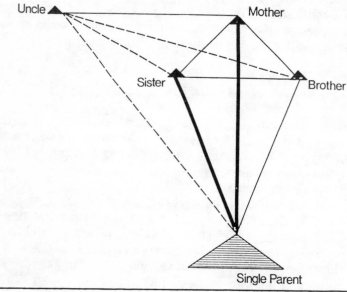

Figure 2.1 Kin Network

other. These can indirectly affect the single mother. For example, while the single mother has only a weak direct tie to her uncle, he is closely linked to her mother (his sister). It may be that he provides strong help to the mother, thus bolstering her ability to support the target individual. The ability to see such relational patterning is one of the advantages of network analysis. As Hammer, Makiesky-Barrow, and Gutwirth (1978) argue, network approaches to the study of support are heuristic and yield more powerful explanation of social processes than do investigations of individual differences alone.

In addition to her kin ties, the single mother also has links to other groups including various friends, coworkers, and neighbors (diagrammed in Figure 2.2). Some of her relationships are stronger sources of support than others, depending on such factors as the opportunities for interaction, and the extent of multiple role attachments that exist in any single relationship (for example, a neighbor may also be a coworker who attends the same church, which increases time for communication and the number of shared interests). The frequency of communication and the multiple types of role connections in various relationships show the potential for mutual influence across the cliques. Isolated as well as clustered relationships come to have meaning for the single mother in context. These can affect her subsequent communication behavior (such as how frequently interactions occur, under what circumstances, and with what kinds of intent).

Finally, in the course of time and events, members of one group in the single mother's network may meet those of another, thus "blending" some divisions. Coworkers may develop connections with the target individual's family, neighbors may become acquainted with friends, and so on. Figure 2.3 represents the overall network structure at a particular point in time for our single mother. The most important feature illustrated is the extent of overlap among the ties the single mother has to different sectors of her network. This image reflects the ways communication networks come to enmesh the individual in ever-widening social circles.[1]

Relevant Theoretical Frameworks

Theory does and should play an important role in the study of support networks. But research has been largely a descriptive enterprise. Few theory-driven predictive studies have been undertaken to explain the impacts of communication networks on individual behavior. The development of a shared code of meaning is at the heart of human communication. This in turn affects cognition, emotion, and behavior. But when it is chained out at an aggregate level, it is a process in need of explanatory foundations.

However, at least two frameworks in the literature have been helpful for understanding network structures and functioning. These include the "convergence model of communication" (Rogers & Kincaid, 1981), and the "social feedback model" (Hammer, 1981). While some may argue that these are more organizational devices

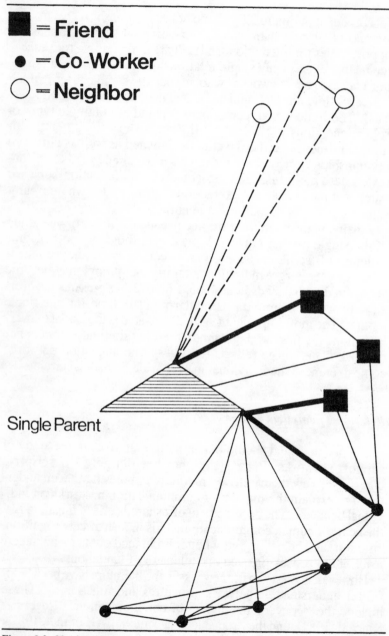

Figure 2.2   Multiple Networks

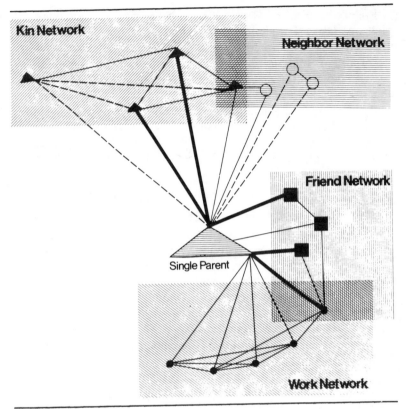

Figure 2.3 Overlapping Networks

than formal theories, they do extend the theoretical perspective on support framed in Chapter 1.

The convergence model. The convergence model discussed by Rogers and Kincaid (1981) supplements our earlier discussion of support as a communication process. Rogers and Kincaid termed the communication occurring within network relationships as one of the creation and sharing of meaning between participants. Drawing from such theorists as Bateson (1972) and Wittgenstein (1958), their model was used to describe how relational clustering occurs in network structures. The exchange of symbols to which people attach meaning will bring them to points of convergence or divergence in their perceptions of reality.

Rogers and Kincaid (1981) argue that there is never total or complete overlap in shared meaning and understanding. Rather, mutual uncertainty is reduced to acceptable levels. The degree to which uncertainty is tolerated is based on such factors as situational exigence, background, and experience. As they note:

> By means of several iterations or cycles of information exchange, two or more participants in a communication process may converge toward a more mutual understanding of each other's meaning, obtain greater accuracy, and come within the limits of tolerance required for the purpose at hand. (p.64)

This model is relevant to our discussion of the development of social support networks because of the inherent dual-level perspective. Given that networks are the macro-level manifestations of dyadic-level interactions (Mehan, 1978), areas of affiliation or clustering on a network map represent converging among network members around symbolic meanings of support. The drive of this model (and the point of our discussion in Chapter 1) is that communication involves the mutual influence of partners in interactions. At issue, then, in the study of social support networks should be the range of mutual effects on both providers and recipients, and the ways that together they reduce uncertainty and construct meaning together in order to exchange support. Research designs limited to exploring recipient effects easily miss many of the important, complex dynamics of support. A simple linear conceptualization of supporter-recipient effects (rather than a transactional perspective of mutual effects) ignores recipients' influences on providers, providers' effects on themselves, or secondary effects on individuals who are not the primary targets of support (see Rogers & Kincaid, 1981, pp. 70-71) and so on. In taking a communication perspective, the unit of analysis for the study of support shifts from the level of the individual to the level of the relationship.

Social feedback model. While the convergence model is a useful illustration of our framework of support as a communication process of uncertainty reduction in the search for shared meaning, Hammer's (1981) social feedback model is applicable to our discussion of support as a means for uncertainty reduction and enhanced control. Specifically, Hammer's notion of social feedback is a device for describing how support networks can function through influence and uncertainty reduction to control community problems (such as social deviance and disease).

Essentially networks are seen as structured channels for information that function to deter mental illness and deviant behavior in the community (Hammer, 1981). Thus the model is consistent with our theme of communicative influence; social attitudes and behavior are shaped over time through feedback communicated from one's fluctuating structure of ties. The communication process occurring in networks is the means to acquire and reinforce social skills. These skills are grounded in appropriate behavioral norms in the community. The organized network plays a significant role as a mechanism for absorbing uncertainty in the community about socially acceptable behavior patterns (Albrecht & Adelman, 1984).

Hammer also cited Cassel (1976) in describing a second specific function of network feedback: the controlling of disease and other physiological disorders. Adequate feedback reinforces a pattern of behavior and performance leading to normal health and development. Inadequate networks provide either a lack of reinforcement or information distortion. These produce disturbed behavior and physiology, both of which increase susceptibility to disease and illness (p. 407). A primary way this occurs is that individuals in a network may feel pressured to behave as other network members. Depending on the behavior, "groups or networks have the potential to be either health-promoting or not, and this may influence the health status of individuals" (Berkman, 1984, p. 429). Eating disorders in adolescents, for example, may originate in family and friend network influences as well as from strictly psycho/physiological abnormalities in the individual. Problematic eating patterns may develop when the adolescent is routinely permitted to eat alone, without the presence of family members. The problem is most likely in families where members do not eat together at regular intervals and do not integrate the family meal as a time of social/emotional bonding. Because eating is a pleasurable activity, one may need a social level of control to regulate possible overindulgence or aberrant behavior (DuPont, personal communication, June 25, 1986).[2] Family members operate in this instance to give feedback to the individual on the appropriateness of his or her actions. Social restraint at regular intervals from the family helps to shape and guide the child's long-term behavioral patterns.

Social feedback for norm reinforcement may also explain the inhibiting function of highly dense kin networks. Given that close kin are more likely to provide single mothers with tangible support (e.g., child care, money, housing; Henderson, 1980), obligatory demands from the network may mean that mothers are constrained from experimenting with alternative life-styles or associating with persons who are not approved by network members.

Similarly, networks of deviant subcultures can operate to impose a negative peer influence, preventing the successful adjustment of members to the larger community. Coates, Miller, and Ohlin (1978; see also Whittaker & Garbarino, 1983, p. 341) reported that delinquent youths who maintained former gang ties were generally bound to continue their deviant behavior patterns. Conversely, youths who had opportunities for interaction and positive reinforcement from supportive new ties in the conventional community were less likely to return to delinquency (Hawkins & Fraser, 1983).

This model illustrates specific ways the individual is inextricably tied to his or her social field. The prediction from the model is that the function of support at the network level is to maintain norms that preserve the community. The individual's behavior is regulated though he or she may not necessarily benefit from this pattern.

It is important to recognize that network members attempt to invoke feedback as a deterrent to the experience of uncertainty caused by behavior outside of rule-governed bounds. This is also evidence that the *lack* of a socially shared attributional framework for causes and effects can lead to aberrant psychological and behavioral consequences.

Dimensions of Support Networks

Most of the studies on support across disciplines have been oriented around network *properties* (e.g., variables such as density, reciprocity, size, and multiplexity). While it is easier to organize our review of the literature around these variables, it is also important to study support structures in terms of different levels of analysis, including the individual-network interface, the relationship or dyad, the group/clique level, and the macro network structure.

Below is a brief description of each level of analysis, followed by a review of the network literature organized around major structural properties. The types of network variables used to study support at each level are shown in Table 2.1. (See also the Appendix at the end of this chapter for definitions of each network construct.)

Levels of analysis. Studies at the micro level are investigations of the effects of sets of ties on the *individual*. (For a discussion of whether these effects are direct or buffering of stress and pathology, see Chapters 3 and 8.) For example, individual difference studies of child abusing versus nonabusing mothers are in this category (e.g., Gaudin & Pollane, 1983; Salzinger, Kaplan, & Artemyeff, 1983). Typically, study findings have been used to describe the differences between distressed and normal persons based on their ranges of network support.

Studies of support networks at the *dyadic* level are focused on structural characteristics of individual links between persons. Functional and dysfunctional properties of relationships have been examined, as well as how those relate to the well-being of the individuals involved.

The *group/clique* level of analysis is focused on the dense regions of connections among members of a network. Primary support groups are usually kin and close friends and represent the strongest structural ties and the closest interpersonal communication in an individual's life. Secondary groups are often ties to persons outside of the primary group, and open up one's range of contact to supportive, but distant, noninterpersonal links. The group may be described by structural properties, as well as the position of the group in the overall network. Most studies on support examine either the structure of communication in formal "support groups" or the correlates of group properties on individual-level adjustment, coping, and well-being.

Finally, analysis of overall support *networks* include studies of differences in structures of ties based on social class (Berkman & Syme, 1979; Hammer, 1983; Pool & Kochen, 1978) and comparison studies of community support systems in related geographical areas (e.g., Warren, 1982). Less frequent but equally interesting research has been the study of smaller, contained networks and the relationship to stress and illness. Hansell (1985) studied the entire population of adolescents in a private school to determine the positioning of students and the general relationship to mental duress

TABLE 2.1
Selected Network Constructs for Analysis of Support Networks

Level	(aka)[a]
Individual Level	
network role	
—liaison	linker/nonlinker
—bridge	
—group member	
—isolate	
—primary	
—broker	
—sycophant	
centrality	
zone size	reticulum (first order)
integrativeness/	density
range/diversity/span	
over/under reporting of links	
accessibility	reachability
radiality	dispersion
Dyadic Level	
strength of tie	frequency/rate of comm./intensity
strong/weak ties	primary/secondary links;
	direct/indirect
reciprocity	equality of interaction
symmetry	
uniplexity/multiplexity	
mode of comm.	
stability	
homogeneity/heterogeneity	
proximity	
openness	
path distance	
"Simmel measures"	
Group/Clique Level	
size	
density	interconnectedness
dominance	anchoring
homogeneity/heterogeneity	
reciprocity	
mode of comm.	
frequency of comm.	
primary/secondary support groups	
openness	
liaison linkage	
bridge linkage	

TABLE 2.1 (Continued)

	(aka)[a]
Macro Level	
size	
homogeneity/heterogeneity	
dominance	
reachability	compactness
fit	network overlap
stability	
clustering	
density	interconnectedness
degree	

a. *aka* refers to constructs that are "also known as" other terms. The network literature spans several disciplines; such breadth inevitably brings overlap and inconsistent use of terminology across the research.

and illness. Studies of macro networks give insights into prototypical patterns of functional and dysfunctional arrangements (e.g., Warren, 1982). These are helpful because the boundaries of the networks are extended outward for a fuller view (Hammer, 1983).

Critical Properties of Support Networks

Our review of network properties (see Table 2.1 and Appendix) includes many more constructs than are typically found in most social support network studies. Below is a sampling of research studies (though the chapters in Part II of this volume will include additional reviews of network studies that are more context bound).

The properties most often used in research designs have been *size* (the number of people in the focal unit), *homogeneity/heterogeneity* (the similarity or diversity of persons in the network), *reciprocity* (the degree support is given and received), *over time changes* in the network, *multiplexity* (the extent of multiple contents of communication occurring in the link), and *density* (the interconnectedness of contacts).

Size. Researchers have generally found that normal persons differ from psychotic, disturbed individuals in the size and mix of their networks (see Hammer, 1963-1964; Lipton, Cohen, Fischer, & Katz, 1981; Sokolovsky, Cohen, Berger, & Geiger, 1978). Mitchell (1982) found that the simple number of ties to intimates (reported by clients in counseling) related to problem solving (r =

.50), and psychopathology ($r = -.31$). Phillips (1981) reported data from one of the few large-scale studies of support, showing that network size had the strongest relationship with happiness for men and the number of social encounters had the highest correlation with happiness for women. Though her correlations were low, the author reasoned that increased rewards were available to women who were socially active, whereas larger networks for men probably reflected a healthier balance between professional and social contacts.

A significant comparison study of size and social class was reported by Pool and Kochen (1978). Though their data were not based on supportive ties per se, the results are suggestive of relative differences in the potential support available to blue-collar versus professional classes. Working-class individuals reported seeing a median of 140 persons during a 100-day period, while professionals reported about 540 contacts. As might be expected, blue-collar workers communicated much more often with their network members. Commenting on these data, Hammer (1983) notes:

> For the blue collar workers, there is a relatively bounded set of people, a large proportion of whom are seen with high frequency; for the professionals, there is a much larger, more open set of people, relatively few of whom are seen with high frequency. One might expect that at times of life transition (e.g., marriage, early parenthood, job change) or other sources of rapid change, these forms would have different strengths and vulnerabilities in providing feedback from and access to others and in the ease of maintenance and especially replacement of core network members. (p. 410)

Those who communicate frequently with fewer network contacts may realize a stronger sense of self-identity and community, stable norms, and more resources during uncertain periods of life. But for reasons outlined in the properties below, such network patterns may also be restrictive, providing limited opportunities for change and growth.

Homogeneity/heterogeneity. Normal persons have been found to have primary network clusters of about 25 ties to heterogeneous configurations of family, relatives, friends, neighbors, and coworkers (Pattison & Pattison, 1981). "Normals" have been found to communicate with their contacts frequently, and have a balanced reciprocity of affective caring and instrumental assistance. In contrast, disturbed populations such as schizophrenics have smaller networks (8-12 persons) of shorter relational duration, with low reciprocity and low affect. These findings have been somewhat corroborated in descriptive studies (though of small sample sizes) of psychotics. Disturbed persons were found to have homogeneous networks (mostly family members) less than half the size of nonpsychotics, more imbalanced dependence on others for affect and instrumental support, and fewer multiplex relations (Cohen & Sokolovsky, 1978; Tolsdorf, 1976). Also included in the disturbed populations studied have been child abusers (see Salzinger et al., 1983). Gaudin and Pollane (1983) found the size and strength of the mother's network was negatively related to the likelihood of child abuse ($r = -.39$). When combined with stress, strength explained 24.6% of the variance in abuse. Abusive mothers gained little from their networks to ease the uncertainty they faced, nor to assist them in better controlling their domestic situations. In fact, they lacked direction from their contacts for dealing with stressful situations:

> Mothers living in high situational stress situations who perceive their social networks to be weaker, less supportive, can be expected to have high levels of anxiety and fewer adaptive responses to stressful situations. . . . Social networks that are perceived . . . weak, non-supportive, do not provide mothers with clear, unambiguous feedback, emotional support, and assistance with parenting tasks needed to effectively cope. . . . The lack of adaptive responses to a high stress parenting situation raises the likelihood of mothers becoming abusive. (Gaudin & Pollane, 1983, pp. 98-99)

In an intriguing, macro-level descriptive study, Warren (1982) reported data on network patterns of helping behavior in several Michigan communities. He examined the diversity of links in "problem-anchored helping networks" (PAHNs) and found that the healthiest communities (ones with the most variety of helping resources: relatives, friends, neighbors, coworkers, spouses, and so on) were those where the use of one source for support did not preclude the use of others. Warren examined the network patterns of individual help-seeking and then aggregated the data to look for dominant trends in each of the communities. He then contrasted the communities according to whether the use of one support source correlated (positively or negatively) with the use of other sources. A representative finding was that the use of the spouse as a helper in one community tended to deter reliance on a range of other sources of support, including agencies, friends, relatives, neighbors, and coworkers. Low diversity and heterogeneity of supporters can become a fortress that segregates the individual, barring access to a range of strong and weak ties that could provide more comprehensive support and assistance (see also McKinlay, 1973).

Reciprocity. Reciprocity of emotional and instrumental aid also has been found to be generally necessary for healthy, lasting relationships. Reciprocation in relationships has an important personal function of preserving self-esteem in some groups (such as the elderly) (Wentowski, 1981). The perceived ability to give in exchange for receiving helps prevent feelings of inadequacy, uselessness, and lack of control in communicating in order to have positive impacts on others. In contrast, the inability to give and receive in network links overburdens and strains supportive relationships (and networks), resulting in disrupted and broken ties. This particularly entraps the psychotic or disturbed individual in a vicious circle. As the psychosis increases, overdependence on others increases, straining and fracturing ties at the time the individual is most in need of support (Pattison & Pattison, 1981; Politser, 1980).

Over-time changes. Most studies on the ways support systems expand or shrink in size have been based on cross-sectional data, which limits the conclusiveness of the results. However, some interesting findings have emerged. Stigmas (such as divorce or mental illness) tend to precipitate network deterioration. Rands (1981) found that spouses lost almost half of their contacts after divorce or separation for reasons including family disapproval (Kitson, Moir, & Mason, 1982) and divided loyalties among friends (Wilcox, 1981). Parents of mentally retarded children found that as their children grew older, the negative reactions of network members intensified (Suelzle & Keenan, 1981). Parents of younger children communicated more with close network ties and used more services than did parents of older children, who were in need of greater help but were left feeling more isolated (which presumably served then to increase the amount of uncertainty and anxiety they experienced as the children grew older).

In one of the few longitudinal studies, Kaplan, Robbins, and Martin (1983) found evidence for the substitutability of support relationships over the life cycle. They interviewed adolescents (n = 1,633) in the seventh grade and again 10 years later, finding an expected shift in primary networks from kin-dominance to peer-dominance. More longitudinal data are still needed to clearly document the life cycles of relational patterns for a variety of age segments.

Density. A final important characteristic of support networks has been density (also termed *integration*—the interconnectedness among a set of ties). The term *density* is analogous to a web of ties that enmesh the focal individual in helpful and possibly harmful ways. The basic generalization from the research is that individuals who have low density, heterogeneous network structures are likely to fare better than those who do not (Albrecht & Adelman, 1984). However, there are some important benefits from high network density. Low dense structures are helpful for enhancing personal control by facilitating stress coping and role transition, and by opening up information paths for obtaining needed health and welfare referrals. In contrast, high density is helpful for reinforcing positive social identity and obtaining tangible services (Hamburg & Killilea, 1979; Hammer, 1983).

One important way to reduce overall density in a network is to segregate the total range of links into more or less independent sectors of relationships. For example, segregating ties (and thus lowering density) among kin, outside friends, and acquaintances was most helpful for the stress coping of cardiac patients (Badura & Waltz, 1982). Without some network partitioning, the strain of care or overprotection by family-dominated networks can reinforce negative self-perceptions of patients. Hirsch (1981) found that low density among friend and kin contacts was related to social reinforcement and higher self-esteem during final exams. He reasoned that low-density networks provided greater opportunities for support (e.g., when one sector was in conflict or stress, the student could turn to other sectors of the network for help). Network differentiation fostered diverse feedback; more channels existed for a greater variety of satisfying norms to emerge. Politser (1980) hypothesized that shared communication and disapproval in a dense network would lead to rejection of a disturbed family member. Such a breakdown in support would produce either a "social insatiability" or "social ambivalence," thus exacerbating the mental problems (see pp. 80-83).

Low-density networks are functional for facilitating cultural assimilation, and role transitions for those undergoing life change. Garrison (1978) found that low-density networks facilitated cross-cultural adaptation. In comparison, women who had tightly knit kin and friendship ties had more mental problems (including schizophrenia) and greater difficulty in adjusting to the new city. Dense, restricted networks reinforced language and cultural barriers that precluded effective socialization to the new environment.

Highly segregated networks allow greater freedom for the individual to develop and change because ties are less encumbering and provide more opportunities for experimenting with life-style and self-image. Low-density contacts were found to be functional for recently divorced women who wanted to learn and try new roles and behavior patterns (Wilcox, 1981) and McLanahan, Wedemyer, and Adelberg (1981) reported a similar finding for single mothers establishing new role identities. Such links helped these women by providing new information, models for change, and increased social contacts. And heterogeneous networks of low density but multiplex links were most supportive for young widows and older women returning to college (Hirsch, 1980). They reported greater satisfaction with support, more positive moods, fewer symptoms of illness, and greater self-esteem. Hence differentiated networks tend to enrich the personal lives of people by affording opportunities to be in control of desired variations in their life-styles.

Finally, low-density networks can provide greater opportunities for instrumental support in the form of institutional resource referrals and aid. Pattison and Pattison (1981) argued that the schizophrenic's support structure is a collusive, closed system, isolating the individual from external social contact (see also Pattison, Llamas, & Hurd, 1979). Alternatively, low dense structures have been found efficient for channeling information about support agencies and resources in the community. Horowitz (1977) and McKinlay (1973) found that those with low network integration most readily sought psychiatric help and health and welfare services. Those with strong kin support but lacking outside friendship circles were dysfunctionally insulated from obtaining referrals. Indeed, the family system would attempt to contain and shield the psychosis, often until advanced, highly disturbed stages. A different problem but an equally startling finding by Mitchell and Hodson (1983) showed that battered women in tightly knit social networks lost major portions of their social ties if they separated from their husbands. One could speculate that a reason some women continued to endure the situation was knowledge that they would find themselves and their children bereft of significant network ties if they severed the spousal relationship, however abusive it might be. Certainly their situations could be aided and access to help achieved if from the start their networks were disjunctive from their husbands'.

In sum, dense networks have been generally stifling for those experiencing mental illness and undergoing life change or conflict. Highly dense ties may create a group influence effect that entraps a person, particularly devastating in times when group members collectively reject the individual (Politser, 1980). Stable, highly connected relationships can produce a "fortress" effect, deterring the acquisition of new self-identities, personal growth, and blocking pathways in the community to new information and treatment (for example, the "trapped" effect adolescents experience in a drug culture that envelopes them and sanctions efforts to change their life-styles).

However, we acknowledge several positive effects of high interconnection of contacts. Close-knit ties can be helpful in several ways without *necessarily* stifling one's needs for growth and new information. Indeed, highly integrated ties can prevent feelings of anomie, especially in populations whose living situations are highly mobile and temporary (see Parks, 1977a) and help the psychological adjustment of those in posttrauma conditions (see Kadushin, 1982, for a discussion of the benefits of social density for the mental health of Vietnam combat veterans). High density also aids in coping with particular types of job stress, particularly for those experiencing uncertainty from organizational change or professionals in human service work who often work in the field outside of formal organizational boundaries (see Szilagyi & Holland, 1980; Albrecht, Irey, & Mundy, 1982; see also Chapter 8 in this volume). At least for the short term, highly dense organizational networks can be more efficient for assimilating newcomers in the organization. Greater interconnectedness among organizational members can help meet needs for information and uncertainty reduction of newly hired individuals (see Wilson, 1986).

Finally, a particularly poignant application of the density concept is the analysis of the concealment and protection of the Danish Jews from the Nazis during World War II (see Yahil, 1969). Network terms were not used in the historical account, but it was clear that the geographically small, closely knit structure of the Danish population enabled efficient, swift communication about impending dangers to the Jews and cooperation in their rescue efforts. The physical density also helped reinforce a communal sense of honor and collective defiance toward the enemy.

In short, density is a major structural variable in the study of support networks. It is a particularly critical feature to measure; problems with density can, as Pattison et al. (1979, p. 66) argue, "produce stress because they offer ambiguous and conflicting emotional responses and either social isolation or social collusion" (also cited in Gaudin & Pollane, 1983). We have suggested elsewhere (Albrecht & Adelman, 1984) that differentiated clusters of differing types of contacts may be most functional for individuals (see also Hamburg & Killilea, 1979; Warren, 1982). Such structures provide breadth for contact, freedom of expression, and information, yet retain anchoring qualities that enable the individual to feel a sense of reinforcement, belonging, and commitment. (For a summary of the studies cited in this section on network properties, see Table 2.2.)

Concluding Note

Whether one is considering the supportive ties of single mothers or the helping linkages throughout a community, a network perspective is useful for describing the shape, size, and functions of these micro to macro systems. The network approach enables mapping of the direct and indirect connections among a collection of individuals; the growing list of network properties facilitates complex analysis of the map at multiple levels of analysis.

Clearly, the proliferation of network terminology and research across disciplines is evidence that this is one perspective that can unite diverse thought and findings. Yet the continued development of relevant theoretical frameworks and clarification of structural

TABLE 2.2
Summary of Selected Studies Grouped by Network Properties

Size	Homogeneity/Heterogeneity	Reciprocity	Over Time	Density
Hammer (1963-1964)	Pattison & Pattison (1981)	Pattison & Pattison (1981)	Rands (1981)	Hamburg & Killilea (1979)
Lipton et al. (1981)	Cohen & Sokolovsky (1978)	Polister (1980)	Kitson et al. (1982)	Hammer (1983)
Sokolovsky et al. (1978)	Tolsdorf (1976)		Wilcox (1981)	Badura & Waltz (1982)
Mitchell (1982)	Salzinger et al. (1983)		Suelzle & Keenan (1981)	Hirsch (1981)
Phillips (1981)	Gaudin & Pollane (1983)		Kaplan et al. (1983)	Politser (1980)
Pool & Kochen (1978)	Warren (1982)			Garrison (1978)
				Wilcox (1981)
				McLanahan et al. (1981)
				Pattison & Pattison (1981)
				Pattison et al. (1979)
				Horowitz (1977)
				McKinlay (1973)
				Mitchell & Hodson (1983)
				Politser (1980)
				Parks (1977)
				Kadushin (1982)
				Szilagyi & Holland (1980)
				Albrecht et al. (1982)
				Wilson (1986)
				Yahil (1969)

properties will be essential for broadening the kinds of empirical
claims that can be made.

Appendix:
Summary of Definitions
for Major Network Properties

Individual-Level Constructs

network role: usually defined as liaison, bridge, group member, or
isolate; terms are used to indicate the extent to which individual
has extensive cross-clique or network links (liaisons or bridges) or
is embedded in single cliques (group members); those with extensive, differentiating links are also termed "linkers" as opposed to
"non-linkers" (Albrecht, 1984; Richards, 1975; Rogers & Kincaid, 1981); other recent terms used for roles include "primary
roles" (high prestige, usually perceived as leaders, with high rates
of nomination as contacts), "brokers" (have a large number of
unreciprocated links to those in primary roles, but also are highly
nominated as contacts), and "sycophants" (unreciprocated contacts to prestige persons and receive a negligible proportion of
nominations in the network) (Hansell, 1985)

centrality: extent to which one is at the cross-roads of information flow
in the network (Farace et al., 1977); the minimum distance between
an individual and all other persons in the group (Brass, 1984)

zone size: refers to the range of direct or indirect contact of an individual; first-order zones in one's support network would be a sphere
representing all direct links of support; a second-order zone
includes all direct links of contacts not shared by the focal individual (these second-order links are indirect contacts for him or
her) (Mitchell, 1969; Farace et al., 1977)

connectedness: the range of contact of an individual (usually expressed
as a ratio of number of actual to possible linkages) (Farace et al.,
1977; Tichy, Tushman, & Frombrun, 1979)

integrativeness/density: the extent to which one's support contacts communicate with one another (expressed as a percentage of actual to
possible links) (Berkman, 1984; Richards, 1975; Tolsdorf, 1976)

range/diversity of links/span: the extent to which one's links are heterogeneous in character (Thurman, 1979/1980)

over/underreporting of links: a perceptual variable, refers to the extent a focal person over- or underestimates the range of his or her support network (Farace et al., 1977)

accessibility: the ease of contact between a focal individual and his or her support network members (Berkman, 1984)

radiality: the extent to which an individual's links are dispersed; one operationalization is the ratio of the number of second-order links to the extent of first-order interconnection (Lester, 1981)

Dyadic-Level Constructs

strength of tie: usually refers to the frequency and rate of communication (may also be weighted by perceived importance of link) (Richards, 1975)

strong/weak tie: "strong ties" are often close, interpersonal relationships with one's primary group of friends/kin; "weak ties" are either direct links to individuals outside of one's primary support group or indirect links through others to outside contacts (Granovetter, 1973, 1982)

reciprocity: generally whether there is mutual exchange of affect or instrumental support (often measured as individual perceptions of the link as mutual; (see Adelman, 1986; Berkman, 1984; Pattison & Pattison, 1981); also defined as the extent to which two people independently agree they have a link, is used as indicator of measurement reliability (Richards, 1979; Hansell, 1985)

symmetry: the extent to which exchange between two people is on an equal basis.

uniplexity/multiplexity: the extent to which multiple message contents are exchanged in a supportive relationship (e.g., business-related and personal information) (Minor, 1983; Rogers & Kincaid, 1981)

mode of communication: the predominant type of channel used in communicating supportive messages (face-to-face, telephone, and so on).

stability: the length of duration of the link (usually associated with multiplexity, reciprocity, and strength)

homogeneity/heterogeneity: the similarity of support partners on various characteristics (usually demographic) (Berkman, 1984)

proximity: the physical distance between partners

openness: the range of contact to outside links

path distance: the shortest link(s) between two persons (Alba, 1982)

"Simmel measures": the degree of intersection (the number of distinct persons contained) of the support groups of two individuals (Alba, 1982)

Group/Clique-Level Constructs

size: the number of persons in the support group/clique

density: the ratio of actual to possible within-group links

dominance: the members to whom most interaction is directed (Farace et al., 1977).

homogeneity/heterogeneity: the degree of similarity/disimilarity among members

reciprocity: the ratio of reciprocated to unreciprocated links in the group

mode of communication: the predominant channel of communication among members

frequency of communication: the amount of interaction occurring in the group

primary/secondary support groups: primary support groups are generally dense clusters of closest friends and kin (strong ties); secondary groups are usually noninterpersonal contacts

openness: the degree of network contact to the larger network

liaison linkage: the extent of contact between group members and liaisons (usually expressed as a percentage compared to other group/liaison contact) (Farace et al., 1977)

bridge linkage: the extent of group member contact with members of other groups (usually a percentage compared to other group contact) (Farace et al., 1977)

Macro Network-Level Constructs

size: the number of people in the network (Mitchell & Trickett, 1980)

homogeneity/heterogeneity: the degree of similarity/disimilarity among network members

dominance: point of anchoring/direction of greatest contact in network

reachability: the "compactness" of the network; may be operationalized as the average distance (or number of links) between any two members of the network

fit: the overlap between two support groups; also discussed as the comparison between perceived networks and "ideal" networks (Farace et al., 1977; Farace, Taylor, & Stewart, 1978)

stability: the degree to which membership in the network changes over time

clustering: the number of groups/cliques dense regions in the network (Tichy et al., 1979)

density: the extent of interconnection among members; also, the extent of connection between members from different groups

degree: the average number of contacts network members have with other network members (Thurman, 1979/1980)

NOTES

1. The above example is simply an illustration of the network configuration of a single mother as it develops and meets her needs for support at home and work over a relatively short time span. Kahn and Antonucci (1980) encourage an even broader conception of support networks. They argue for a view of support in terms of support systems or "convoys" that evolve over the entire life cycle of the individual.

2. The need for a "reaffirmation of social control" for those engaging in eating disorders, drug abuse, and personal safety carelessness has been discussed extensively by Robert L. DuPont, Clinical Professor of Psychiatry, Georgetown Medical School and the Center for Behavioral Medicine.

3

Measurement Issues in the Study of Support

TERRANCE L. ALBRECHT
MARA B. ADELMAN

There is no doubt that support has a quantitative element. . . . But merely counting people and computing ratios concerning density and other structural variables does not touch the depth of the concept "support." A large, interconnected family can be mobilized for support, but also for condemnation and ostracism. Social support must therefore be seen as the availability of helping relationships and the quality of those relationships. (Leavy, 1983, p. 5)

Recently others have joined Leavy (1983) in his call for the study of *relationships* in the empirical investigation of support (see Gottlieb, 1985). At issue in the study and treatment of support is the distinction between an emphasis on the process of supportive relationship building and the effects of support on individual health and well-being. Our emphasis in this volume is on understanding the dynamics of supportive interactions within the spectrum of relationships in a person's life.[1]

Central Issues in Measurement

The Interplay Between Theory and Methodology

Interdependence usually exists between a researcher's theoretical perspective and the types of methodological choices faced in the investigation. The theoretical emphasis may direct the selection of methods, while the types of methods used may limit or enhance the interpretations drawn that confirm or fail to confirm the original theory. This has been especially true in the study of support. Various perspectives and accompanying methodological strategies have engendered debates on the veracity of claims drawn from studies about the phenomenon of support. Among the most notable illustrations of this issue has been the "buffering versus direct effects" controversy (e.g., Aneshensel & Stone, 1982; Bruhn & Phillips, 1984; Dean & Lin, 1977; House, LaRocco, & French, 1982; Jayratne & Chess, 1984; LaRocco, 1983; LaRocco, House, & French, 1980; Schaefer, 1982; Seers, McGee, Serey, & Graen, 1983; Thoits, 1982, 1983). While we refer the reader to the extensive commentary on the buffering versus main effects discussion, we raise it here as an example of the theory-methodology interdependence and what it has meant for the etiological assessment of support and the relationship to pathology.

A basic attraction of the "buffering hypothesis" is the parsimonious explanation of the relationship between life stress and social support. The main proponents, LaRocco, House, and French (1980) argue that the interaction effect between stress and support is weaker for those with high levels of support. Stressful events that occur while an individual enjoys high support should produce less distress than if they occur during times without support. However, others (e.g., Aneshensel & Stone, 1982; Schaefer, 1982; Thoits, 1982, 1983, 1984) argue that the effects of support on stress symptoms, illness, and strain are direct, that instead of shielding an individual from the negative impact of stress, support may be important for decreasing stress symptoms.

However, inconsistent evidence for interaction effects has meant a serious need for conceptual specifications (Seers et al., 1983) and this is where the interplay between theory and methodology becomes critical. Seers et al. (1983) argued that the "coping hypothesis" is a more theoretically plausible description of *how people use* support to manage stressful circumstances. House et al. (1982) suggest that given support does *not* buffer some stress-strain relationships, theories should pinpoint the *sources* and *types* of support that buffer the specific kinds of stressors and under what types of conditions. Finally, Schaefer (1982, p. 98) has suggested we need to know more about the *processes* that occur when people use their relationships during stressful events, the processes that prompt people to respond supportively, and how such processes affect health and well-being.

Certainly a communication approach is useful in sorting many of these issues. For example, studies should focus on the interactional processes and subsequent effects on recipients' (and providers') uncertainty reduction and control levels. Examining sources in terms of levels of relationship development can better frame the nature of providers and the types of support rendered. Finally, how support is transacted in the relationship can be studied as a function of stressors, timing, nature of the relationship, and the context. Whether the effects are direct or indirect is a subordinate question guided by the overarching theoretical questions being asked about the communication relationship. As Thoits (1983) notes, a test of the buffering hypothesis is whether the individual is able to maintain a high level of support during crisis periods. Hence, to the extent interaction patterns remain stable, the individual should be able to cope with crisis events.

Retrospective Versus Longitudinal Designs

Related to the above debate is how patterns of support relate to stress symptoms and illness over time. A persistent call for longitudinal work has been echoed by numerous researchers (e.g., Bruhn & Phillips, 1984; Dean & Lin, 1977; Frydman, 1981; Henderson, 1980; Wortman, 1984).

Whether the research design is retrospective and cross sectional or prospective and longitudinal has implications for the legitimacy of drawing causal claims about the effects of support on stress. Leavy (1983) criticized reliance on retrospective designs, arguing that researchers are forced to depend on data that could be distorted by deficient memories, particularly in clinical populations where psychological disorders can affect accuracy. Henderson (1980) aptly pinpointed this as a difficulty in sorting causal links to explain the role of communication networks in schizophrenia. Much of the research has been either a post hoc comparison of the social networks of disturbed and normal patients or a retrospective accounting of relationship patterns before the illness. However, he argued a prospective design is necessary to track the network relationships of those at high risk for the illness *before* the onset of symptoms. Unfortunately, even with this effort, confounding effects can occur in the data if the disorder was prematurely displayed in impaired communication skills. (And whether this had happened in a given case would be difficult to determine; see Henderson, 1980.)

But how long is longitudinal? Depending on the population, "longitudinal" has been data collection at two points in time (e.g., Albrecht, Irey, & Mundy, 1982), over the course of an illness or major life stress event (e.g., Burgess & Holmstrom, 1978), or life span data covering as long as nine years (e.g., Berkman & Syme, 1979). Confirmation or disconfirmation of the mechanisms of social support or the buffer or direct effect question will depend on "when and how social support is measured: before, after, or independently of the occurrence of life changes" (Thoits, 1982, p. 153). Indeed, Depner, Wethington, and Ingersoll-Dayton (1984) argue that longitudinal designs should be used only after the researcher has conducted preliminary work to determine major times during the stress experience when measurement should take place.

Attention to the cooccurrence of change in social support during a stressful event is particularly needed. Thoits (1982) illustrated this problem with the study of support patterns during divorce. Such a life change alters support systems in ways that may deprive an individual of important relationships while other new ties may be formed. If support is measured only after the divorce, results may present a distorted picture of the causal directions between support and stress events.

In short, prospective and longitudinal designs are costly and difficult, but there is consensus that they are essential if we are finally to specify with any empirical rigor the depth of causality between support and outcomes on health and well-being.

Measurement of Supportive Functions

Since the late 1970s, the number of scales for measuring the functions of support has multiplied (House & Kahn, 1985). (See, for example, scales by Dean, Lin, & Ensel, 1981; Flaherty, Gaviria, & Pathak, 1983; House, 1981; Norbeck, Lindsey, & Carrieri, 1983; Pollack & Harris, 1983; Procidano & Heller, 1983; Sarason, Levine, Basham, & Sarason, 1983.) Almost all are self-report scales targeted for individuals. Self-report assessments are used on the grounds that the support that counts is the behavior perceived by the subject as supportive. The subject is argued to be the most reliable source for determining helpfulness (as opposed to the researcher who may observe a behavior and label it as an instance of support or nonsupport, Bruhn & Phillips, 1984; House, 1981).

Cautions toward traditional approaches. Behavior perceived to be supportive is usually measured as helpful behavior that has been experienced directly from a set of supporters. It could also be based on attributional judgments about future behavior from sources that are expected to be helpful (Antonucci & Depner, 1982). Either way, two concerns are apparent that should be considered in the study design. First, supportive behaviors cannot be categorized and measured without accounting for the nature of the relationship and the interactions in which support took place. Whether support is perceived is inextricably tied to the way the relationship is defined and the way the specific encounter was experienced. The ability to borrow $10 from a friend is evidence that tangible assistance could be available. But it should not necessarily be measured as "potential" support. It may be that expectations exist that such a transaction could also mean possibilities of loss of face and indebtedness, prices too high to be worth the support.

House and Kahn (1985) also point out a second serious flaw to be considered in such studies. Asking people to list the number of persons in their support networks can lead to distortion in the data. When the overall measures of different support functions are based on the numbers of persons identified, network size confounds the functional qualities of the support relationships. Simply adding the responses for each person named in the network produces high intercorrelation among measures of support functions (see pp. 96, 100). A better alternative might be to use direct magnitude estimation to measure the quantity and perceived helpfulness of support independently of the number of sources.

Most scales incorporate measures of the more commonly discussed functions of support, subsumed under various labels with either tangible assistance, emotional nurturance, and in some cases mastery emerging as central (e.g., Cohen, Mermelstein, Kamarck, & Hoberman, 1985; House, 1981; House & Kahn, 1985; Norbeck et al., 1983; Procidano & Heller, 1983; Schaefer, Coyne, & Lazarus, 1981; Ward, Sherman, & LaGory, 1984). However, related to the above concern is the failure of many researchers to sort out differences between types of support (House & Kahn, 1985). Results of several studies have shown clear distinctions between tangible and emotional support. But high correlations do appear among emotion-related functions. House and Kahn attributed the problem primarily to methodological difficulties (e.g., artificial results based on indexing, confounded measurement).

However, we argue that much of the overlap is due to an underlying conceptual overlap among the variables. For example, House (1981) and House and Kahn (1985) identified four types of support: emotional support (esteem, affect, trust, concern, listening); appraisal support (affirmation, feedback, social comparison); informational support (advice, suggestion, directives, information); and instrumental support. The reduction of uncertainty about self and circumstances is a pronounced theme in appraisal support and informational support and the reduction of uncertainty about one's relationship is gained through emotional support. It is not surprising then, that these dimensions are not orthogonal. (See Table 3.1 for a selected compilation of representative approaches and scales for studying support.)

Uncertainty. While the theme of uncertainty reduction is implicit throughout various measures of support, it has been directly addressed in a few select research schemes. Researchers have measured the level of uncertainty or ambiguity experienced and then correlated increases or decreases with the presence or absence of quantified support. For example, in their classic analysis, Kahn, Wolfe, Quinn, Snoek, and Rosenthal (1964) measured work role stress in terms of role ambiguity and role uncertainty. Recently, Mishel (1984b, 1985) reported acceptable validity for her uncertainty scale composed of item clusters for ambiguity, complexity, deficient information, and unpredictability. Both scales are intended for specific populations and contexts (members of organizations and clinical patients undergoing diagnosis and treatment) but could be adapted for wider use. Included in the assessment could be direct magnitude estimations of the level of attributional confidence regarding stressful life events. Central to any precise measurement will be items that tap the extent to which persons feel they

TABLE 3.1
Methodological Approaches to the Study of Social Support[a]

Methods	Technique	Author(s)	Sample/Key Questions	Scales/Indices[b]
Large-scale mailed questionnaire	Mailed self-report questionnaire	House & Wells (1978); see House (1981)	(n = 1,809) Male factory workers/ Effects of support on job stress and health	Social support measures designed by authors
Interview questionnaire	Focus interviews, questionnaires administered	Barrera (1981)	(n = 86) Pregnant adolescents/ Scale development, social support as moderator of health	Negative Life Events ASSIS (Arizona Social Support Interview Schedule) ISSB (Inventory of Socially Supportive Behaviors)[b] (.92) Brief Symptom Inventory
Longitudinal study (4-6 years)	Longitudinal study using focused/ open ended, face-to-face and telephone interviews	Burgess & Holmstrom (1978)	(n = 92) Rape victims/ Relationship between prior stress in a victim's life, and patterns of recovery after rape (including role of support)	
Contextual study/ multiple methods	Participant observation, logs of daily activity, interviews	Cohen & Sokolovsky (1978)	(n = 44) Experimental residence for released psychiatric patients/ Described the social networks of schizophrenic ex-patients	
Scale development	Self-report questionnaire (27 items) (used several psychological and personality measures	Sarason et al. (1983)	(n = 602) College students/ Scale development and correlation with personality measures	Social Support Questionnaire (.97)[b]

a. The following studies were selected on the basis of diverse methods, populations, and scales in order to give the reader a sampling of approaches that have been used in the last decade for studying social support.
b. Internal reliability coefficients for scale cited in the study.

can explain the events around them in cause-effect terms. The extent to which this changes as reflected in supportive transactions with others could then be analyzed.

Personal control. Most studies of the relationship between support and control have used various scales to measure locus of control. Given that measurement issue is to assess the extent to which persons believe that their communication behavior can produce desired outcomes, measurement needs to extend beyond simple psychometric testing of the locus dimension. Included in these studies should be evaluations of the extent to which behavior is perceived to have stable and general outcomes in light of stressful events. Comparative links could be drawn between the content of supportive interactions that reduce uncertainty and the subsequent actions of the individual that he or she perceives to affect the stressor conditions.

The Measurement of
Supportive Communication

The study of supportive communication is the study of transactional and reciprocal processes occurring within emergent network patterns. Measurement of communication processes and patterns should include assessment specified at the following levels: (1) the nature of supportive messages exchanged between interactants and the type of relationship that exists between them (the level of interpersonal/noninterpersonal depth), and (2) the characteristics of the network structure embedding the interaction.

Supportive Message Transactions
and Relationships

Few studies have been based on attempts to document what it is that people *say* to each other when engaged in supportive episodes. In surveying the literature, one is struck by the lack of research attention paid to measuring the specific factors that make a message or message sequence "supportive." And, of course, a key factor in determining whether a message is perceived to be supportive is the type of relationship presumed to exist between parties (that encompasses the message exchange). Certainly much interpretation or sense-making of messages is based on judgments of the type of relationship in which they occur. In other words, the message is often interpreted to be supportive or nonsupportive, depending on the state of the relationship one has with the source of the message (the content and relational notions of messages described in Chapter 1). One may expect more sensitivity and support in a crisis, for example, from a close friend. But if the level of sensitivity and understanding from that person seems inadequate, one may make a more extreme judgment of low support from the friend and question the status of the relationship in general.

Supportive messages (as noted in Chapter 1) have at least one or more of the following characteristics: (1) convey information for cognitive reframing of personal cause-effect contingencies; (2) provide information for an instructional purpose (to enhance the skill level of the other); (3) provide confirmation of other's self-concept (offer acceptance or reassurance); (4) provide openers for other's ventilation; and (5) include a nonverbal accompaniment conveying positive tone and gestures of reassurance.

Analysis of direct interactions of message exchanges can be accomplished in laboratory settings. Realistic transactions can be set up between confederates and subjects and then taped for later coding and analysis. An example of such work related to the support area by Samter and Burleson (1984) showed differences in the elaboration of "comforting" message sequences between high and low cognitively complex subjects (using college students). Confederates were trained to disclose personal problems in one-on-one encounters with subjects. Scripts were designed to elicit natural messages of consolation from the subjects. The interactions were taped, transcribed, and coded according to a hierarchy of increasing perspective taking (see Chapter 1).

Analysis of such messages should include coding of the presence or absence of the supportive quality and then rating of the extent to which the supportive quality is helpful for uncertainty reduction and enhanced control. Including multiple vantage points in data collection strategies could provide valuable comparison. Augmenting ratings by observer groups with reactions to the sequences by the participants themselves (playing either the roles of providers or recipients) could illuminate aspects of the process and provide the self-report check of perceived helpfulness (see House, 1981).

Certainly field studies of support often pose challenges to the direct taping and analysis of supportive interactions. Role plays could be set up between spouses, partners, and the like and then taped. Droge (1983b) reported a study of a self-help group of epileptics where meetings were taped and later analyzed for disturbances in communication patterns. Of course some interactions will not be accessible, making necessary the reliance on participant recall for the presence and ratings of support.

Measurement of relationships. Perceptions of relationships are grounded in the attributional judgments made by both parties. Researchers have generally presented these to subjects as established role categorizations of friend, spouse, acquaintance, bartender, coworker, supervisor, and so on.

However, additional measures of relational distance, uncertainty, and attribution of motive can further specify dimensions of the attachment. As discussed in Chapter 1, communication relationships can be interpersonal or noninterpersonal, depending on the level of discrimination possible toward the relational partner apart from his or her role, group membership, or cultural background (Miller & Steinberg, 1975). Drawing from uncertainty reduction theory, the more extensive communication is between partners, the more likely the relationship will develop and endure (Berger & Bradac, 1982; Berger & Calabrese, 1975; Parks & Adelman, 1983). Finally, attribution of the cause or motive for the other's supportive behavior (e.g., internal or external stimulus) provides a way to understand the perceptions of types of support in terms of the relationship. It is a way to lodge action within the bounds of the tie between the supporter and receiver, and to assess how that fits with expectations for the supportive behavior. Hence analysis of supportive messages will encompass the ways the content is evaluated in terms of the relationship.

Several strategies are available to measure relationship ties at the levels noted above. Distance can be assessed in terms of magnitude estimation judgments of the relative psychological "closeness" or "distance" perceived by the source and receiver toward one another. Magnitude distances could be indicators of the degree to which supporters and recipients identify with each other. Discrepancies in their independent judgments could be not only a further indicator of the distance but an indicator of the reliability of the estimates.

Recent measures of relational uncertainty (based on the original theoretical work by Berger & Calabrese, 1975) focus on the extent to which interactants can predict one another's behaviors, feelings, attitudes, and so on. An example is an eight-item scale by Parks and Adelman (1983) that included such questions as how confidently one felt he or she could predict the other's behavior, attitudes, values, preferences, and responses, how well one understood the partner's behaviors, how frequently the partner's verbal or physical behavior is surprising, and so forth.[2]

Attributional judgments of motive could be based on external/internal causes of behavior. Internally driven causes would be most likely attributed to sources with whom the receiver has an interpersonal tie. For example, I am likely to expect my mother or my best friend to be supportive because we are close and they personally want to help me. In contrast, if I feel my best friend is just helping because she feels obligated as my friend (external attribution), I am more likely to perceive the supportive behavior as less helpful (and perhaps even toxic to our relationship). Conversely, motives would be most likely ascribed to external inducements (such as role obligations or cultural norms) in more distant, noninterpersonal relationships.

Communication Network Analysis

As noted in Chapter 2, the study of support networks is a complicated analysis of data representing many structural properties. In this section, we move beyond discussion of specific architectural features of support networks to a review of critical and interrelated methodological issues that emerge. These include the study of the range of network contact versus network integration and qualitative versus quantitative approaches to data collection, interpretation, and analysis.

Range of contact versus integration. Researchers who study support networks often ask respondents to report the number of supporters they have along a set of indicators (see, for example, Ward et al., 1984). However, the study of communication networks is the study of scale as well as the *integration* among a set of contacts. Integration (or density) is the extent to which those identified in a support network are connected to one another.[3] As was demonstrated in our review of the network literature in Chapter 2, whether

one's support contacts are densely linked/integrated has important positive and negative implications for the focal individual's
well-being.

However, integration can be estimated in at least two ways, each
of which has a distinct conceptual impact on the nature of the findings. The simplest method is to have the respondent evaluate how
well his or her contacts know and interact with one another. This is
easily handled by presenting the respondent with a grid or matrix
of contacts listed by column and row and having him or her fill in
the extent of connection perceived among all possible pairs.

This method provides a measure of subjective integration, or the
respondent's viewpoint on the clustering among his or her respondents. It is useful for the researcher in understanding how knowledgeable subjects are of their communication environments and
their subjective assessments of the functionality or helpfulness of
their perceived relational arrangements. This method is also instructive to respondents by increasing their awareness of the nature of
their networks and relationships. This can give greater insight into
the ways their individual relationships overlap, help or hinder one
another, and whether network extensions to other groups would
broaden one's visibility and access to new ideas, and provide greater
freedom or personal control in one's life.

This method does not usually include verification of interconnectedness from the personal reports of contact from each member
of the support network. Many respondents do not know or over- or
underestimate the interrelationships among their supporters. Certainly their perceptions are often what is most useful in understanding the meaning of support to them. While gathering data from the
network members of the focal subject is costly in terms of time and
resources, it may be essential for some respondent groups and
research questions. Populations such as psychotics or the elderly,
for example, may have impaired memories that distort their reports
of their kin and friends. Direct interviews with network members
will be critical for the researcher who is seeking a more objective
measurement of the coordination among an elderly widow's ties
(to stay with her during her grief periods, help with moving, financial expenses, and in developing a new social pattern). Thus the
reports of connection among a set of ties are best evaluated by interviewing each contact person in the network to examine their
reports of relational ties. This also helps to gain an assessment of

second-order zones (those persons to whom the focal individual is indirectly connected through his or her direct links) to understand the potential of broader channels of support. Clearly, research designs that encompass assessments of density/integration from both the respondent and contacts provide comparison opportunities to explore areas of data convergence and divergence.

Quantitative versus qualitative studies. The study of support networks also depends on the perspective one takes in the research. Most quantitative studies involve survey administration to large respondent samples. The self-report measurement yields data about respondents' perceptions of their range of contacts and characteristics of their networks. The benefits of these strategies include *efficiency* (the time and cost of collecting and managing large data sets is manageable and rapid); *comprehensiveness* (whole systems such as self-help groups or organizations can be studied at individual, dyadic, group, or macro levels); and *stability* (such procedures facilitate multiwave administration of network instruments to assess the degree of change perceived among relationships in the system).[4] However, if these techniques are conducted as the lone measurement of support networks, disadvantages include *recall difficulties* (if not cued properly, respondents can have difficulty remembering the nature of their contacts with others, particularly if they are disabled or experiencing stress); *respondent suspicion* (subjects may be reluctant to cooperate with the researcher's efforts because in naming support contacts they may feel they violate a sense of trust through lack of anonymity); and *lack of interaction and nonverbal data* (the lack of process data precludes insight into ways that providers and recipients structure their network relationships).

To the extent that support networks are socially constructed phenomena, a viable research goal that falls under the rubric of interpretive research is to understand the complexities of becoming a member of a particular social unit (Albrecht & Ropp, 1982; Van Maanen, 1981). To do so, the researcher must use operations of sufficient scope and flexibility to match the phenomena (Albrecht & Ropp, 1982; Daft & Wiginton, 1979). Qualitative methods including nondirective and directive one-on-one and focus group interviewing, participant observation and naturalistic structured observations can assist the researcher in looking for "deep structures" to explain functional or dysfunctional patterns in support networks.[5]

Of course there are drawbacks to these methods, chiefly that they are time-consuming and limit one's focus in assessing the array and scope of a support network. A central problem with some qualitative/interpretive studies is also the lack of a coherent theoretical framework to drive the observational process, data reduction and analysis procedures, and interpretation of the data. Without a strong theory for explanation, the researcher is left with making sense of a bank of data with little to guide the claims drawn and perhaps stumbling from overreliance on intuitive and primitive analyses (see Miles, 1979).

If possible, the collection of both quantitative and qualitative network data could improve the knowledge gained from the research process. One can more easily verify individual perceptions of links, and tie the nature of the communication in the network more directly to the context (Sokolovsky & Cohen, 1981). For example, one's questions can better account for features of the setting in which supportive interactions usually occur (for example, the home, organization, or meeting house) that may affect the interaction. More respondent perspectives (in addition to the researcher's observations) can be drawn into the data pool and intensive follow up questions can be framed from information gleaned at the broad quantitative level (see a discussion of this in Albrecht & Ropp, 1982).

In addition, a qualitative research component can round out the quantitative network evaluation by enabling subjective evaluations of the network ties. Some researchers have used respondents' identification of their support networks (often based on quantitative survey data) as the single criterion for evaluating the presence of affiliation and network bonding (Sokolovsky & Cohen, 1981). However, as shown in research by Ward et al. (1984), subjective evaluations of each network relationship can have stronger empirical relationships with well-being than mere assessments of the quantity of social involvement.

Concluding Note

In highlighting some central measurement issues we argue that support comes in many forms (through interaction and relational structure) and the interpretation of that support is based on perceptions of one's needs and relational partner. Hence measurement that assesses the role of supportive communication in a person's life should analyze over time the "net effect" of support[6] in terms of the uncertainty reduced and the control that is increased.

Of course, these issues of interaction, change, and effect cannot be assessed without a focused attention to the ways the population-specific or setting-specific contexts influence the communication process of support. As Eckenrode and Gore (1981) note, context needs to be a consideration in interpretation of support given that the surrounding frame gives meaning to the encounter (see Part II in this volume). The trade-off of precise description is that contextual embeddedness of findings limits generalizability. But such detailed knowledge may be the answer to understanding the complex causal aspects of the relationship of support to well-being.

NOTES

1. Several helpful reviews of social support methodology have been published recently in the literature, including papers by Bruhn and Phillips (1984), Cohen, Mermelstein, Kamarck, and Hoberman (1985), Depner, Wethington, and Ingersoll-Dayton, (1984), House and Kahn (1985), Lin, Dean, and Ensel (1981), and Tardy (1985).

2. Parks and Adelman (1983) reported internal reliability coefficients for this scale at .80 and .81.

3. Often expressed as a ratio of actual to theoretically possible links. A value of 0.0 would represent no interconnectedness among a set of contacts while a value of 1.0 would represent perfect connectedness.

4. See Albrecht and Ropp (1982) for a larger discussion of the strengths and weaknesses of quantitative and qualitative network data.

5. See discussions of qualitative/interpretive research methods by Miles and Huberman (1984), Light (1979), and Adelman (1986).

6. We acknowledge Professor Edward Gross for his comments on this notion of "net effects" of support (from Dept. of Sociology, University of Washington).

PART II:

Contexts of
Supportive Communication

4

Support in Family Ties:
Stress, Coping, and Adaptation

LEONA L. EGGERT

Families, we've found, really do make it easier to live a healthy life. Beyond their general power to help deal with stress, families can help people make very specific changes. . . . The people closest to us may be able to do the most for us. (Gurin, 1985, p. 40)

When family members interact in ways that nourish and sustain—socially support—one another, they create an essential building block of the larger social order. Despite a voluminous general family literature, studies of the family as a support system have been infrequent and weakly conceptualized (Dean & Tausig, 1986). Moreover, though family communication is a central construct in most family perspectives, these frameworks have largely ignored communication theory.

Of particular interest here is the accumulation of evidence linking a family's ability to cope with stress as a function of its social support patterns (see McCubbin, Cauble, & Patterson, 1982).[1] Most family theories posit family communication as a central facilitating dimension between stress and health (Epstein, Bishop, & Baldwin, 1984; Olson, Russell, & Sprenkle, 1984). Accordingly,

AUTHOR'S NOTE: I wish to acknowledge the extensive editorial and expressive support of Annalee Luhman in the preparation of this chapter and the helpful comments of Teri Albrecht and Mara Adelman.

this chapter provides a selective review of theory and research examining the association between communicated kin support, family stress, adaptation processes, and family well-being. This review reflects my three goals for the chapter: first, to discuss the family as a special context for studying social support; second, to offer a synthesized family support process model useful for integrating research in the communication of family support; and finally, to summarize theoretic and research challenges central to the study of family support. An in-depth literature review is not claimed; rather, the goal is to model the process of family support.

Overview of the Family

Although families have been variously defined, most definitions of the modern family are consistent with that offered by Fitzpatrick and Badzinski (1985, p. 687): "a small kinship structured group whose primary function is the nurturant socialization of the newborn." More useful for our purposes, Bochner's (1976, p. 382) definition underscores the importance of communication to how a family comes to be defined:

> An organized naturally occurring interactional system, usually occupying a common living space over an extended time period, and possessing a confluence of interpersonal images which evolve through the exchange of messages over time.

The important notion is that family members have life-long involuntary ties and mutual obligations: "Families can't dissolve as easily as friendships" (Argyle & Furnham, 1983, p. 483). There are indicators, however, that the modern family is less stable than in previous times and survives because it has adopted new forms (Pilisuk & Parks, 1983; Sussman, 1980).

The contemporary family is a critical context for the study of support. Historically, families were multifunctional, economically interdependent units. Described as "emotional icebergs," nineteenth-century family members were assigned highly instrumental roles in order to survive as self-sufficient units. By comparison, today's families are left with only three major functions: *child care and child rearing, facilitating members' psychological well-being*, and *giving economic assistance* (Malson, 1983). Moreover, these functions are no longer the family's alone. Peers also socialize adolescents (Adelson, 1980; Eggert, 1984; Schwartz & Baden, 1973) and the government increasingly assumes responsibility for the aged (see Brubaker, 1985). Indeed, in view of continuing societal changes, Fitzpatrick and Badzinski (1985) go so far as to argue that families have in fact only one job left to them—that of providing emotional care for their members. There is some consensus for this view; Malson (1983, p. 46) suggests that "the most important function of social support systems may be to provide someone to rely on, to listen to, and offer advice about problems and concerns."

Family Support Functions and Health

Family support is the communication—verbal and nonverbal—between family members that reduces uncertainty about routine and stressful family situations, individual family members, or family relationships. It functions to enhance perceptions of personal and family control in the member-to-family and family-to-community fit (see also Chapter 1).

A review of the literature shows that family support functions to fulfill basic human needs for attachment (Bowlby, 1977), dampen the effect of physical illness (Gallagher, Beckman, & Cross, 1983) and depression (Lin, Dean, & Ensel, 1986), ward off stress and enhance family adaptation (McCubbin & Patterson, 1983b; Pearlin, 1984), and provide cues for general social role performance (Kagan, 1977) and positive parenting (Brandt, 1984). Numerous correlational studies show a positive association between social support and mental health. Longitudinal studies demonstrate the predictive power of social support and future psychosomatic symptoms, psychologic complaints, and depression (Cutrona, 1984; Holahan, 1983; Lin, Woelfel, & Light, 1986; compare Biegel, McCardle, & Mendelson, 1985). Finally, Caplan (1976) claims, based on empirical evidence, that family support functions as a feedback guidance loop, source of ideology, problem-solving guide, concrete source of aid, haven for rest, reference and control group, and validator of identity.

The emphasis in the research findings on support and health outcomes is that people in supportive social environments "are in better health than their counterparts without this advantage" (Kessler, 1982, p. 261). This research is grounded in both complementary and competing theoretic models. Despite differences among models tested and modified, most posit family communication as the critical dimension between stress and health (see Olson & Miller, 1983, 1984).[2]

Of course it is through communication that families create meaning and coherence in daily life, celebrate life's joys, adapt to life's sorrows. Instruction, support, self-identity, ideology, and philosophy are all accomplished through communication. This brief review of the family support literature and the narrowed family responsibilities noted earlier underscores the need for a better understanding of family communication, stress and adaptation.

Family Stress and Adaptation

One list of the top ten stressors challenging modern families includes the following:

(1) economics, finances, budgeting
(2) children's behavior, discipline, sibling fights
(3) insufficient couple time
(4) lack of shared responsibility in the family
(5) communicating with children
(6) insufficient "me" time
(7) guilt for not accomplishing more
(8) spousal relationship (communication, friendship, sex)
(9) insufficient family playtime
(10) overscheduled family calendar (Curran, 1985)

Certainly stressful stimuli confronting families are not limited to major crises such as hunger, serious illness of a family member, or death. Finite resources, small annoyances, conflicting goals, and difficult interpersonal communication situations are the daily bread and butter for the family (Burgess, 1981). Minor but continuous stressors can take on an exaggerated importance and ultimately "pile up" to levels of conflict or crisis proportion (McCubbin & Patterson, 1983b). Indeed, mounting stress and conflicts may lead to greater negative family interactions implicated in "the dark side of families" (see Bolton & Bolton, 1986; Finkelhor, Gelles, Hotaling, & Straus, 1983; Gelles, 1979, for reviews on family violence). Hence it is the confrontation of both normative and nonnormative problems that typically require adjustments and adaptations by the family.

We know much about family adaptive processes as a result of the recent theoretic advances of researchers who have systematically tested systems models.[3] Many of these models identify communication as a central dimension and thereby set the stage for isolating the role of communicated support in adaptive family processes. Of particular value here is the Family Adjustment and Adaptation Response (FAAR) model (McCubbin & Patterson, 1983a, 1983b) of family functioning in response to life stressors.

The Family Adjustment and Adaptation Response Model

McCubbin and Patterson's (1983b) FAAR model, based on longitudinal studies of families under stress, represents synthesis of several lines of research, integrating work in family systems (e.g., Olson et al., 1984), critical family transitions (e.g., Mederer & Hill, 1983), family paradigms and problem solving (e.g., Reiss & Oliveri, 1983a, 1983b; Klein, 1984), adaptive coping and support processes (e.g., Menaghan, 1983; Pilisuk & Parks, 1983). Hill's (1958) ABCX family crisis model variables are redefined and family response processes are included. The following demonstrates a family's response to typical strains and stressors according to this model.

Family stress and crisis. McCubbin and Patterson's (1983b) redefined double ABCX model is summarized by two conceptual equations:

Precrisis Equation:

A (stressor event) × B (existing family resources) × C (family perception and definition of the event) ⟶ X (the crisis) ⟶ (Postcrisis Response)

Although the first equation depicts a crisis outcome, the crisis need not occur if the family can use existing resources and define the situation in a way that maintains family stability. For example, say a family has a heated argument over their son Brett's (age 15) plummeting grades (As to Ds) on entering high school (factor A). The parents are emotionally distraught (factor B). With the help of Brett's counselor, they confirm the situation as serious but correctable (factor C). They hire a private tutor for sessions three times each week, even though this means stretching financial resources (factor B). This situation is *stress*—that is, it is a subjectively upsetting event (Pearlin & Schooler, 1978), demanding adjustment in existing family resources, both financial and emotional. Thus stress is a *"demand-capability imbalance."* A crisis would occur, for instance, if the parents incur many financial debts because of the private tutor, or should they find their son is not attending the tutoring sessions, becomes implicated in drug use, is suspended from school, and threatens to run away. Hence a crisis is a demand-capability imbalance plus a *family instability phenomenon* calling for restructuring or new coping strategies.

If a crisis does occur, the postcrisis equation applies:

Postcrisis Equation:

aA (pile-up of stressors) × (bB [existing and new resources] × cC [perception of X + aA + bB], where bB × cC is defined as "coping") ———→ xX (Maladaptation)

Here again, maladaptation (xX) does not necessarily result if the crisis is resolved. Bonadaptation can occur if the family coping element (i.e., bB × cC) functions to resolve X (the crisis) and reduce aA (the pileup of stressors or family demands). Thus family stability could be restored.

Family adjustment and adaptation phases. In a further expansion of the double ABCX model, McCubbin and Patterson (1983b) integrate *process components* of family responses to stressors and crises. These variables and processes are illustrated in Figure 4.1 and describe how families manage life's hardships. This model provides the arena for later defining communicated family support in relation to its central variables and processes.

In Figure 4.1, note first that the family response is best viewed in the same two phases already described—the *adjustment phase* (as the response to a stressor) and the *adaptation phase* (the response to a crisis). The adjustment phase depicts the process dimension of resistance; the adaptation phase describes the processes of restructuring (at level 1) and consolidation (at level 2). The A, B, and

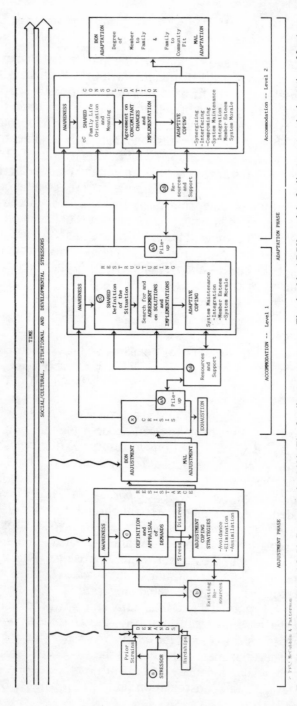

From H. I. McCubbin and J. M. Patterson (1983b). The family stress process: The double ABCX model of adjustment and adaptation. *Marriage and Family Review*, 6, p. 23. Copyright 1982 by Haworth Press. Reprinted by permission of Haworth Press, New York.

Figure 4.1 FAAR: Family Adjustment and Adaptation Response

C factors change over time. A family begins by appraising and adjusting to demands (C). Should maladjustment occur here, a new "shared definition of the situation" becomes necessary (cC). Finally, the crisis event and restructuring prompts consolidation in the "family's life orientation and meaning" (cC). Similarly, different steps of the problem-solving process and discrete coping strategies appear in the resistance element of the adjustment phase, and in the restructuring and consolidation elements of the adaptation phase. When the outcome of the adjustment phase is maladjustment, or when a major crisis event occurs, the adaptation phase becomes operative. Restructuring and consolidation become necessary during the adaptation phase and lead to a final outcome of bonadaptation to maladaptation. Pearlin and Schooler (1978, p. 6) hypothesize that bonadaptation is facilitated by supportive

> (1) responses that change the situation out of which strainful experience arises; (2) responses that control the meaning of the strainful experience after it occurs but before the emergence of stress; and (3) responses that function more for the control of stress itself after it has emerged.

Finally, McCubbin and Patterson (1983b) point out the cyclical nature of family adjustment and adaptation processes. If bonadjustment is the outcome of the adjustment phase, only this phase is repeated. Families can keep repeating the adaptation phase, where maladaptation can recycle directly back to crisis, or to consolidation, consolidation can cycle back to restructuring, and restructuring can return to a crisis state. A severe family crisis or a "revisiting" of old unresolved crises may result in "exhaustion" as an exit mode, and family dissolution could be one concomitant outcome.

The FAAR model is useful for integrating communication theory (for example, see Dance, 1982) in the adaptation process. The model accounts for the influence of time, sociocultural, situational, and developmental stressors and can thus incorporate research efforts about critical family transitions or life stages and studies focusing on social problems facing the family. Studies of message patterns and sequence (e.g., Street & Cappella, 1985) could be pursued in relation to these. In addition, much of the work on family paradigms and attributional processes explains differences in the C and cC elements of the FAAR model (such as the influence of the family's perception and definition of minor and major family life events). This element could benefit from "coordinated management of meaning" (Cronen, Pearce, & Harris, 1982), uncertainty reduction (e.g., Berger & Bradac, 1982; Berger & Douglas, 1982), or constructivist (Delia, O'Keefe, & O'Keefe, 1982) communication theory. And the research results explaining family problem solving and family adaptive coping strategies informs our understanding of how families resolve crises, why some families adapt well, and how and why some families survive despite hardships while others adapt poorly. Finally, research on family problem solving and crisis resolution would benefit from small group communication perspectives (e.g., Fisher, 1982; Hirokawa & Poole, 1986; Poole & McPhee, 1985; Scheidel & Crowell, 1979).

In sum, the resistance, restructuring, and consolidation elements of the FAAR model are clearly family communication phenomena—for example, how a family defines and interprets stressful situations, how members decide a course of action, how members stabilize meaning and implement solutions—all are constituted by *family communication*. These adjustment and adaptive coping mechanisms are a function of resources and support.[4] The adjustment and adaptation continuums represent the health outcome factor in our global model (see Figure 4.2).

The Family as a Communication Support System

Efforts at defining and operationalizing family social support have proliferated during the past ten years.[5] Family researchers have often tested their conceptualizations of support by studying people in ordinary and stressful life events, observing what support was given and received, by and to whom, for what purposes or problems. These "content by source by situation" matrices consistently showed that social support is exchanged across situations by communication between people, providing both support givers and receivers with specific outcomes.

Four major premises can be drawn from the extensive investigations of support: (1) Most family support occurs through communication; (2) the mere existence of family ties (relationships) is considered social support; (3) the content of family ties (messages that get exchanged) can be on a supportive/nonsupportive continuum; and (4) communicated support modifies such family functions as nurturing, instructing, socializing, and family accommodation/adaptation responses to family stressors. These empirical and theoretic efforts also suggest four essential components of any conceptualization and operationalization of communicated family support: (1) a *support component* or the content of support exchanged; (2) a *social network component* or the nuclear and extended family relationship ties, the family resources; (3) the *support process;* and (4) *outcomes* of family support. Having explicated family adjustment/adaptation as outcomes, the other three components warrant clarification and discussion.

Support Dimension

Lin (1986b) operationalized and confirmed two dimensions of support: that is, *expressive and instrumental,* while Brown (1986a) tested House's (1981) conceptualization, finding a global (unidimensional) rather than a multidimensional construct. Building on these, I extend their definition to include information, advice, and affirmation, and advance the following claim: *expressive* support indicators include affectional, affirmational, or esteem-enhancing communication, whereas *informational/instrumental* support includes informational, guidance/problem-solving communication, and instrumental interaction time. Whether these expressive and informational provisions are actual or perceived is important in both routine and crisis life events. For instance, Brett may be receiving considerable actual positive reinforcement (expressive support) from his parents to improve his grades, and tutoring assistance (informational support) for the same purpose. However, he perceives this help as pressure and negative feedback and decides his parents think him inadequate and a "loser." He concludes he is not getting much support. However, our calculation would show *perceived* support at one end and *observed* support at the other end of the continuum[6] (see also Chapters 1 and 3).

Table 4.1 shows a synthesized conceptualization of the *support* dimension based on the empirical and theoretic literature reviewed. Expressive communication indicators (input and output) for amount

TABLE 4.1

Conceptualizing the Support Dimension

Support Elements	Input	Communication Indicators	Output
Expressive Support Element	Perceived and Actual: Amount of Interaction/Companionship • Shared leisure activities • Frequency of communication Affective Quality of Interaction: • Frequency of positive versus negative exchanges • Frequency of conflicts, disagreements • Tension management communication Level of Intimacy/Affection • Messages of love, liking, comfort • Messages of affirmation, positive reinforcement Level of Commitment • Expressed bonding/binding • Expressed trust		Communication development/nondevelopment Relational development/disengagement Esteem enhancement/esteem loss Expressive support competencies
Informational/Instrumental Support Element	Perceived and Actual: Amount of Informational Support • Advice, suggestions or directives • Specific information • Guidance feedback • Problem-solving exchanges Amount of Instrumental Support • Participation in child-rearing/care • Participation in routine household tasks/problems • Participation in crisis resolution, important life events		Adequacy of information processing Adequacy of guidance/problem solving Informational support competencies Adequacy of routine and crisis support Instrumental support competencies

90

of interaction, level of intimacy, and level of commitment are depicted and closely parallel those identified by Fitzpatrick and Badzinski (1985) and in two confirmed measurement models of relational development by Eggert and Parks (in press), and Parks, Stan, and Eggert (1983). Besides these typical provisions we add an affective quality of interaction indicator to measure tension management and the ratio of positive to negative exchanges—predictors of marital development/disengagement and satisfaction (Burgess, 1981; Gottman, 1979). Thus expressive support (sometimes called emotional support) is a set of messages exchanged rather than a psychological property of persons (see Gottlieb, 1985). Informational/instrumental family support indicators are also primarily constituted by communication. As evident in the FAAR model, much of what support resources affect are the family's appraisal process and information processing/problem solving used to select courses of action and coping strategies. At its heart then, the support construct is conceptualized as a communication phenomenon.

Social Network Dimension

The *social* aspect of family support means access to and use of family network support sources. This definition is consistent with social resource theory and network perspectives (Cobb & Jones, 1984; Gottlieb, 1981; House, 1981; Lin, Dumin, & Woelfel, 1986; Mueller, 1980; Pearlin, 1984; Turner, 1981; Wellman, 1981) that focus on internetwork relationships and structural variables (Hammer, 1981b; Pearson, 1986).

In Table 4.2, and following Eggert (1984), LaGaipa (1981), Lin (1986a), and Parks et al. (1983), the social dimension of family support is separated into layers: the *confiding partners, social networks,* and *community-at-large* levels. Departing from Lin, we divide the social network level into *nuclear family* and *extended family* sources to reflect primary and secondary groups (Homans, 1950). Each social network level is further defined by various family subsystems including dyads, primary family triads or larger clusters, and secondary family clusters. Each contributes to the total support resources available within a family. The community level is a "resource pool" from which intimate partners develop and where families become integrated.[7]

TABLE 4.2

Conceptualizing the Family (Social) Network Dimension

Social Network Elements (Support Resources)	Indicators
Intimate Confidant Relationship(s): Adult/Adult forms • Marital couple • Cohabiting pairs Other family dyadic forms • Sibling-sibling • Parent-child	Perceived and Actual: Range of "confiding" relationship(s) Anchorage (duration and complexity) of relationship Availability for routine and crisis support Frequency of contact/shared activities
Nuclear Family Household Form: Family unit forms • Single career family • Dual career family • Single-parent household • Remarried nuclear family • Remarried bihousehold family • Intergenerational kin family • Experimental family Dyadic subsystems • Parent-child–e.g., mother/daughter or son, father/daughter or son, parent/adopted daughter or son • Sibling-sibling–e.g., brother/sister, sister/sister, brother/brother, twins, siblings due to remarriage, adopted sisters, brothers • Intergenerational dyads–e.g., adult child/parent of origin, adult child/ inlaw parent, grandparent/ grandchild, etc. Triadic/cluster subsystems–e.g., • mother-father-child, • mother-infant-toddler, • father-child-adolescent, etc.	Perceived and Actual Network structure (size, density) Range of direct contacts Anchorage of relationships Availability for support Frequency of contact/shared activities
Extended Family Network Form: Total specified family unit Subsystem clusters–e.g., nuclear units Dyadic subsystems–e.g., adult child/ parent or inlaw parent or grandparent/ or grandchild, aunt or uncle/ nephew, niece, and so on Triadic subsystems–e.g., mother/ mother-in-law/infant, father/ mother-in-law/father-in-law, and so on	Perceived and Actual: Network structure (size, density) Range of direct contacts Anchorage of relationships Availability for supportive exchanges Frequency of contact/shared activities
Community Network Form: Friendship involvement Coworker involvement Neighborhood involvement Other nonkin involvement	Perceived and Actual: Network structure (size, density) Range of direct contacts Anchorage of relationships Availability for support Frequency of contact/shared activities

Contemporary families consist of at least six forms (Feldman & Feldman, 1985; Skinner, 1982; Sussman, 1980): the single career family, intact nuclear family with husband as provider (13% of all households fit this definition); single-parent households (16%); remarried nuclear families (11%); and experimental families (multiadult households or cohabiting pairs [4%]). In addition, there are growing numbers of binuclear families—postdivorce families that span two households (Hayes & Hayes, 1986). Previous a priori definitions of the nuclear family are inadequate. The modern American kinship pattern is not necessarily an isolated nuclear unit, but neither is it one of extended kinship. Rather, families define themselves by commitments to procreation *and* chosen ties, varying cross-culturally and intergenerationally (Bilge & Kaufman, 1983; Eiduson, 1980; Fischer, 1985; Gilford & Bengtson, 1979; Hoyt & Babchuk, 1983; Leigh, 1985; Turner, 1980).

Some of the assumptions underlying family support processes are reflected in the qualitative expressive and informational elements of the support dimension—that is, "relationships involving consensus (shared values, attitudes, and interests), obligation (feelings of mutual responsibility), and affection" (Pearson, 1986, p. 390). The network indicators of family support include reachability, content, function, and structure of contacts with each layer of resources.

Family Relationships

The *strength* of family tie supports (according to Lin, 1986a, and Weiss, 1974) includes *belonging ties* (to community networks), *bonding ties* (to family networks), and *binding ties* (to intimate family confidants). (See Table 4.3.) The strongest family tie support usually comes from intimate pairs such as marital couples and/or cohabiting partners (Burgess, 1981). The degree of proximity, accessibility, commitment, interdependence, and opportunity for intimacy is highest within the family, particularly within the marital dyad (Gottlieb, 1985). It is the intimate family couple that has the greatest potential for the widest range of support provisions (Argyle & Furnham, 1983; Weiss, 1974). But because the defining characteristic of strong-tie support is the "confiding" nature of the relationship (Lin, 1986a), strong-tie support can also come from other family members such as siblings. (See Adelman

TABLE 4.3
Linking the Support and Social Dimensions of Family Support

Family Network Elements	Support Elements		Output
	Input		

Intimate Partner Relationship(s):
• Marital couple/cohabiting partner
• Family member confidant
	Perceived and Actual:
	Range of "Confiding" Relationship(s)
	• Expressive support exchanges
	  (availability, reciprocity,
	  amount/frequency)
	• Informational/Instrumental messages
	  (availability, reciprocity,
	  amount/frequency)
			Adjustment/Adaptation Levels:
			Marital status satisfaction
			Expressive support adequacy
			Instrumental/Information
			  support adequacy
			Relational satisfaction
			Relational commitment

Nuclear Family Form:
• Specific family unit
• Dyadic subsystems
• Triadic subsystems
	Perceived and Actual:
	Strength of Strong-Tie Family Support
	• Expressive support exchanged
	  (amount, availability, reciprocity)
	• Informational/Instrumental exchange:
	  (amount, availability, reciprocity)
	Structure (size, density)
	Range of Direct Contacts
			Adjustment/Adaptation Levels:
			Family solidarity
			Family support satisfaction
			Member to family fit
			Parental satisfaction

Extended Family Form:
• Specified family unit
• Dyadic subsystems
• Triadic subsystems
• Subsystem clusters
	Perceived and Actual:
	Strength of Weaker-Tie Kin Support
	• Expressive support exchanged
	  (amount, availability, reciprocity)
	• Informational/Instrumental exchange:
	  (amount, availability, reciprocity)
	Structure (size, frequency of contact, density)
	Range of Direct Contacts
			Adjustment/Adaptation Levels:
			Family solidarity
			Family support satisfaction
			Family to family fit

Community Network Form: • Family friendship network • Family neighborhood network • Other nonkin networks	Perceived and Actual: Involvement with Friends and Other Nonkin Home-Based vs. Community-Based Activities Structure (size, frequency of contact, density) Range of Direct Contacts		Adjustment/Adaptation Levels: Family to community fit Support satisfaction

and Siemon, 1986, for a review of the binding ties between twins.) Weaker-tie support usually comes from ego-distant network resources such as extended kin or community members and may typically be more uniplex (expressive or instrumental/informational) in nature.

Primary family ties are usually multiplex, expressive-informational exchanges. *Informational* support probably involves using family resources to achieve both routine family adjustment and crisis family adaptation goals—getting a ride to work, solving son Brett's school difficulties, gaining information about collecting unemployment benefits (cf. Lin, 1986a). *Expressive* support probably involves using family ties both as a *means* and an *end* in the FAAR processes—ventilating frustration, finding meaning in grandpa's death, affirming one another's self-esteem.[8]

Across dyadic, primary family, and extended kin network forms or subsystems, the *type of family relationship* should affect the amount and availability of support exchanged. The greater the shared characteristics of the interacting parties, the greater the likelihood of access to and use of each other for support (the homophily principle; see Eggert, 1984). Shared characteristics influencing homophily among individuals in family networks would include *gender* and *age* of members, *shared interests* and *activities* (e.g., church attendance, participation in sports), *shared role responsibilities* (e.g., parenthood), and *shared communication patterns,* among others.

Space limitations prohibit full treatment of influencing factors; however, a few illustrations emphasize how the availability and amount of support exchanged may vary because of homophily and other moderators. First, *gender* predicts which family members are most likely to give and receive support. Female kin are sought as confidants (Fischer, 1985), and as major providers of family health (Cooke & Lawton, 1984; Gurin, 1985; Pleck, 1985) and well-being (Argyle & Furnham, 1983; Reis, 1982). Second, differences in support exchanges across *intergenerational family ties* can be explained as a function of age similarity or perceived similarity of values and attitudes (Eggert, 1984; Rogers, 1980). Third, unique *family roles and interaction patterns* can influence the reciprocity of confirming versus confrontive support exchanges (Ting-Toomey, 1983) and functional versus dysfunctional parent-child interaction forms having positive versus negative consequences for support (Burgess, 1981). Fourth, geographic *proximity* can affect family interaction and use of the extended family for support; whereas some investigators found geographic distance and interaction negatively related (Leigh, 1985; Malson, 1983), others found "the car keys in our pockets and the telephones on our nightstands . . . alter how people help each other" (Fischer, 1985, p. 459). Similarly, close proximity may mean greater exchanges of support, however, it may also mean greater environmental stress (Holahan, 1983), conflict (Braiker & Kelly, 1979; Rozenblatt, Johnson, & Anderson, 1985), and need for greater use of tension management systems (Gottman, 1979).[9] Finally, the *family developmental life stage* and critical transitions can strongly influence the support process. Results of work focusing on these variables are summarized in Table 4.4.

Related research needs include both large surveys and small intensive comparative studies across different family forms. Social support theory will be enhanced by studying mutual-support systems during different life-cycle stages, in single-parent, dual career, and remarriage families, and families of differing cultures. Also, little is known about the benefits and costs of giving and receiving support from family.

A Proposed Model of the Structure of Family Social Support

In this section I address the dual issues of how family support functions to influence adjustment/adaptation in the Family Adjustment and Adaptation Response (FAAR) process (McCubbin & Patterson, 1983b), and why positive *family* relationships and social support are beneficial for health and well-being.

Supportive communication in the family functions to enhance perceptions of personal and family control in the member-to-family and family-to-community fit. Personal control theory posits that negative effects of family life stressors can be reduced by achieving personal control over stressful situations (Moos, 1981). Personal control is defined cognitively "as the way an individual interprets a threatening situation" and behaviorally "as the availability of a response that can directly modify a threatening event" (Holahan,

TABLE 4.4
Critical Family Life Stage, Transitions, and Family Support:
A Select Review

Family Life Stage/Transition	Family Network/Support Findings
Establishment Stage and Family Support	
Burgess, 1981	• adjustment to marriage required, perhaps espepecially by women; marital satisfaction begins to decline soon after the newly wed period
Milardo, 1984	• new couples socially withdraw from individual separate networks and simultaneously construct joint, couple-centered networks
First Parenthood and Family Support	
Brown, 1986a	• support activities during pregnancy may indeed be varied or a dominant unidimensional construct in pregnant couples
Brown, 1986b	• satisfaction with partner support, with other persons' support, stress, and chronic illness were important explanatory variables of health and differed for expectant mothers and fathers
Cutrona, 1984	• support appeared most strongly linked to depression and lower levels of stress in the transition to parenthood
Family with Preschooler and Family Support	
Fawl, in Burgess, 1981	• child-induced family conflict greatest with preschool children
Garbarino and Stocking, 1980	• re social context in child maltreatment, they suggest it influences parenting functions and coping abilities; necessary factors are enduring interpersonal relationships outside the immediate family, dependency needs satisfied, help in controlling impulses
Family with School Child and Family Support	
Brandt, 1984	• negative response style of maternal discipline was reduced when the mother felt supported
Cooke and Lawton, 1984 Seligman, 1985	• mothers bear the major burden of child care and housework, families with disabled children do not receive as much support from relatives, friends, and neighbors, as some previous studies of children with particular disorders have suggested
Family with Adolescents and Family Support	
Cauce et al. 1982	• found differences in the perceived helpfulness of the support dimension as a function of adolescents' age, sex, and ethnic background

(continued)

TABLE 4.4 Continued

Family Life Stage/Transition	Family Network/Support Findings
Eggert and Parks, in press	• strong positive associations between family social support and both friendship and dating relationship development
Family as Launching Center and Family Support	
Parks, Stan, and Eggert, 1983	• predominant relationship between social support and romantic involvement was positive and linear; greater romantic involvement meant greater contact with each other's family and friendship networks
Family in Retirement and Family Support	
Cheal, 1985	• (1) "the obligation of older actors to transfer resources to younger actors is stronger than the obligation of younger actors to transfer resources to older actors; • (2) the fulfillment of obligations is contingent upon the availability of transaction capacities; • (3) in contemporary North America, action capacities decline with advancing age at a faster rate than do financial capacities" (p. 500)
Cicirelli, 1985	• present support behaviors (helping, attachment) of adult children to elderly parents strongly influenced commitment to provide future help
McAuley, Jacobs, and Carr 1984	• older wives were more likely than older husbands to provide assistance to spouse and others
Stueve, 1983	• most elderly maintain involvement in social exchanges, particularly with those closest to them
Brubaker, 1985	• the fact is that American families are growing old; more reach this stage; they are "alive and well"
Bengtson and Robertson, 1985	• on grandparenting
Peterson and Quadagno, 1985	• on social bonds in later life and role of network in intimate relationships and social supports
Family Divorce—A Most Important Life Event	
Hetherington, in Burgess, 1981	• children find transition from 2-parent to 1-parent family difficult
Weiss, 1974	• kin groups often help out by providing companionship, lending money, extending a hand with child care and making homes available
Lin, Woelfel, and Light, 1986	• marital disengagement may substantially disrupt one's network to the point of making it incapable of providing necessary supports • recent marital disengagement linked with using new ties; whereas recently divorced used ties of longer duration (e.g., siblings)

1983, p. 550). Family control is thus the way the family interprets a threatening event and responds to modify it.

Family support functions to ameliorate stressors, helping members to perceptually control stress or crisis. Family adjustment or adaptation outcomes are thus modified. How family support influences adjustment/adaptation is modeled in Figure 4.2. The support resources component includes the four levels of possible social relations available to ego. These support resources link with support processes to reflect the availability and use of expressed and informational support from each source. These in turn are reflected in salience levels of actual (behavioral) and perceived (cognitive) support for either routine demands or the crisis depicted in the FAAR model. It is this salience level that reduces uncertainty and gives family members a sense of personal and family control. The control ratio influences and is influenced by the family's awareness of the demands, the definitions, and appraisal of the demands, and the resulting adjustment/adaptive coping strategies. Finally, the effectiveness of the coping strategies adopted to manage both routine and crisis events in turn determines the family location on the bonadjustment/-adaptation versus maladjustment/-adaptation continuum. In summary, the family resource elements combine with the support elements (expressive and informational) and function to enhance personal/family control and effect a reality-based (1) awareness of the demands or crisis, (2) accurate definition and appraisal of the demands, and (3) selection of adjustment-oriented and adaptive-oriented coping strategies.

The central hypothesis from this model is that defining and appraising the stressful events (and agreeing on appropriate adaptive coping and implementation strategies) are directly influenced by the control ratio (personal or family). These are linked with family support resources and processes in the model. Enhancing personal and family control thus facilitates acquisition of adjustment and adaptive coping strategies and competencies, and thereby enables family health and well-being (bonadjustment and bonadaptation) (see also Table 4.5).

Control perceptions and behaviors are viewed as outcomes of reduced uncertainty arising from the expressive and informational/instrumental support constituted in family relationships. When personal/family control *desired* does not equal control *possessed,* individual family members and nuclear units access and use kin

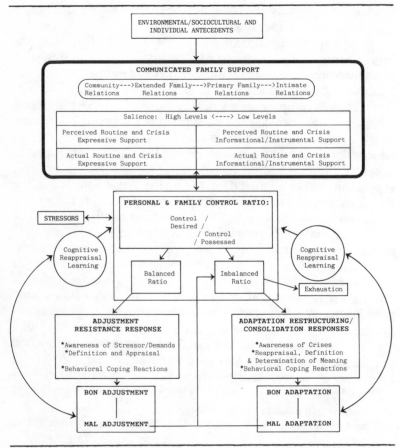

Figure 4.2 Dynamic Model of Family Social Support Structure, Process, and Outcome

for support in the adjustment and adaptation processes. Feedback from the experiences of family cognitive processing and meaning-making, as well as the effectiveness of behavioral coping strategies reinforces personal/family control and communication support competencies. The greater the uncertainty associated with a stressor or crisis event, the greater the salience of the event and need for family support. Such salience leads to attributions of causality for the event, changes in personal/family control ratios, and move-

TABLE 4.5

Uncertainty Reduction as an Explanatory Framework:
Predicting Outcomes of Family Support

Expressive Support—Personal/Family Control

Reduced Uncertainty and Family Intimacy/Affection and Commitment
Knowledge that one is loved; nurturing competencies
Basic sense of security; security promoting competencies
Related to individuation, shared family life, and socialization—member-to-family fit

Reduced Uncertainty and Family Interaction—Quantity and Quality
Individual developmental mastery—Identity
general personal competence
related to mental health
Social developmental mastery—Relational
interpersonal competence
community/societal competence
related to social health
Related to member-to-family and family-to-community fit

Instrumental Support—Personal/Family Control

Reduced Uncertainty and Family Informational and Appraisal/Guidance Support
Problem appraisal and problem solving framework
Problem solving competencies
General attribution-making competencies
Related to individuation, shared family life and socialization—member-to-family and family-to-community fit

Reduced Uncertainty and Family Instrumental Support
Routine family care and household maintenance
Practical service/aid competencies
Related to individuation, shared family life and socialization—member-to-family and family-to-community fit

---

ment to the resistance and/or restructuring phases of family adjustment and adaptation. The greater the known strengths of the family support processes, the greater the perceptions of personal/family control and the greater the likelihood of bonadjustment and bonadaptation effects.

In the early stages of appraisal of the stressors and/or crisis events, family members' attributions of the likelihood of bonadjustment/-adaptation outcomes will be positively affected by the strengths and deficiencies in the family support system (see Gottlieb, 1985). The greater the uncertainty of strengths and the greater the certainty of deficiencies, the greater the opportunity for maladjustment/-adaptation outcomes or learned helplessness (see Chapter 1).

Following Gottlieb (1985), the greater the certainty that family members can draw on their "savings account" of family support if necessary, the greater the likelihood of personal control and the less the need to make "a withdrawal." The *belief* that one has support available *if needed* raises self-confidence and a greater sense of mastery than would have occurred had one actually used the support. The greater the certainty of support resources, the greater the benign appraisals of family contextual threats and the greater the family's coping competency. Family communication thus shapes family support; family support shapes our competencies; family competencies shape our lives, philosophy, and our general health and well-being.

But families do not exist in a societal vacuum. As one of the "basic threads which tie the individual psychologically to the wider society" (Hooper, 1982, p. 522), the family is influenced by that wider society. Indeed, as family members share a variety of experiences—living in substandard or elegant accommodations, being a part of the cultural mainstream or periphery, their need for and ability to provide social support varies as a function of these intra-family and external environmental factors. While close physical proximity, frequent and extended interaction, life-span involvement, and shared meanings and values are characteristic of much family life, several *antecedent factors* may differentially affect the access and use of expressive and informational support across various family network members.

Socioeconomic status is a powerful predictor of the nature and extent of life crises a family must confront and often endure. It can also influence resources members are able to provide. Fischer (1985) found that as the education level of a family increases, members of that family become more dispersed and rely less on kin for support. Afro-American or black families, who are one of the most socioeconomically disadvantaged groups in America, form more support ties with kin than with friends because economic barriers restrict their geographic mobility (Malson, 1983).

Cultural variation, often in combination with the socioeconomic factors identified above, appears to reflect differing antecedent norms and values for the instantiation of kin support. Peters and

Massey (1983) characterized the social environment confronting blacks as a mundane, extreme environment "where racism and subtle oppression are ubiquitous, constant, continuing" (p. 195). This emphasis on persistent oppression—as opposed to an occasional crisis or misfortune—may explain differences in kin support patterns among blacks, as one case in point. Hence convergent or divergent levels of family support may well occur as a result of powerful socioeconomic and sociocultural antecedents.

In summary, I attempted to present a model of the role of communicated family support in the processes of family adjustments and adaptations to normative and nonnormative life stressors. The task ahead is to test empirically the structure and processes depicted. Throughout the chapter, an agenda of research needs and suggestions was developed; the list is long indeed. However, greater knowledge and understanding of how communicated support/nonsupport occurs in family relationships will mean knowing how families can make it easier, or more difficult, to live a healthy life.

NOTES

1. Inventories categorize and update this vast family literature on a yearly basis (see Olson & Markhoff, 1985, and the Family Resource and Referral Center's collection of bibliographic data).

2. Paradoxically, the scholars who make this conceptual link do not generally incorporate communication theory in their work. Conversely, neither have traditional communication scholars utilized the family as a context for study. Bochner's (1976) call for such attention notwithstanding, few studies have been published since (see Knapp & Struck, 1983); but see Fitzpatrick and Badzinski (1985) for a recent review of family communication.

3. See Burr (1982), Epstein et al. (1984), Feldman and Feldman (1985), Holman and Burr (1984), McCubbin et al. (1980, 1982a, 1982b, 1983a, 1983b), Miller (1986), Miller and Olson (1985), Olson and Miller (1983, 1984), Olson and Markhoff (1985), and Pratt (1982) for reviews and commentaries on the state of the art.

4. Several instruments are available to measure variables of the FAAR model, including the following:

FILE (Family Inventory of Life Events and Change): 71 items designed to measure a family's level of stress (normative and nonnormative life events experienced in previous 12 months), producing an index of family "pile-up"

FIRM (Family Inventory of Resources): 61 items in 5 major scales tapping family strengths, health, social support, and financial well-being

CHIP (Coping Health Inventory for Parents): 45 items tapping responses to managing disturbances in family functioning

5. Scholars as diverse as Brandt (1984), Brown (1968), Caldwell and Bloom (1982), Caplan (1976), Cauce, Felner, and Primavera (1982), Cobb (1976), Dean and Lin (1977), Dean and Tausig (1986), Eggert and Parks (in press), Gottlieb (1978), House (1981), Hammer (1981a, 1981b), Kahn and Antonucci (1980), Lin, Dean, and Ensel (1986), and Weiss (1974) have each tested and clarified this elusive construct. Still, consensus on what social support is has not been reached.

6. Both cognitive and behavioral approaches are meaningful methodologically and conceptually, thus important to measure when possible. We can begin to explain the effects of social network involvement on the individual or family only by measuring both actual and perceived levels (see Dumin & Woelfel, 1986; Eggert, 1984). These two variables may or may not be positively correlated, according to the literature. Some scholars suggest that cognitive perceived support may reflect the meaning to an individual whereas behavioral support reflects the "outsider's" view. Both can thus be treated as separate indicators of support, or the discrepancy could be reflected in a ratio variable of actual to perceived support.

7. The *family* as a unit of analysis has received little attention (see Fitzpatrick & Badzinski, 1985; Miller, 1986), with most researchers still studying individuals (e.g., Lewis, 1986; Poresky & Atilano, 1982; Pleck, 1985), marital dyads (e.g., Burke & Weir, 1982), or parent/child dyads (Eiduson, 1980), and triads (West et al., 1986).

8. When examining family support we advocate measuring family support content exchanged within *each* relationship type—including dyadic pairs, triads, and primary and secondary groups. Even a cursory understanding of the implications of this conceptualization can be gained by looking at some family relationship variables and predicting the differential levels of expressive and informational support available in each.

9. Cramped physical surroundings or extremely close proximity also have been implicated in family violence (Bolton & Bolton, 1986; Gelles, 1979).

5

Supporting Friends in Need

MARA B. ADELMAN
MALCOLM R. PARKS
TERRANCE L. ALBRECHT

Friendship is for aid and comfort through all the relations and passages of life and death.

It is fit for serene days, and graceful gifts and country rambles,

but also for rough roads and hard fare, shipwreck, poverty, and persecution . . .

So that a friend may well be reckoned the masterpiece of nature.

(Ralph Waldo Emerson, in Wilson, 1960, p. 44)

We have a need to talk about our problems and share our misfortunes. And the people we most often go to first are our close friends and intimates (Young, Giles, & Plantz, 1982). Developing close relationships with others is a central activity from birth to death (Angyal, 1965; Lowenthal & Haven, 1968). Whether transient or enduring, support from friends is profoundly linked to our sense of belonging and social integration (Parks, 1977a; Thoits, 1985), our ability to cope with the major life crises and transitions (e.g., Brown & Harris, 1978; Cobb, 1976; Silver & Wortman, 1980; Stroebe & Stroebe, 1985), and our overall sense of self-worth (e.g., Brown & Harris, 1978; O'Conner & Brown, 1984).

In order to delineate the support functions of close friendship we begin by comparing close friendships with other close relationships such as those with family and kin. Second, we set close friendships within the broader context provided by recent literature on the development of close relationships in general and apply that literature toward an understanding of how the giving and taking of support fits into the overall development and dissolution of friendships. Third, we extend this understanding to the role of friends in coping with major life crises and transitions such as physical and mental illness, old age, and, bereavement. While friends obviously provide routine social support, we believe that life crises and transitions provide paradigm cases in which the dynamics of social support in friendship can be seen most clearly. Finally, the chapter closes with an attempt to focus our appreciation of the supportive role of friendship even more sharply by examining recent research on loneliness and the absence of supportive, close friends.

The Nature of Friendship

Friendship is a slippery concept. Even if we limit the problem of defining friendship to North American and Western European models, consensus regarding the nature of friendship exists only at the most general level. Reisman (1979, p. 108), for example, defines a friend as "someone who likes and wishes to do well by someone else and who believes those feelings and good intentions are reciprocated." Argyle and Henderson (1985, p. 64) can be no more specific than to define friendship in this way:

> Friends are people who are liked, whose company is enjoyed, who share interests and activities, who are helpful and understanding, who can be trusted, with whom one feels comfortable, and who will be emotionally supportive.

The difficulty with such definitions, of course, is that they do not neatly differentiate friendship from other close relationships. In fact, most of the characteristics of friendship can, to one degree or another, be found in other close relationships (see Argyle & Henderson, 1985). Given this ambiguity, we believe that concepts like "friend" and "close friend" are best treated as social and cognitive labels. Their meaning is derived from the individual's act of labeling a relationship as a friendship rather than from some unique and theoretically specified conceptual domain.

Friendship is also a slippery concept because it is both a type of relationship and a quality that people attribute to other types of relationships. For example, people often view other types of close relationships as if they were friendships (e.g., "She's my cousin, but mostly she's my friend" or "My wife is my best friend"). People frequently count kin among their close friends. Conversely, people often treat close friends as if they were members of the family (e.g., "You're like a brother to me").

None of these observations should suggest that the vessel of friendship is an empty one, only that many other relationships also carry its cargo. Perhaps friendship can be distinguished from other relationships by negation. Marriage, for example, carries all of the expectations of friendship, but friendship does not carry all of the expectations of marriage. This naturally begs the question of what the expectations and characteristics of friendship are. Our admittedly nonexclusive manifest of characteristics includes the following factors: (1) voluntariness, (2) status equality, (3) assistance, (4) activity sharing, and (5) confidentiality and emotional support.

Voluntariness. We are born into a family, but we choose our friends. The perception of choice distinguishes friendship from most family, kin, and work relationships. No other close relationship except marriage contains such a strong aura of voluntariness. The perception of voluntariness may give the support received from friends enhanced value just because the recipient knows that it was given more as a matter of choice than of obligation. However, even this perception is subject to restrictions. The amount of contact one has with kin becomes increasingly a matter of choice in adulthood (Argyle & Henderson, 1985). Moreover, because friendships are often developed within a network of other friendships, one's actual freedom of choice may be bounded by definite social pressures to either develop or to maintain a given friendship within the network.

Equality. Close friendships are usually based on the shared perception that the participants are social equals (Reisman, 1979, 1981). In her study of adult friendship choices in the United States and Germany, for instance, Verbrugge (1977) found that equality in social status was a major factor in close friendship choices. Less developed friendships, on the other hand, need not always be among equals. Many relationships growing out of work settings are "mixed friendships" in that they contain both elements of equality and inequality. Superiors and their favored subordinates, for example, often mix both a work relationship and a friendship. Elaborate rule systems are often needed to signal shifts from one relational domain to another. In general, however, the closer the friendship is perceived to be, the more equality the participants will perceive.

Assistance. Most studies of friendship emphasize that friends are people who help each other (e.g., Argyle & Henderson, 1985; Crawford, 1977; Parlee, 1979; Reisman, 1981; Reisman & Shorr, 1978). In contemporary U.S. and Western European cultures, however, there are definite limits to the amount of tangible and task assistance expected from friends. As Allan (1983) notes, friends typically "care about" rather than "care for" each other. While short-term and minor assistance can be expected, long-term and significant assistance must usually come from kin or public agencies. In a study of men who had suffered from myocardial infarctions, for example, Croog, Lipson, and Levine (1972) found that support from friends was more of a supplement to support from family rather than a primary or compensatory form of support.

Activity sharing. Argyle and Henderson (1985, p. 84) observe that "above all we need friends to do things with, especially leisure activities, going out, and having fun." Obviously marital and family relationships also engage in activity sharing, but many of these shared activities are experienced with a sense of obligation rather than sharing for the joy of the activity alone. Shared leisure activities among friends can be more easily enjoyed purely for their intrinsic value. Friends also provide opportunities to share activities that are less enjoyable to the spouse or to other family members. Thus friends support us by giving us an outlet for activities not shared with family members and by giving us opportunities for enjoying activities without the larger relational implications so frequently a part of family life.

Confidentiality and emotional support. A major theme in the social support literature on friendship is the provision of emotional support, intimate confiding, and felt attachment (e.g., Allan, 1983; Argyle & Henderson, 1985; Bankoff, 1981; O'Conner & Brown, 1984; Quam, 1983). Friendships may serve as the primary sources of emotional support for unmarried persons, for adolescents experiencing the stresses of developing an independent identity, for men and women whose spouses are unsupportive, and for the elderly who have no kin living nearby (Argyle & Henderson, 1985). Friends may therefore at least partially compensate for inadequacies in other types of relationships. Even for those with many close family relationships, however, friends may serve as important sources of emotional support for at least two reasons. Because friendship networks tend to be less densely connected than family networks, individuals have a generally easier time keeping information confidential. Concerns for confidentiality and privacy figure prominently in people's subjective definitions of friendship (Argyle & Henderson, 1985; Crawford, 1977; Reisman & Shorr, 1978). In addition, friendships are sometimes more easily terminated than family and kin relationships. This fact provides individuals with a kind of "emergency exit" when the issues raised by the pursuit of emotional support become too disruptive to the relationship.

Dimensions of Relationship Development

Most of the literature on social support is based upon a tacitly static view of human relationships. The giving and taking of support are usually studied apart from the larger evolution of the relationships in which support occurs. Relationships are usually assessed in terms of the support they can provide with comparatively little attention to the consequences of the support process for the overall development of those relationships. We believe that such an approach results in an inherently limited view of the support process.

In the last decade or so, communication researchers and social psychologists have increasingly turned their attention from what might be called "single process" concerns (e.g., attraction, disclosure) to the broader question of how personal relationships develop and dissolve over time (see Altman & Taylor, 1973; Berger & Bradac, 1982; Berger & Calabrese, 1975; Burgess & Huston, 1979; Duck & Gilmore, 1981; Huesmann & Levinger, 1976; Kelley, 1979; Kelley & Thibaut, 1978; Knapp, 1984; Miller & Steinberg, 1975). Though a thorough integration of this literature with the literature on social support is beyond the scope of this section, we can draw on this rapidly expanding literature to identify the major dimensions of relationship development and to explore their implications for the process of social support.

What does it mean to say that a relationship has "developed"? Relationships "develop" in several directions at the same time and so there is no one answer to such a question. However, we believe that the following six dimensions provide a relatively comprehensive view of relationship development. Personal relationships can be said to develop as (1) intimacy and emotional attachment increase, (2) the breadth or variety of interaction increases, (3) the degree of interdependence or contingency increases, (4) communication codes become specialized, (5) cognitive uncertainty about the self and other decreases, and (6) the participants' social networks become intertwined. Changes in each of these factors are presumed to affect the others. Moreover, while our primary concern is with the development of friendships, these dimensions of development are general ones that can be applied to the development of virtually any close relationship.

Increasing intimacy and attachment. The most obvious and researched aspect of relationship development is self-disclosure and intimacy. This is the "depth" dimension of relationship development (Altman & Taylor, 1973; Levinger & Snoek, 1972). As a relationship develops, the participants typically disclose more personal information, express more positive and negative feelings, and express praise and criticism more openly (Altman & Taylor, 1973; Huston & Burgess, 1979). At a general level, this implies that the value or magnitude of rewards and punishments exchanged tends to increase as a relationship develops (e.g., Altman & Taylor, 1973; Aronson, 1970; Hatfield, Utne, & Traupmann, 1979; Huesmann & Levinger, 1976). In a longitudinal study of friendship development, Hays (1984), for example, found that development was associated with increases in the intimacy of behaviors exchanged. At a more specific level, the depth dimension implies that the intimacy of participants' conversations increases as their friendship develops (e.g., Altman & Taylor, 1973; Naegele, 1958; Parks, 1976). Interaction becomes more oriented around the distinctive characteristics of the individual than around the more generalized characteristics they may stereotypically share with others (Miller & Steinberg, 1975).

Along with increases in the intimacy of interaction come increases in a series of affective variables such as liking and loving (e.g., Huston & Burgess, 1979) and a number of cognitive variables associated with them. In one recent study of friendship development, for instance, Eggert and Parks (in press) found strong positive correlations among measures of liking, love, intimacy, perceived similarity, satisfaction with communication, and the expectation that the friendship would continue into the future.

These findings suggest that the depth dimension of friendship development is reciprocally related to social support. As a relationship develops, the opportunities to provide the more intimate forms of social support such as emotional support increase and the participants place greater value on the support they receive. And as the opportunity for and value of support increases, the development of the relationship is spurred onward.

Increasing breadth or variety of interaction. As a friendship develops, the participants come to interact not only about increasingly intimate concerns, but also about an increasing variety of concerns. This is the "breadth" dimension of relationship development (Altman & Taylor, 1973). Disclosure and conversation occur along a greater variety of topics (e.g., Altman & Taylor, 1973; Naegele, 1958; Parks, 1976). In the parlance of exchange theory the variety of resources exchanged increases as a relationship develops (e.g., Hatfield et al., 1979). This point is nicely illustrated by Hays's (1984) longitudinal study of same-sex friendship development. Hays found that pairs whose friendship developed tended to engage in more behaviors in more categories of interaction (i.e., activity sharing, task assistance, mutual disclosure, expressing emotion) than did pairs that terminated or failed to become closer over the three month period of the study. These findings suggest that closer friendships provide more different types of social support for the individual and that the ability to provide such variety contributes to the overall development of the relationship.

As a relationship develops, the participants also tend to interact in an increasing variety of settings and contexts (e.g., Huston & Burgess, 1979). Closer relationships are more portable, less dependent upon the particular situational context. This implies that close relationships can serve as sources of social support in a greater range of settings than can "weaker," less developed relationships (see Chapter 6 this volume).

Increasing interdependence and contingency. Relationships develop to the degree that the participants become increasingly interdependent (see Kelley, 1979; Kelley & Thibaut, 1978). What each receives becomes more contingent upon the actions of the other. Their individual goals and actions become more synchronized and intermeshed (e.g., Altman & Taylor, 1973; Huston & Burgess, 1979). Indeed, if the participants believe that the benefits of the relationship can also be obtained from a variety of other sources, the relationship is less likely to develop (Huston & Burgess, 1979).

Interdependence and contingency have several implications for the social support process. First, increasing interdependence creates increasing substitutability in the resources or types of social support. The individual who gives support in one area may be repaid by support in another area. Less developed or "weaker" social ties, on the other hand, tend to operate more often on a give and take of like resources (Hatfield et al., 1979). While this characteristic makes the coordination of a close relationship a more difficult task, it also increases the range of behaviors that can be used to reciprocate support and thereby decreases the probability that an inability to reciprocate with like resources will disrupt the overall relationship. In addition, increasing interdependence is usually associated with a lessening concern for immediate repayment of favors and assistance received. Close friends tend to be more tolerant of inequities in the support taken and given because, unlike those in less developed relationships, they can believe that they have a good deal of time and many ways to restore equity (Hatfield et al., 1979). Finally, these characteristics of interdependence imply that methodologies that examine only those support requests that are immediately reciprocated with similar resources will miss much of the richness of the support process in close relationships.

Increasing communication code specialization. Relationship development is not only characterized by an increasing depth and breadth of communication, but also by changes in the structure of communication. Waller and Hill's (1951, p. 189) comments about the communication of courtship pairs apply equally well to the communication of close friends:

> As a result of conversations and experience, there emerges a common universe of discourse characterized by the feeling of something very special between two persons. . . . They soon develop a special language, their own idioms, pet names, and jokes; as a pair, they have a history and a separate culture.

Code specialization occurs at several levels (Bernstein, 1964; Hopper, Knapp, & Scott, 1981; Knapp, 1984). Private slang or jargon may be developed. Conventional language forms may be given new meanings that are fully understood only by the participants themselves. Verbal statements may become abbreviated, incomplete. Or that which used to be verbally communicated may become communicated nonverbally.

Code specialization has both methodological and substantive implications for the study of social support. Observers given the task of coding interaction for its support value may simply miss much of what is happening in a close relationship unless directly aided by the participants. Moreover, the presence of a specialized or "restricted" code implies that the conversation of close friends subtly reinforces and supports their relationship in an ongoing way that is independent of its overt content (see Bernstein, 1964). However, because so much is implicit in these codes, their presence can also be a barrier to renegotiation and change when partners have difficulty talking about their relationship (metacommunicating) at a more explicit level (see Adelman & Siemon, 1986).

Decreasing cognitive uncertainty. Humans have a deeply set need to "make sense" of their social interactions (Heider, 1958). Much of what happens as a personal relationship develops is therefore contingent upon the participants' abilities to predict and explain each other's behavior; that is, to reduce uncertainty (Berger & Calabrese, 1975). Most theories of relationship development recognize the centrality of uncertainty reduction processes either explicitly or implicitly. As Parks and Adelman (1983, p. 56) point out, "No theory presumes that interpersonal relationships can develop when participants are unable to predict and explain each other's behavior." And, as we have emphasized elsewhere (see Chapter 1, this volume; also see Albrecht & Adelman, 1984), uncertainty reduction processes are also at the heart of the process of social support.

Uncertainty reduction involves creating the sense that one knows how to act toward the other, knows how the other is likely to act toward the self, and understands why the other acts the way he or she does (Berger & Calabrese, 1975; Berger, Gardner, Parks, Schulman, & Miller, 1976; Parks, 1976). As uncertainty is reduced, predictive and attributional confidence grow. So, too, do most other dimensions of the relationship between the participants. Measures of uncertainty reduction have been empirically linked to increases in the breadth and depth of communication, the frequency of communication in general and metacommunication in particular, measures of emotional attachment and attraction, contact with and support from the partner's network, perceived similarity, relationship satisfaction, commitment to the future of the relationship, and even with the overall stability of personal relationships over time (e.g., Berger & Calabrese, 1975; Berger et al., 1976; Eggert & Parks, in press; Parks, 1976; Parks & Adelman, 1983).

Increasing network contact and overlap. Whatever our inner experience of them may be, our personal relationships are also social objects existing within the broader context created by our surrounding social networks. How the participants in a developing relationship relate to those networks is therefore a vital dimension of the relationship itself.

The developmental course of a personal relationship is deeply influenced by network factors such as the extent to which the partners create an overlapping network of friends, perceive that each other's friends and family support their relationship, communicate with each other's networks, and are attracted to each other's friends and family. Research on friendship and romantic relationship development has shown that these factors are positively linked with the partners' emotional attachment for each other, their intimacy, commitment, perceived similarity, satisfaction, the frequency of their communication, and the stability of their relationship over time (e.g., Eggert & Parks, in press; Lewis, 1973; Milardo, 1982; Parks & Adelman, 1983; Parks, Stan, & Eggert, 1983).

Distinctive Roles of Friends
in Life Crises and Transitions

The supportive characteristics of friendships and other close relationships emerge most clearly when people encounter the major, seemingly inevitable, crises and transitions of life. These are obviously the times when support is most needed. They are also the times when people are most receptive to the influence and support of others (Caplan, 1964). Close relationships of all kinds serve some common functions in helping people through difficult times. While we will note several of these more common functions in this section, we will focus more on the distinctive ways in which friendships, especially highly developed ones, provide support for three very broad groups of people experiencing major life crises or transitions. These groups are those with physical or mental illnesses, the elderly, and those facing the death of a spouse.

Physical and mental illness. Much of the current interest in informal social support grew out of concerns with the mental and social needs of those afflicted with physical or mental illnesses (e.g., Caplan, 1974; Croog et al., 1972; DiMatteo & Hays, 1981). Beyond recovering from the specifics of the illness itself, patients also have to recover or create new social role relationships and socioemotional capacities (DiMatteo & Hays, 1981). Generally, friends contribute directly to the recovery process by increasing patient morale and responsiveness to rehabilitation (e.g., Finlayson, 1976), expanding social role functioning (e.g., Bloom & Spiegel, 1984), and perhaps even by extending life expectancy (e.g., Weisman & Worden, 1975).

One more specific way in which friends contribute to the recovery process is by referral support. Friendship ties, for example, that are not connected to family members are often valuable sources of referrals to psychiatric services (Horowitz, 1977). Family members and one's closely connected friendship network simply may not possess needed information. Or the individual may find it easier to ask a less connected friend where to get help. By the same token, friends may be a source of referrals for the patient's family as they seek help for the patient or help in coping with the strain of the illness on them.

One of the more pressing challenges facing those with a prolonged or severe illness is the need to make sense of their situation, to assemble ego-fortifying, adaptive cognitive defenses against an intolerable experience. Those close to the patient can be powerful sources for social comparison, validation, and ventilation (DiMatteo & Hays, 1981). Those who can allow the patient to talk freely about the illness and who can be less judgmental are often perceived to be especially supportive by the patient (e.g., Carey, 1974; Finlayson, 1976; Litman, 1966). In a study of men recovering from automobile accidents (Porritt, 1979), for example, the *quality* of contact with friends and other close supporters turned out to be a more critical factor than the sheer amount of contact. Quality of support included factors like empathic understanding, respect, and constructive genuineness. Close friends may be as good or sometimes even better sources of quality support than kin and family. In a study of men recovering from myocardial infarctions Croog et al. (1972) found that friends were considered as important as close kin for moral support. They added that friends may often give more support than some types of family and kin. In some cases, friends are an outlet when family members are unable to discuss the patient's concerns openly.

Friends also contribute to the recovery process by providing short-term physical, financial, or tangible assistance. As we noted earlier, friends are not usually the primary or long-term providers of such support. But to the patient, even small-scale assistance can mean a lot. Friends may have special expertise or resources not available from family or kin (e.g., advice on how to recover your tennis swing after a car accident, keeping track of what's going on at work). If nothing else, friends can help spread the little tasks of recovery around, thereby supporting both the patient and the patient's primary caregivers.

Friends serve as a source of release and reintegration for patients who depend primarily on family members. Family members may become overly protective. The patient may not request as much support as is needed for fear of overburdening family members. In either case, friends get us out of the house. They are valuable intermediaries between the family and the many broader social contexts into which the recovering individual must reintegrate. Indeed, contact with those outside the family is usually associated with positive recovery outcomes (e.g., Garrity, 1973; Hyman, 1971; Lewis, 1966).

Friends contribute to the recovery process not only directly, by helping the person afflicted with injury or illness, but indirectly, by helping family members who are taking the primary responsibility for the patient's recovery. Friends offer a release, if only temporary, from the strain and drain of caring for an ill person. They are especially useful when they can empathize with the family's plight either because of close personal association with both the family and the victim (e.g., Chesler & Barbarin, 1984) or because they are experiencing the same situation in their own families as in the case of friends made in self-help groups (Bloom, 1982; Fengler & Goodrich, 1979; see also Chapter 7). Support for the family may in turn help the patient. Schizophrenic children, for example, appear to make better progress when their parents have social outlets such as those to friends (Brown, Birley, & Wing, 1972). In fact the entire family seems less affected when the caregiver has these outlets (Mitchell, 1982).

The elderly. Old age is typically viewed as a period of social disengagement characterized by shrinkage in the size of friendship networks and by diminishing activity with friends (Argyle & Henderson, 1985; Cumming & Henry, 1961; Dickens & Perlman, 1981; Riley & Foner, 1968; Rosow, 1970). However, this view is subject to so many limitations that it is perhaps best left as a stereotype. The extent of disengagement appears to depend heavily on factors such as age, sex, marital status, social class, income, access to transportation, housing and neighborhood type, and health status (e.g., Antonucci, 1985; Dickens & Perlman, 1981; Chown, 1981). We know little about the relationships among or interactions between these variables because of limited theoretic development and limited use of multivariate analysis.

Recent reviews also contain no shortage of findings that either directly disconfirm or support a much more restricted version of the disengagement hypothesis (Chown, 1981; Antonucci, 1985). For example, Kahn and Antonucci (1983) found no differences in network size or the amount of support received when comparing subjects ranging in age from 50 to 95. They did find, however, that the number of people to whom one gave support declined with age. Moreover, it may not be so much a matter of sheer network size as having even a single close confidant to shield against the "insults" of aging (Lowenthal & Haven, 1968). Still other studies suggest that satisfaction with close relationships, including friendship, may actually be as high or higher among the elderly as among younger groups (e.g., Harris, 1975; Kahn & Antonucci, 1983; Veroff, Douvan, & Kulka, 1981). Further evidence indicates that serious social isolation is relatively rare and that many of those who are isolated were already isolated before they became elderly (e.g., Antonucci, 1985; Chown, 1981; Kahn & Antonucci, 1980).

Perhaps the best that can be said based on available research is that, while the image of widespread social isolation is undoubtedly exaggerated, disengagement and isolation are nonetheless real phenomena that exist in varying degrees for an undetermined number of people. More useful generalizations will come when researchers move beyond simple concerns with variables like network size to a more in-depth analysis of factors such as the degree of relationship development and the specific ways in which social support is communicated. Although friends appear to play all of the same support roles they played prior to old age (Antonucci & Kahn, 1983), they may also serve some roles more or serve distinctive roles. Friends, for example, may play a greater role in supporting one's perceptions of self-reliance during old age. Because it is a voluntary relationship emphasizing common interests and equality, friendship "sustains a person's sense of usefulness and self-esteem more effectively than filial relationships" (Blau, 1973, p. 67). Family and kin contacts, though they too become more important with age, may not be as satisfying as more voluntary, self-directed relationships like friendship (see Wood & Robertson, 1978). Certainly self-reliance suffers if one becomes too dependent upon friends, but a wide range of social support is available even within the restricted expectations of friendship:

> Older people and their friends and neighbors visit together, escourt each other to doctors, help out during emergencies, and assist with shopping. Above all, friends and neighbors provide important sources of socialization and affective supports, including tension reduction, over and above that supplied by the kinship system. (Cantor & Little, 1985, p. 758)

Friendship networks also play special compensatory functions for the growing number of "familyless elderly" (Cantor & Little, 1985; Cohen & Rajkowski, 1982; Stoller & Earl, 1983). Cantor and Little (1985), for instance, found that inner-city elderly without families had more extensive contact with friends and neighbors for social interaction and received a higher level of assistance than elderly with families.

Friends are significant even for those with families. In addition to the special potential of friends to sustain self-reliance as we already noted, friends are indirectly significant because of the support they can provide family members who care for the "frail elderly." Many of these family members are caught in the middle between the demands of caring for their elderly parents and their own children and/or the need to earn a wage (Brody, 1981; Farkas, 1980; Fengler & Goodrich, 1979). Friends help provide socio-emotional supports such as outlets for socializing and opportunities for emotional ventilation as well as instrumental supports such as temporary assistance with care (e.g., Cantor, 1980; Fengler & Goodrich, 1979; Gottlieb, 1983; Lowenthal & Robinson, 1976; Zarits, Reever, & Bach-Peterson, 1980).

Bereavement and widowhood. Losing a spouse ranks among the most stressful events of life (Argyle & Henderson, 1985). In addition to bereavement, the loss of identity, and the need to develop new skills for independent living, the loss of a spouse frequently leads to major realignments in the pattern of friendships. Disruptions in friendship patterns particularly affect widowed men who depended upon their spouse for social involvement and who now find themselves in a social environment with few other single men their age (Blau, 1961; Booth, 1972; Philblad & Adams, 1972).

The activity sharing and limited task assistance typical of friendship take on special importance for the widowed person who is adapting to the requirements of independent living. Friends help without making the widow overly dependent upon family, kin, and public services. Friends are especially supportive for the elderly widowed because, as we previously noted, the voluntary and egalitarian features of support from friends protect the individual's self-esteem and self-reliance in ways that support from family and public agencies can not. Friends who live nearby are the most valuable for the elderly widowed and indeed friendships with neighbors may be more important sources of support for this group than for other groups (e.g., Chown, 1981).

Friends also play a distinctive role in the bereavement process itself. The bereaved person may need to recount memories of their spouse and share feelings of profound sadness. Hirsch (1979) found that widows whose health deteriorated during the first year of bereavement tended to believe that others prematurely focused attention on the present or future without showing sufficient sympathy for their grief. Single and widowed friends may be perceived as better sources of emotional support during this phase of bereavement (Bankoff, 1981). In general, contact with friends appears to be more strongly related to the morale of the widowed than contact with family and kin (Arling, 1976). Friends and neighbors foster a sense of belonging based on reciprocal conviviality and norms of egalitarianism (Arling, 1976; Hess, 1972; Hochschild, 1973). In spite of their good intentions, family members may breed a sense of dependency. This is particularly true of the elderly widowed when previous parent-child roles may reverse.

Finally, friends play a unique role in recovering from the loss of one's spouse. The task of building a more independent life may require new social skills and the development of a new identity. Friends who are not connected strongly to the family network are in a better position to facilitate this process of changing self-perceptions, experimenting with new behaviors, and reintegrating into a broader social world (Hirsch, 1979; see also Chapter 2). Family members and those close to the family, on the other hand, may inadvertently slow the recovery process by reminding the widow of past roles or by failing to support needed changes.

Loneliness and Social Support

Researchers have increasingly recognized the mutual relevance of research on loneliness and research on social support (e.g., Gottlieb, 1985; Jones, 1985; Rook, 1985). Each research area is concerned with the profound consequences of deficits in close relationships for physical and mental health. Their complementarity illuminates future directions for theoretical and applied development. As Rook notes (1985), social support research has emphasized the "help-providing functions," while research on loneliness has focused more on the "pleasurable companionship and intimacy" found or not found in social relationships. Jones (1985, p. 225) contrasts research on loneliness and social support in the following way. While the former "begins with the subjective impressions of the lonely person and then looks outward for explanations of the discomfort"; the latter examines "issues from the outside inward," taking as its starting point the effects of the social network on recipient outcomes.

Loneliness is typically defined in terms of qualitative and quantitative deficits in the individual's social relationships (Perlman & Peplau, 1981). It is measured as both emotional and social isolation (Russell, 1982) and exists along a continuum ranging from the short-term to the chronic (Suedfeld, 1982). We believe the research on loneliness sharpens our understanding of the support process by delving into the personalities, the social skills, and the network structures of those who may be least capable, and therefore in greatest need, of developing close, supportive relationships.

Personality correlates of loneliness. Loneliness is more than simply being alone. It involves broader aspects of personality that influence not only the lonely person's behavior toward others, but also the lonely person's perceptions of others' behavior toward him or her (Peplau & Perlman, 1982). It includes "the way in which lonely people perceive, evaluate, and respond to interpersonal reality" (Jones, 1982, p. 244).

A large number of studies have examined the personality correlates of loneliness (for reviews, see Jones, 1982, 1985; Peplau & Perlman, 1982; Stokes, 1985; Watson & Clark, 1984). These studies typically characterize the lonely person as introverted, shy, low in self-esteem, socially anxious, susceptible to symptoms of depression and neurosis, and easily upset or distressed.

Watson and Clark (1984) have merged several of these personality correlates into a more general construct they call "negative affectivity." They note that people who are high in negative affectivity "tend to be distressed and upset and have a negative view of self" (p. 465) and tend to dwell "on their failures and shortcomings . . . to focus on the negative side of others and the world in general" (p. 483). Lonely people experience greater negative affectivity toward themselves, those with whom they interact, and toward people in general (Stokes, in press; Wittenberg & Reis, 1986).

Perhaps the most telling implication of this research for the social support process is that lonely people not only seek out social support less, but are also less "supportable." Their own negativism engenders negative responses from others. It also leads them to misinterpret and reject even sincere attempts at support. It is therefore self-perpetuating (see Wittenberg & Reis, 1986).

Social skill correlates of loneliness. One reason the chronically lonely have difficulty initiating and sustaining satisfying, supportive relationships is that they may lack the requisite social skills or, more properly, communication skills for doing so (Bell, 1985, in press; Jones, 1982; Jones, Hobbs, & Hockenbury, 1982).

Lonely people, for example, have difficulty initiating and managing self-disclosure (Stokes, in press). They tend to anticipate rejection and therefore share less of themselves with others (Jones & Briggs, 1983). Lonely people also respond in inappropriate, self-defeating ways to the disclosures of others, thus creating negative responses from others.

The general, communicative style of lonely people is characterized by low levels of attention and involvement. Jones et al. (1982), for instance, found that when lonely subjects interacted with strangers they made fewer references to their partner, were less likely to pursue topics initiated by the partner, and asked fewer questions. Bell (1985) found that lonely subjects were basically passive interactants. They talked less, interrupted less, gave less support through the use of vocal back-channels, and generally remembered less about the interaction.

In short, interactions with lonely persons frequently fall into the realm of forgotten or forgettable encounters as a result of the lonely person's lack of communicative skill. On a more positive note, social skills training has met with at least short-term success in improving the communicative involvement of lonely individuals (e.g., Jones et al., 1982).

Network correlates of loneliness. Loneliness is commonly associated with social isolation, but equating the two confounds the subjective experience of loneliness with the objective qualities of aloneness. Loneliness occurs when one's expectations for social contact are not met, while *aloneness* refers to the degree of social isolation that may or may not invoke feelings of loneliness (Peplau & Perlman, 1979).

Nonetheless, it is not difficult to identify conditions under which isolation or aloneness would also breed the subjective state of loneliness. Fischer and Phillips (1982), for example, identified two such conditions in their study of people who were severely isolated or who had only minimally rewarding social encounters. One of these was isolation from networks of work relationships. Fischer and Phillips found that nearly six times more nonworking males than working males were severely isolated. In addition, Fischer and Phillips found that geographic mobility created social isolation among newcomers during the first year of relocation. While this isolation lessened over time, even temporary removal from familiar networks can create both social isolation and loneliness. Similar effects might be observed among young adults making the transition to college life (e.g., Shaver, Furman, & Buhrmester, 1985).

Network density is also a correlate of loneliness. Indeed research suggests that it may be a stronger predictor of loneliness than network size because it provides "a sense of community, . . . of belonging to a group, which tempers feelings of loneliness" (Stokes, 1985, p. 988).

Summary

Friendship is among the most malleable of human relationships. It is best understood as a social and cognitive label given to relationships that are characterized by relative voluntariness, perceived equality, the give and take of assistance, sharing activities, confidentiality, and emotional support. While the labor and tangible assistance provided by friends is usually less than that from family and kin, friends are a major source of emotional support as well as a less dramatic, though no less significant, form of support, such as sharing a favorite activity or helping with daily tasks.

Not all friendships are the same. Studies that equate the number of friends with the amount of support miss the developmental dynamics of personal relationships that in turn ultimately reflect and shape the support process. Nor is it sufficient to evaluate the supportive resources of friendship the same way one might size up the goods on a market shelf. Simply assessing the degree to which certain types of support are available ignores both the impact of the developmental process on the provision of support and the effects of the support process on the life of the relationship. Relationships, like persons, develop and change over time. In order to better describe how friendships develop, we drew upon recent literature in communication and social psychology to identify six interrelated dimensions of change. Close personal relationships such as friendship develop as (1) intimacy and emotional attachment increase, (2) the breadth or variety of interaction increases, (3) the degree of interdependence or mutual contingency increases between the participants, (4) communication codes become specialized, (5) cognitive uncertainty about the self and other is reduced, and (6) the participants' social networks become more intertwined and overlapping.

Some of these dimensions have rather straightforward implications for the support process. The intimacy and breadth dimensions, for example, imply that the value and variety of supportive resources available to the participants will increase as a friendship develops. Other dimensions have more complex implications for the support process. Increases in mutual interdependence, for instance, facilitate support exchanges by allowing participants to repay interpersonal debts of one type with supportive resources of another type. However, increases in mutual interdependence also increase the time and energy required to manage the relationship. Increases in code specialization can have similar two-edged effects on the support process. While code specialization increases the efficiency of interaction and provides implicit ongoing support for the relationship, the implicit nature of specialized codes can make it difficult for participants to negotiate change openly and explicitly.

The distinctive contribution of friendship to the support process emerges most clearly when we consider the needs of those experiencing major life crises and transitions. We explored the role of friendship in coping with three general types of crises and transitions: physical and mental illness, old age, and bereavement. These are obviously not the only crises and transitions we face, but they are among the more common and typical. There are also obvious individual differences within each of these categories. Stereotypic images of a "generic elderly," for example, are rapidly becoming inaccurate.

Nonetheless, our analysis revealed distinctive functions of friendship that cut across the variety of major life crises and transitions. We call these distinctive functions the "four Rs" of friendship: referral, relief, reintegration, and reliance. Friends are often vital sources of information and referral support for those experiencing physical and mental illness and for their families. Friends may be close enough to the problem to be well informed, but not so close as to be immobilized. Friends also serve a relief function. They provide minor, but vital, physical assistance and tangible support as well as major social outlets for those strained by the demands of caring for the ill and the frail. Friends can also offer relief and release for those directly experiencing crises and transitions by giving them social and emotional outlets that family and kin may be unable to provide. Recovery from a major crisis or passage through a life transition usually entails some sort of social reintegration. Friends are often in a distinctive position to bridge the gap between the sometimes suffocating world of the family and the frequently frightening world of new behaviors and new relationships. By the same token, friends can provide assistance that reinforces the suffering person's sense of self-reliance and control. Because friendships are voluntary and based on equality and common interests, asking for help from friends is often less damaging to perceptions of personal control and self-reliance than asking for help from family and kin.

Finally, no discussion of friendship and social support would be complete without at least brief reference to those who have the most difficulty making and maintaining friendships, the chronically lonely. Lonely people evaluate themselves and others in negative terms. Their low self-esteem is reflected by social anxiety and distress. Their low level of communicative skill is reflected in poor attention to the dynamics of interaction and reduced ability to manage the give and take of interaction in general and self-disclosure in particular. Their loneliness is exacerbated by external events that shrink the size of their networks and by low-density networks that fail to provide a minimal sense of involvement and belonging. Sadly, the chronically lonely emerge as people who desperately need the support of others, but who behave in ways that make them unsupportable and who are likely to devalue what little support they do receive.

6

Beyond Close Relationships:
Support in Weak Ties

MARA B. ADELMAN
MALCOLM R. PARKS
TERRANCE L. ALBRECHT

As a waitress you really get to know the "regulars" around here—
what they eat, their little habits, daily ups and downs. Between
pouring cups of coffee you share bits of gossip, local news, details
from their fishing trips. And even though you don't have a close
relationship—they notice if you've been away from work. I like
that. And when they're sick, you kind of miss them, too. (interview
with a waitress)

"Help is where you find it" (Cowen, 1982, p. 1). The sorrow
revealed to a passing stranger, the spiritual guidance obtained from
a priest, the consolation offered by a waitress are all exemplary of
the types of social support found beyond our circle of family and
close friends. Whether central or peripheral in our lives, these
weaker social linkages extend the range of social support tradition-
ally found among closer relationships.

The term *weak ties* refers to an umbrella concept that covers a
wide range of potential supporters who lie beyond the primary network of family and friends. The term was apparently first coined
by Granovetter (1973) to describe relationships that lacked the intimacy and frequency of interaction characteristic of stronger ties to
family and close friends. We shall use the concept of weak ties to

include the spectrum of informal sources of social support found within the community. Our use of the concept is generic and shall include others' labels such as "other-helpers" (Gershon & Biller, 1977), "urban agents" (Kelly, 1964), and "natural caregivers" (Collins, 1973).

Much of the current interest in weak ties stems from the recognition that professional health care delivery systems are unable to reach large segments of the population suffering from psychological distress (President's Commission on Mental Health, 1978). While recognizing the natural limits of private and governmental agencies is surely one reason for focusing greater attention on weak links, there are also other compelling reasons for our concern with weak links. Beginning the chapter with a section on the general significance of such ties, we go on to examine the features of weak links in greater detail. Next we develop an enriched theoretic perspective for social scientific study by examining their distinctive functions. Finally, we elaborate on the current literature by cataloguing many of the various types of weak links that so frequently provide direct and indirect social support in the life of the individual.

Significance of Weak Ties

Comparatively little attention has been devoted to the ways that less highly developed, weaker relationships can and do provide support in our daily lives (Cowen, 1982). The vast bulk of the research and commentary on social support has focused on the stronger, closer ties characteristic of family and kin relationships, marital relationships, and close friendships. In part this bias toward the study of close personal relationships probably reflects a more general "ideology of intimacy" (Parks, 1982; Sennett, 1977) that often devalues the significance of weaker, more impersonal relationships. It may also partially reflect the fact that stronger ties are more memorable and identifiable for the subject and researcher alike.

Whatever the reasons for paying less attention to weak ties, it is now clear that they play unique roles in the provision of social support and in the development of social support networks. At a minimum, weak ties are significant in a developmental sense because all strong ties were once weak ties. Even if one is concerned only with the most developed, intimate relationships within a support network, a comprehensive understanding will require examining how weak ties develop into strong ones (see Chapter 5, this volume). This is particularly true given that most personal networks experience a certain amount of turnover in membership and therefore experience an ongoing need to replace stronger ties from the ranks of weaker ones.

In addition, weak ties often provide support during periods when our stronger ties are disrupted. Crises like the death of a family member, sudden unemployment, divorce, and long-term illnesses usually result in disruptions in the network composed of stronger ties. Divorce, like the death of a family member, directly eliminates close potential supporters (e.g., Rands, 1981). Other crises simply reduce the amount of support available across the close network (e.g., Eckenrode & Gore, 1981). Still other life transitions such as geographic mobility can limit access to strong links at the very time when they are most needed (e.g., Fontaine, in press; Shuval, 1982). In all of these cases, weak ties assist people through times of crises in ways that their stronger ties can not.

For many people, weak ties provide compensation, albeit limited, for a lack of strong ties. The current emphasis on close, intimate relationships ignores the fact that many people either do not desire strong ties or are incapable of developing them. Weak ties may provide a vital lifeline to those who lack the requisite social and cognitive skills for intimate relationships. Those clinically identified as socially avoidant or extremely shy probably fall into this category. So, too, may those suffering from a variety of mental illnesses but who are outside of an institutional setting (e.g., noninstitutionalized schizophrenics, see Cohen & Sokolovsky, 1978). We might include some of the more mobile homeless in this category as well. Still others may deliberately avoid close ties as a result of personal beliefs in independence, self-reliance, and the desire for an eccentric life-style. For example, Lally, Black, Thornock, & Hawkey (1979) found that older women living in SRO (single-room occupancy) hotels often viewed themselves as self-sufficient and therefore not particularly in need of close relationships with others. Weaker links to hotel staff were frequently vital for these women who avoided more involved relationships.

Finally, and perhaps most importantly, only weak ties can transcend the limitations of our stronger, more enduring social ties to family and friends. These limitations of strong ties can take many forms. Networks of strong ties may act as "barrier forces" that limit individual freedom and action (Levinger, 1979). For example, a person experiencing a religious conversion may seek support from weaker, newer ties to counteract united opposition from his or her network of strong ties. Strong ties may be suffocating. Albrecht and Adelman (1984), for instance, note that the acquisition of new information and social identities is discouraged by "fortress families" whose tight interconnections retard change and innovation. Dependence on highly insulating social networks can prevent individuals from reaching out to needed physical and mental health professionals (Freidson, 1970; Horowitz, 1977). Moreover, strong ties are often limited by the expectation of mutual reciprocity. Those suffering from chronic illnesses, for example, sometimes react to support attempts by close friends and family with discomfort and anxiety because they do not believe that they will be able to reciprocate (Froland, Pancoast, Chapman, & Kimboko, 1981; Greenberg, 1980). For such people, support from weaker links will not create such intense discomfort. The expectations of weaker links are generally less extensive and more easily reciprocated (see also Chapter 2 in this volume).

Thus our weaker social relationships contain the seeds of stronger, more intimate relationships, help compensate during times of crisis when our close relationships are disrupted, are accessible to those with lower levels of communication skill, and can liberate us when our circle of intimate relationships proves too confining. We shall now turn to a more detailed examination of the features and functions of weak links to illustrate how weak links provide these benefits.

Features of Weak Ties

Weak ties are limited relationships. More specifically, such links are limited along three general dimensions: their internal or dyadic features, their relationship to other sectors of an individual's social network, and their physical and temporal context. Ironically, these very limitations yield the accessibility, predictability, and freedom from which the various benefits of weak ties flow.

Dyadic features. Close relationships develop in part (as we discussed in more detail in Chapter 5), as a result of increases in the degree of mutual interdependence and the intimacy and variety of interaction between the participants. Weak ties, being less developed relationships, typically exhibit lower levels of interdependence, intimacy, and variety (see Huston & Burgess, 1979; Kelley, 1979). Mutual interdependence is lessened because what is rewarding or costly is more easily identified and because "payment" for goods and services is expected rather immediately. Interaction in weak ties usually emphasizes resources whose value is commonly understood and easily negotiated (see Hatfield, Utne, & Traupmann, 1979). While strong ties usually develop strong emotional attachments and interact about intimate topics regularly, such attachments are lacking in weak ties and discussion about intimate topics occurs only sporadically within highly limited contexts. While strong ties interact about a wide variety of topics and exchange a wide variety of resources, the interaction of weak ties is usually restricted to fewer topics and a narrow range of resources. Weak ties are "noninterpersonal" in the sense that interaction is based on rather stereotypic information concerning the other person's cultural and social background. The fact that weak ties can operate effectively with such generalized information reduces the amount of energy that must be expended to obtain support and thereby extends the range of people from whom we can draw support (Miller & Steinberg, 1975; see also Chapters 1 and 5).

The way in which these characteristics of exchange and interdependence among weak ties minimize obligation and relational development can be seen in Wentowski's (1981, p. 603) description of immediate exchange in the social support networks of the elderly:

> Exchanges are instrumental—a means to an end. . . . Individuals often verbally spell out what they expect ("Drive me to the airport and I'll pay for your gas"). In the folk taxonomy of network helpers, immediate exchange is practiced between the least involved categories of individuals (often labeled as "friendly acquaintances," "social friends," and "neighbors who speak" . . .). The medium of exchange is impersonal—often money, sometimes goods or objects whose exact market value can be calculated. People feel little obligation beyond the immediate transaction.

Strong and weak links can also be distinguished by the manner in which uncertainty is reduced. Uncertainty is reduced in close relationships by extensive exchanges of personal information, similarities, and interaction with the other person's network (e.g., Berger & Calabrese, 1975; Parks & Adelman, 1983; see also Chapter 5). However, in less developed, weaker social links uncertainty is reduced as a function of highly constrained role definitions and well understood limits on the scope and duration of interaction (Albrecht & Adelman, 1984).

Finally, the use of specialized communication codes differs in strong and weak links. The distinctive personalities and experiences of the participants in a close relationship breed specialized ways of communicating verbally and nonverbally (e.g., Knapp, 1984; see also Chapter 5). While specialized codes also occur in weak ties, they are more frequently a function of the participant's roles and contexts rather than of their personal characteristics. The technical jargon of health professionals, for example, says less about the personality of any one user than it does about broader roles and contexts.

Network features. Perhaps the most distinctive feature of weak ties is their placement within the broader personal networks of individuals. Weak ties are more likely to be unfamiliar with each other and with the individual's strong ties. That is, the density of parts of a network containing strong ties is typically much higher than the density of parts of a network containing weak ties (Granovetter, 1973). Put another way, the social fabric of a person's communication network is woven far more tightly in those sectors composed of strong ties than in those sectors composed of weak ties.

The generally lower density of the weaker links within the individual's network facilitates uncertainty reduction and the pursuit of social support in several interrelated ways. Because weak ties tend to be more or less safely detached from the hub of the individual's social circle, they have less potential to transmit information back to the individual's primary network of strong ties. This network distance enhances perceived anonymity and allows people to seek information and support without having to deal with the uncertainty of how those in primary relationships might respond. The sexually active female teenager, for example, may avoid discussing issues of contraception with close friends and family, but may safely discuss contraception with weak links who are socially distanced from her primary network. Weak ties also provide contexts in which the individual may experiment with new behaviors and new identities without the burden of being held accountable by those one sees more regularly. Finally, because of their relative detachment of strong ties in a network, weak ties serve to extend the range of information to which the individual has access. More people can be reached indirectly through one's weak ties than through one's strong or more intimate relationships (Granovetter, 1973; Rapaport & Horvath, 1961). Thus access to new ideas and people is facilitated more by one's weak ties than by one's strong ties.

Contextual features. In addition to their distinctive internal structure and placement within the participants' broader communication networks, weak links may be distinguished from strong links in terms of a series of contextual factors. First, most weak ties exist within a more restricted range of contexts than most strong ties. That is, many weak ties have interaction in only one place. Talk with the hairdresser always occurs at the salon, confession occurs only at church, a visit to the physician always occurs at his or her office, and so on. Strong ties, on the other hand, have more portable relationships. Their behavior will, of course, be contextually influenced, but not to the degree it will among weak ties. In fact the influence of the physical context may be so profound that interaction becomes difficult when weak ties are encountered outside their normal surroundings. Running into your physician's nurse at the supermarket, for example, may result in a momentary failure to even recognize the person and then in uncertainty as to what to say or do.

Most weak ties also exist within a restricted temporal context. Interaction has a clearly understood time limit. In stronger, more intimate relationships, however, it is often assumed that discussion about a given topic will continue until the topic is exhausted. If an interruption should occur, it is assumed that the topic can be taken up again at a later time. Weak ties often do not share these expectations for returning to the topic. While this obviously limits the breadth and depth of conversation, it also provides a sense of freedom and relative anonymity that often allows individuals to disclose far more than they otherwise would.

Finally, many weak ties can exist within a more restricted range of communication channels than strong ties. Intimate relationships usually require at least some face-to-face interaction in their development and maintenance. Many weak ties, however, develop within the electronic context of telephone services, computer bulletin boards, and a host of other emerging technologies currently being laid over more traditional restricted channels like the mails. The use of restricted communication channels in weak ties obviously extends individuals' access to information and social support far beyond what might be gained purely through face-to-face contact. Restricted communication channels such as letters or the telephone also provide individuals with a comparatively anonymous way to disclose highly personal or potentially embarrassing information (e.g., Albrecht et al., 1986; Shapiro, 1980).

The Distinctive Functions of Weak Ties

The distinctive features of weak ties breed distinctive functions in the social support process. In this section we apply and extend previous theoretic work (Granovetter, 1973; Parks, 1982) in order to identify four special support functions of weak ties: (1) extending access to information, goods, and services, (2) promoting social comparison with dissimilar others, (3) facilitating low-risk discussion of high-risk topics, and (4) fostering a sense of community.

Extending access to information, goods, and services. While the number of close relationships one has is typically rather small, the number of weak ties is often extremely large, running into the hundreds if not thousands. Thus weak ties provide greatly extended access to information, goods, and services by virtue of their greater number alone (Parks, 1982). However, the role of weak ties in extending access is enhanced even more by virtue of their special position within the individual's social network. Because weak ties tend to be less connected with one's strong ties and with each other, they reach much further out into the community than do strong ties alone.

"Community agents" and "urban agents" such as clergy, teachers, retail salespersons, bartenders, hairdressers, and lawyers demonstrate the reach of weak links in our lives. Gurin, Veroff, and Feld (1960), for instance, found that 42% of adults report seeking out clergy when dealing with personal problems. Clergy are typically trained in assessment and intervention methods and have extensive contacts to use for the purposes of referral. Given these skills and the fact that one's link to clergy is relatively confidential, the clergy can offer "stigma-free assistance" (Brodsky, 1968; Gershon & Biller, 1977) and function as gatekeepers to formal health care and social services.

Some "agents" such as hairdressers, bartenders, and shopkeepers represent much less formal weak links. Nonetheless, they acquire bits of information related to their neighborhood that enable them to function as conduits of social support. We know of one colleague, for example, who got a management position in a bank when her local bartender reported to her that one of his other customers was planning on leaving the position.

Perhaps the most explicit examples of how weak links function to extend access to information and services can be found in volunteer agencies. Telephone hotlines for cancer patients, for instance, often put cancer victims in touch with very specific information such as where to purchase wigs, to get assistance writing a will, or to purchase cookbooks for those undergoing chemotherapy. They often provide direct referrals to counselors who specialize in life-threatening issues.

Promoting social comparison with dissimilar others. Social comparison is a process through which we create and evaluate our own perceptions against the background of others' situations and experiences (Festinger, 1954). Wills (1983) has observed that those seeking support use social comparison as a means for both self-evaluation (i.e., using others for normative comparison) and self-enhancement (i.e., using others for enhancing self-esteem).

Close relationships tend to develop between people who are perceived to have similar values, attitudes, and life-styles (e.g., Altman & Taylor, 1973; Berger & Calabrese, 1975; Berscheid & Walster, 1978). Therefore it is not surprising to find that networks of strong ties tend to be rather homophilous groups (Erickson, 1982; Granovetter, 1982; Schlenker, 1984). Weak ties, on the other hand, do not depend on similarity as extensively for their development and maintenance (Granovetter, 1973, 1982; Parks, 1982). The restricted relational structure and context of weak ties as well as their comparatively disconnected position within the individual's larger network tend to ease the need for similarity. Thus our weak ties open into a world of distinctive perspectives and reference points and of people who differ not only from the self, but from each other as well.

Because they bring us into contact with dissimilar others, social comparisons to weak ties play a special role in the support process. Self-evaluation is facilitated by comparison to weak ties because they provide a greater variety of information and thus a better ability to judge how typical or normal our own behavior is. Moreover, weak links may give better, more accurate comparison information when they involve experts or specialists whose knowledge goes beyond that of ourselves and those with whom we have close relationships (Parks, 1982).

Social comparison to weak ties can also serve the self-enhancement function identified by Wills (1983). Self-esteem tends to be less damaged by negative comparisons to dissimilar others than to similar others (Hakmiller, 1966; Mettee & Smith, 1977; Parks, 1982; Wills, 1983). One of the most common ways self-enhancement occurs is by downward comparison to those whose circumstances are worse than our own. We are regularly urged to "count our blessings" by comparing our lot to that of people less blessed. Such comparisons can be comforting even for individuals facing a life threatening crisis. Taylor (1982), for instance, found that cancer patients sometimes coped by comparing themselves to other cancer victims who were not doing as well.

Facilitating low-risk discussion of high-risk topics. In recent years it has become increasingly common to view the self-disclosure process as part of a larger process of personal and interpersonal boundary regulation (e.g., Altman, 1975; Derlega & Chaikin, 1977; Parks, 1982). Weak links, as we have noted, tend to be bounded relationships. They may be bounded by their role expectations, by their comparative lack of connection to the rest of the individual's network, or by restricted physical and temporal contexts. All of these factors combine to produce a set of boundaries within which high-risk topics can often be discussed at low risk. Thus high-risk topics are often raised with bartenders and cab-drivers because the individual knows that the role of each implies distinct limits on the range of response, that the information is not likely to get back to friends and relatives, and that whatever the other person's response the relationship is easily terminated.

Several of the characteristics of weak links also combine to reduce the individual's concern with saving face when disclosing risky or negative information. Concern with saving face is less when listeners are unlikely or unable to pass their evaluations along to others, when their evaluations can be more easily discounted, and when the disclosure does not have to interact with those listeners in the future (Brown, 1968; Brown & Garland, 1971). These factors are more likely to be found among weak ties than among strong ties. Thus, as Shapiro (1983) points out, communication with weak ties allows individuals to seek social support for issues that are simply too threatening to raise with stronger ties.

Fostering a sense of community. The concept of "community" is an unusually elusive one. It has been the ideological vehicle for those who wish to reject the present either by longing for a safer, simpler time or by dreaming of future utopias (Fischer, 1977). It has been raised to mythical proportions by countless advertisements and commercials tugging at our emotions with images of life along tree lined streets, neighbors who are like family, and families who are too perfect to be ours. Therefore it is probably inevitable that most people's everyday sense of community is a psychological one, a perception.

The perception of belonging to a community is aided in at least two ways by weak links. First, interactions with weak links promote psychological attachment or identification with one's community. Because of their ability to bring us into contact with diverse groups, weak links extend our knowledge and our sensitivities to those who reside beyond our primary networks (Granovetter, 1973). Weak links spread information about communitywide concerns and triumphs to those who are not directly involved and thereby create a sense of larger identification. We may identify more strongly with the accomplishments of a local sports team, for example, when we know somebody who knows one of the players. By the same token, we may identify more strongly with the tragedies of others when we know people who know the victims.

Second, weak links contribute to our sense of community through their role in fostering collective action. Stripped down to the level of their close relationships, most personal networks lack the resources to alleviate problems like crime, poor schools, inadequate laws, commercial encroachment on residential areas, or pollution. This is not to suggest that there is nothing the individual can do about such problems, only that the individual who attacks these problems with the greater resources reached through weak links will be more effective.

The special value of weak links can be seen even in relatively simple collective actions such as block watch programs aimed at alleviating neighborhood crime. By allowing residents to reach beyond those neighbors, if any, with whom they have close relationships, weaker neighborhood linkages can tie a far greater number of people into the program, thereby increasing its effectiveness and reliability.

What holds for the microcosm of the neighborhood community also holds for the larger communal sense of a city, state, or nation. As Blau (1974, p. 623) emphasizes, our individual connection to these larger entities is based primarily on weak ties:

> Weak social ties extend beyond intimate circles and establish the intergroup connections on which macrosocial integration rests. The social integration of individuals in contemporary society is no longer based exclusively on the support of particular ingroups but in good part on multiple supports from wider networks of less intimate relations.

A Catalogue of Weak Ties

The various features and functions of weak ties discussed so far burst forth in an incredible variety of relationships. Our goal in this section is to further explore several major categories of weak ties including neighborly ties, familiar strangers, strangers-on-the-run, urban agents, and ties by telephone. Almost any effort to create a typology of weak ties is bound to be incomplete given the variety of weak ties and the fact that they receive so little research attention. Nonetheless, even the few types discussed here reveal the way in which the features and functions of weak ties combine to make a crucial contribution to the process of social support.

Neighborly ties. Nearly 20 years ago, Keller (1968) observed that the sentiment many people attached to the concept of their neighborhood had been transformed "from a neighboring of *place* to a neighboring of *taste.*" Contemporary neighboring typically does not result in the sort of densely linked communal solidarities so typically envisioned by either those who long to restore a lost sense of community or those who dream of social utopias (Wellman, 1979). Instead both the strong and weak links of a neighborhood have been liberated from their physical setting by easy travel and communication. Personal tastes may now influence our choices of those with whom we associate as much or more than any sense of obligation to place. While this may ultimately extend our sense of community, it also means that ties with neighbors must compete with the time given to those who reside beyond the immediate locale (Fischer, 1982).

Although neighborhoods rarely represent highly solidified communal enclaves anymore, the people next door, down the street, and around the block still perform individual and collective support functions for each other. Unger and Wandersman (1985, p. 141) reaffirm the importance of neighbors in our lives:

> Neighbors often serve as support systems of individuals, providing emotional and material aid. They may foster a sense of identification and serve as a buffer from the feelings of isolation often associated with today's cities . . . serve as referral agents . . . join together to exercise their political skills.

In the same vein, Litwak and Szelenyi (1969) note that neighbors provide material and human assistance in times of need, connect the individual to the more structured services of the community such as police protection and child care, and socialize newcomers into the larger community.

Many of the features and functions of weak links can be seen in neighborly relationships. The content and structure of exchange is usually restricted. Most relationships are limited to the exchange of information such as news of people in the neighborhood, reports of impending changes in the neighborhood, and referrals to community services. Even when goods and services are exchanged, transactions tend to be explicit and repaid quickly. The provision of emotional support, when it occurs at all, is usually limited to neighbors who have become close friends or to relatives in the neighborhood (see Keller, 1968; Unger & Wandersman, 1985; Warren, 1963). Temporal and contextual restrictions also shape neighborhood interaction. Thus some neighborhoods have extensive interaction during the winter holidays and during the summer, but only minimal interaction at other times. Even in the course of a day, interaction may be structured by the time the mail is delivered or the times when children make their way to and from school. And, of course, neighborhoods differ from one another according to broader contextual factors such as cultural and social homogeneity, length of residence, presence of children, and the viability of community leadership and commercial services (Naparstek, Biegel & Spiro, 1982; Unger & Wandersman, 1985; Warren, 1977).

Nowhere is the importance of the neighborhood as a support system so evident as in the area of crime prevention. Support may be informal as in exchanging keys to each other's home or sharing information. The system may also have more formalized elements such as block watch programs and workshops on crime prevention. It is clear, however, that the support system of a neighborhood is inadequate if it functions only as an information service. That is, sharing information about recent crimes in the area or one's fear of crime only arouses more fear and does not enhance people's sense of control over the situation. Emotional and task support, especially in organized form, is often necessary to decrease feelings of victimization and helplessness (Unger & Wandersman, 1985).

Perhaps the greatest test for the cohesion and sense of belonging to a neighborhood occurs when violent crime or natural disaster hits the area. In such cases, the collective nature of even weak ties can be deeply felt. In our own city of Seattle, the brutal killing of an entire family brought neighbors together for mutual support. Families gathered in a local church to obtain and provide information, to cope with their children's reaction, and to help each other through a painful period of initial shock and then grief. Police officers on the case held a New Year's Eve vigil for the community and concerned area citizens. Later neighborhood events were held to commemorate the family.

Familiar strangers. The term *familiar stranger* appears to have been coined by Milgram (1977) and refers to individuals whom we encounter regularly, but do not know by name and with whom we rarely interact. They are quite different from total strangers, as Milgram's (1977, p. 53) account of regular commuters on a busline indicates:

Many passengers told us they often think about their fellow commuters, trying to figure out what kind of lives they lead, what their jobs are like, etc. They have a fantasy relationship, in which both parties have agreed to mutually ignore each other, without any implication of hostility. . . . The familiar stranger status is not the absence of a relationship, but a special form of relationship that has properties and consequences of its own.

Familiar strangers can probably be found at many points along the route of our daily and weekly routines. Local gathering spots like bus stops, laundromats, bookstores, and coffee shops frequently develop regulars who recognize each other, but do not socialize extensively. Many service attendants, store personnel, police officers, and local officials also fall into this category (Pearce, 1980).

It is difficult to gauge the significance of familiar strangers in the support process because so little research has been conducted. Even so, we believe that these seemingly faint social linkages do make a contribution to the support process in at least two ways. First, familiar strangers may be activated so as to provide small-scale (Pearce, 1980) or emergency assistance (Milgram, 1977). They may help when friends and acquaintances are not available and when total strangers will not help. Familiar strangers have, for example, been known to help victims of street violence when total strangers would not help (e.g., Milgram, 1977). In other cases familiar strangers may be the source of money for a phone call, a newspaper, or a variety of other small-scale services.

Second, we believe that familiar strangers contribute in a vague but vital way to our sense of community well-being. Unfortunately, this level of social integration and identification is usually ignored by researchers who focus instead on the more obvious and readily measured forms of social participation involving neighbors, friends, and family (see House, 1984). Nonetheless, merely seeing familiar faces along one's daily routes can enhance a sense of well-being, security, and belonging. Perhaps the best illustration of this point occurs when people return home after an extended trip. In addition to the overt pleasure of seeing friends and relatives again, there may be a distinct sense of comfort derived from seeing the same people waiting at the bus stop, plodding the supermarket aisles, walking their dogs, and so on. Even without speaking, familiar strangers remind us of the continuity in our lives and that the outer world of strangers need not be so threatening as we sometimes fear.

Strangers on the run. This category of weak ties refers to contact with unfamiliar others in which self-disclosure occurs. These people have also been dubbed "strangers on the train" or "strangers on the plane," although to imply that such relationships occur only during extended travel would be misleading. Disclosure between strangers may occur in almost any situation as long as that situation provides for low levels of reciprocity, minimal expectations for future interaction, and freedom from the fear that what is disclosed will get back to one's everyday network (see Derlega & Chaikin, 1977; Parks, 1982; Rubin, 1975; Simmel, 1950).

Further situational factors augment disclosure. The listener and speaker alike may be temporarily trapped together as in the case of people confined to an airplane or of people sharing the waiting room at the physician's office. Escape may be either impossible or very inconvenient. Self-disclosure is also aided by boredom in many of these situations. Beyond that, the consumption of alcohol, the fear or excitement of the situation, can trigger concerns with self and reduce inhibitions about disclosure.

Although unwanted disclosures from strangers sometimes add to our stress, strangers on the run often engage in truly supportive interactions. Disclosures may be an interesting, if not pleasant, distraction from a boring situation. Participants may gain useful reference points for their own experiences through social comparison. Emotions can be ventilated in relative safety. Participants are also given the opportunity to float a new idea or identity past someone else before they have to reveal it to friends and family. Finally, strangers met on the run may possess useful task or social information such as the cheapest way from the airport to downtown, where to eat, or where to meet people.

Urban agents. The term *urban agent* (Kelly, 1964) covers a wide variety of relationships formed with those working in service roles or with professionals whose jobs imply that they may be good sources for social support. Gershon and Biller (1977) have distinguished between "community agents" (e.g., teachers, ministers, lawyers), whose roles more formally imply a supportive component and "urban agents" (e.g., bartenders, hairdressers, cabdrivers) whose supportive efforts are even less formal. Although we will adopt the term *urban agent* to cover both groups, Gershon and Biller's distinction reminds of us of the great variety of sources from which social support can come.

Empirical research on urban agents has explored groups such as hairdressers, divorce lawyers, bartenders, foremen in job settings, and ministers (Bissonette, 1977; Cowen, 1982; Cowen, Gesten, Boike, Norton, Wilson, & De Stefano, 1979; Cowen, Gesten, Davidson, & Wilson, 1981; Cowen, McKim, & Weissberg, 1981; Doane & Cowen, 1981; Gershon & Biller, 1977; Wiesenfeld & Weis, 1979). Most of these studies have been descriptive, profiling the problems fielded by these caregivers, their help giving behaviors, and reactions to clients, as well as the ecological factors thought to influence the provision of social support (Cowen, 1982).

In a few cases, however, investigators have explored ways in which urban agents could be trained to be more effective providers of social support. Wiesenfeld and Weis (1979), for example, designed a workshop for hairdressers to develop their listening skills and knowledge of community resources. One Seattle area bank has developed a program for bank officers who help people deal with the financial consequences of a divorce, death, or catastrophic illness in the family. Both programs are examples of good social support and good business.

Bartenders represent particularly interesting urban agents because of their prevalence and because they come in contact with a broad cross-section of the community. One survey of bartenders (Cowen et al., 1981) reported that nearly one in five customers raised moderate to serious personal problems with bartenders. Daytime bartenders reported about twice as many disclosures by customers even though, or perhaps because, they serviced many fewer customers. The most common support strategies used by bartenders were to listen attentively, to be lighthearted, and to offer sympathy. The authors comment that these "low-cost strategies" reflect the bartenders' minimal investment of time and energy as well as the hectic circumstances of their jobs. Another study (Bissonnette, 1977) suggests that these strategies may also allow the bartender to maintain control of his or her personal involvement with the customer's problem. One of our own interviews with ex-bartenders reveals the professional skills, forms of exchange, and social boundaries imposed on the bartender's relationship with a customer:

During my training I learned several important lessons. When a customer offers to buy you a drink, it's more than a token tip—he's buying your time and the opportunity to talk. I was told to always pour the drink in front of him, set it there, and try to get back and exchange a few words occasionally. Also, never assume the type of relationship a customer has with another person. He may have spent nights talking about his wonderful wife and five kids, but don't assume the woman he suddenly brings in is her. Finally, what is said one night is often best forgotten by the next.

This advice to a young bartender would serve just as well as advice to a variety of other urban agents. Moreover, in it we see several of the distinctive features of weak links at work. Urban agents often give social support in a hectic setting that limits their attention to any one individual. Their role often presumes tacit agreement not to remember or bring up what was said in the past and this in turn protects the customer and bartender alike. The advice to avoid assumptions about others' relationships reflects a logical response to the socially detached character of the interaction. It is a detachment that both protects the bartender and stimulates the customer's disclosure. Finally, the bartender's provision of support, like that of many other urban agents, remains firmly rooted within the larger framework of the financial exchange.

Ties by telephone. One of the chief virtues of weak links is that they can exist in highly restricted communication channels like those created by telephone hotlines, crisis lines, and talk lines. These telephone services may be staffed to provide either very specific assistance or to deal with a variety of community information and referral needs, or they may be unmoderated, open lines that simply give callers a forum to talk.

Talking on the telephone is usually depicted as a secondary form of human contact, with television commercials reinforcing the idea that the telephone is the "*next* best thing to being there." When it comes to providing social support, however, the contact by telephone is often better than being there. Several writers have, for example, noted the advantage of telephone services over face-to-face counseling services: (1) the caller has more control over the contact, (2) callers can remain anonymous, (3) geographic barriers are eliminated, (4) the caller is able to take greater risks in expressing feelings, (5) hotlines and crisis lines are usually free of charge and provide 24-hour services, and (6) telephones are immediate, allowing people to deal with a crisis as it occurs (Albrecht et al., 1986; Brockopp, 1973; Carothers & Inslee, 1974; Rosenbaum & Calhoun, 1977; Wark, 1982; Williams & Douds, 1973).

A recent study of a telephone hotline for cancer victims and those affected by cancer in their families and work settings reveals how supportive interactions are shaped by the communication channel (Albrecht et al., 1986). For *both* the caller and the volunteer, visual anonymity can be critical in decreasing the profound embarrassment of discussing the physical and emotional devastation of cancer. One volunteer poignantly contrasted the phone with face-to-face meetings with callers:

> You can talk to someone on the phone without seeing their illness. You can almost treat them normally. When you see them face-to-face, you have to come to terms with the illness on a visual basis. You talk to somebody and they tell you, "Well, I'm losing my hair." You don't see it. . . . I walk into a place where somebody has lost their hair and they're very, very skinny and they're obviously dying. The first thing you see is how sick they are as opposed to seeing the person there.

Thus the telephone may not enable one to "see the patient," but it often does enable one to "see the person" behind the disease.

A distinctly different type of program began a few years ago in Great Britain. "Talk About" was an open telephone service in which people could call merely to socialize with others. Approximately two years ago a similar service was introduced in New York City under the label "Talk to a Friend" and since then other services have been tried in other cities under titles like "Talk Line" or "Gabline." These lines typically allow up to a dozen people to talk with one another. The topic of conversation is usually left up to the callers, although some services have experimented with preselected topics and moderators. In some cases, separate lines have been created for particular groups such as teenagers.

Little research has been conducted on these "generic" telephone talklines, aside from the confidential marketing studies of the telephone companies themselves. We do know that talklines have been remarkably popular, especially during their first few months of operation when their novelty value is still high. A talkline in Seattle, for example, logged an average of 8,420 calls per day during its first 20 days of operation. According to the talkline's manager, callers generally fell into one of four groups: (1) those who viewed the line as entertainment; (2) those who were seeking serious discussion of some topic, (3) those who were interested in making new friends, and (4) those who wished to verbally abuse or shock other callers.

One advantage of these talklines over more specialized support lines is the lack of stigma associated with the service. The individual does not have to label himself or herself as needing some particular type of service in order to call. The very ambiguity of the service itself may free people to try it or talk about issues they could not otherwise bring themselves to discuss. Unfortunately we have only anecdotal data thus far on how well these services function to provide support. We do know that they are capable of stimulating face-to-face meetings. One group of callers to the Seattle service, for instance, arranged to meet at a local bar for more direct socializing. We also found examples of serious attempts by callers to give genuine help. In one case, a battered wife who had just viewed *Burning Bed*, a film about spouse abuse, called and received comfort and advice from the anonymous participants. Finally, it seems clear that use of these services is sensitive to more generalized needs for support. Calls to the Seattle service, for example, rose dramatically during a widespread power failure and during the Christmas holidays.

Summary

Weak links are a vital component of an effective, healthy personal network (Albrecht & Adelman, 1984; Parks, 1982). In this chapter we have explored a wide range of weaker support relationships that lie outside our comparatively close circles of family, friends, and close coworkers. We have not examined even weaker types of relationships that exist on the very fringes of the social support process. Two in particular warrant brief mention. One of these types covers the relationships we have with those portrayed in the mass media. Media coverage extends our sense of community identification. Television coverage of happy events such as the return of the hostages from Iran or national tragedies such as the space shuttle disaster, for example, create common identifications among literally millions of people. Moreover, as Friemuth notes in

Chapter 10, people rely heavily on mass media for informational support. In addition, people may derive support or guidance from fictional characters in the media. They often attribute a sort of fantasy-level intimacy or friendship in their "parasocial relationships" with media characters (see Rubin, Perse, & Powell, 1985). Another class of supportive relationships exists between people and animals. While such relationships are social only in the most generous sense of the word, research is beginning to show that contact with animals is useful both for stimulating greater human contact among those with impaired social skills and for compensating for the lack of human contact among those who are socially isolated (e.g., Anderson, Hart, & Hart, 1984; Beck & Katcher, 1983; Fogle, 1984).

Instead of focusing on these more exotic sources of social support, we focus on five of the more common types of weak social linkages. These include neighborly relationships, familiar strangers, strangers-on-the-run, urban agents, and telephone ties. Each of these relationships displays some combination of the characteristics we usually associate with weak ties. Their inner, dyadic structure tends to be at once generalized and restricted. Most operate on stereotypic rather than personalized information. Interaction is usually restricted to the exchange of a limited variety of resources. Weak ties tend to be more or less detached from the individual's network of more intimate relationships. One's weak ties are not only likely to have less interaction with one's intimates, but also less interaction with each other. Moreover, weak ties are typically restricted by their context. While one's stronger ties tend to be more portable, weak ties are often limited to specific physical settings, periods of time, and communication channels.

It is these very limitations that breed the strength of weak ties as sources of social support. We identified four distinctive functions of weak ties in this chapter. First, weak ties can dramatically extend the individual's access to information, goods, and services. This results both from the fact that we have far more weak ties than strong ties and from the fact that the detached character of weak ties within networks brings us into contact with a far greater variety of people and ideas than do our more densely connected strong ties. Second, weak ties promote valuable social comparison processes. Weak ties are usually less dependent upon similarities between people and therefore are excellent sources of contact with those who are dissimilar. Comparison to dissimilar others can assist individuals in judging themselves and protecting their self-esteem in times of crisis. Third, weak ties often provide opportunities for low-risk discussion of high-risk topics. The contextual restrictions of weak ties as well as their more detached network position enable individuals to bring up topics that may be too embarrassing to discuss in more intimate relationships. Finally, weak ties function as a subtle glue holding together and fostering our larger sense of community. Not only are they vehicles for understanding and identification with a larger community, but they forge crucial linkages between clusters of strong ties for the purpose of large-scale collective action.

In spite of the notable virtues of weak ties, it is also necessary to note both the difficulties of researching weak ties and the obvious limits on what they can accomplish. They may not be identifiable or memorable enough to be covered by most standard social support measures (House, 1984). In addition weak ties may be hesitant about discussing their supportive activities because they fear criticism for their informal, untrained support attempts (Gershon & Biller, 1977). Beyond these research difficulties, there are a number of natural limits on the role of weak ties in the social support process. These include limits on the degree and duration of support that can be sought. Just as weak ties can help the individual break out of unhealthy behavior patterns, they can provide an arena in which deviant, unhealthy behavior is reinforced. Nonetheless, weak ties add a richness and variety to the social support process that can not be provided by more intimate relationships alone.

7

Social Support
in Self-Help Groups:
The Role of Communication
in Enabling Perceptions
of Control

PAUL ARNTSON
DAVID DROGE

> You can not tell people what to do,
> You can only tell them parables.
> (W. H. Auden, in Spears, 1963, p. 13)

In *The Theory and Practice of Group Psychotherapy,* Irving Yalom (1975) suggested that therapy groups become "social microcosms" in which group members work out their maladaptive behaviors. It is equally true that planned intervention groups, such as therapy, encounter, and self-help groups, can become "social microcosms" for researchers to see psychological and communication processes unfold over weeks that would normally take years to

AUTHORS' NOTE: This essay is dedicated to the memory of Leonard Borman, whose pioneering work with self-help groups has enriched and enabled both members' lives and our own. The two studies reported here were funded by the Epilepsy in the Urban Environment Project at the Center for Urban Affairs and Policy Research, Northwestern University.

observe in natural support networks. The insights drawn from such groups are evident in the works of Yalom (1975), Lieberman, Yalom, and Miles (1973), and Lieberman and Borman (1979).

Self-help groups in particular can provide researchers with an opportunity to observe social support processes. In the late seventies it was estimated that between 15 and 20 million people were involved in 500,000 self-help groups (Droge, 1983a). Many of these groups were "grass-roots" responses to inadequacies in the members' professional and social networks. Often lay led, these groups are "as much a political and sociological phenomenon as they are a psychological one" (Levy, 1979, p. 34). No one, not even Coates and Winston (1983), would argue with the assertion that self-help groups *can* function as social support systems (Droge, 1983a; Lakin, 1985; Levy, 1979; Lieberman, 1979; Wollert, Levy, & Knight, 1982).

Lieberman (1979, p. 25) has maintained that understanding the impact of self-help groups necessitates a consideration of the "social and psychological dilemmas" surrounding each affliction. The problems associated with having epilepsy make epilepsy self-help groups a particularly relevant context within which to study how communication can engender social support for group members. Unlike many other afflictions, epilepsy is a neurological disorder that can both physically *and* socially disrupt and distort communication. Physically, seizure occurrence quite often means an unpredictable, abrupt loss of control by one interactant in a social encounter. This violation of normal communication rules in everyday interaction can cause social isolation and rejection (Arangio, 1975; Taylor & Harrison, 1976). Socially, the constant attribution of this potential violation of normal communication to people with epilepsy can stigmatize them regardless of their actual seizure activity (Arntson, Droge, Norton, & Murray, 1986). Thus the stigmatized label, "epileptic," with its rejection and social isolation, can lead to a host of psychological problems for some people with epilepsy (Arntson et al., 1986). It is clear that most people with epilepsy require functional social support systems to cope successfully with their physical and social condition.

The research reported here has focused on how communication can function in epilepsy self-help groups to engender social support by increasing perceptions of control for group members. The importance of perceived control in our research on epilepsy self-help groups comes from our reading of previous research on self-help groups and social support and from our experiences in groups. Our research has been primarily descriptive from two interrelated perspectives.

First, we wanted to know what group members said about how their groups functioned. Given that social support is a cognitive variable, asking group members about the social support process in their groups seemed like a good beginning. The two major and most widely cited studies of self-help groups have both asked members to rate the helpfulness of group activities. In the work of Lieberman and Borman (1979), members of five different self-help groups were asked to fill out Yalom's (1975) Curative Factors. These factors, which also have been used in psychotherapy (Yalom, 1975) and encounter groups (Lieberman et al., 1973), showed that feelings of universality (having the same experiences and feelings as others), support, and altruism (helping others) were generally the three most highly rated change mechanisms across the groups. Groups did differ somewhat on which curative mechanisms were most highly rated based on the nature of the group's affliction and on the type of interaction among group members.

Levy and his associates (Levy, 1976, 1979; Wollert et al., 1982) studied 20 self-help groups at one time or another both through observing the groups in action and asking group members to rate how frequently 28 different activities occurred in their group. Based on how members of 8 self-help groups (72 people) rated the activities, Levy (1979, p. 264) suggested that "on the whole, self help groups focus the major portion of their efforts on fostering communication between their members, providing them with social support, and responding to their needs on both cognitive and emotional levels." The number of members in any one self-help group was too small to make valid comparisons between groups. This first research perspective, the group members' perceptions of the self-help process, is a necessary, but not sufficient, condition for understanding the communication process in self-help groups.

Our second research perspective involved observing epilepsy self-help group meetings in order to construct an understanding of how communication functions in these groups. The two research projects cited above again have provided the most information concerning how self-help groups function based on observers' perceptions. Both Antze (1979) and Sherman (1979) have identified peer ideologies that are unique to each self-help group that they studied and observed. These ideologies, or "systems of meaning," can counteract "key attitudes toward the affliction shared" by members of a particular self-help group (Sherman, 1979, p. 305). In studying AA, Recovery Inc., and Synanon, Antze (1979, pp. 304-305) concluded:

> We have seen that each of the organizations considered here achieves its effects by counteracting certain key attitudes that typify its client group. Thus, AA counters the assertiveness of alcoholics by teaching surrender; Recovery, Inc. blocks the habitual surrender of former mental patients by promoting willpower; and Synanon reverses the addict's social and emotional detachment through a process that expresses feelings and strengthens social engagement.

The ideology in a bereaved parents group, Compassionate Friends, is not as easy to identify, according to Sherman (1979). Given the loss of a child, the group's ideology must provide extensive meaning systems for the parents to interact with each other and their social environments. An important aspect of this meaning system is that, "like Recovery Inc., Compassionate Friends stresses the importance of activity and encourages feelings of control and agency" (Sherman, 1979, p. 317). We think that each of these ideologies that Antze and Sherman have identified is primarily concerned with perceived control.

Levy (1979, pp. 245-255) has identified 11 genotypical processes that can account for the effectiveness of the self-help groups that his researchers observed. The first four processes are behaviorally oriented:

(1) both direct and vicarious social reinforcement for the development of desirable behaviors and the elimination or control of problematic behaviors
(2) training, indoctrination, and support in the use of various kinds of self-control behaviors
(3) modeling methods of coping with stresses and changing behaviors
(4) providing members with an agenda of actions they can engage in to change their social environment

Levy identifies the remaining seven processes as being cognitively oriented:

(1) removing members' mystification over their experiences and increasing their expectancy for change and help by providing them with a rationale for their problems of distress and for the group's way of dealing with it

(2) provision of normative and instrumental information and advice

(3) expansion of the range of alternative perceptions of members' problems and circumstances and of the actions they might take to cope with their problems

(4) enhancement of members' discriminate abilities regarding the stimulus and event contingencies in their lives

(5) support for changes in attitudes toward oneself, one's own behavior, and society

(6) social comparison and consensual validation leading to a reduction or elimination of members' uncertainty and sense of isolation or uniqueness regarding their problems and experiences

(7) the emergence of an alternative or substitute culture and social structure within which members can develop new definitions of their personal identities and new norms upon which they can base their self-esteem

Obviously, these processes are not unique to self-help groups, as Levy readily admits. Practically every change process known to social science is on the list. Nor do we find the distinction between behaviorally and cognitively oriented processes to hold when examining the list. Our own analysis of these eleven processes would reduce them to two interrelated processes: uncertainty reduction and developing greater control over one's life and social environment.

Based on the results generated from both perspectives, the importance placed on universality by self-help group members and Levy's observation of social comparison leading to reduction of members' uncertainty and sense of isolation, social comparison would seem to be an inviting process to apply to self-help groups. Recently, Coates and Winston (1983) have done just that. They used social comparison theory to understand the helping process in groups for victims of sexual assault and found that self-help groups do lessen feelings of deviancy among members but not feelings of depression.

However, we would argue that social comparison theory does *not* explain how self-help groups provide social support for members. While increasing feelings of universality and decreasing feelings of being deviant and isolated may result from meeting others with similar problems, there is very little evidence that being with others similarly afflicted will lessen emotional reactions other than fear (Cottrel & Epley, 1977). As a matter of fact, being with fellow sufferers may *increase* emotional reactions, depending on where members are in their group's affliction hierarchy (Brickman & Bulman, 1977; Coates & Winston, 1983). The social support process in self-help groups does not consist primarily of members comparing their emotional reactions with others similarly afflicted in order to validate that their responses are appropriate and normal. Rather we will argue that in epilepsy self-help groups members provide each other with the opportunities, stories, and sets of behaviors in order to increase their perceived control over their physical and social conditions.

Based on the two research perspectives just reviewed, we developed an extensive national survey of epilepsy self-help group members and an intensive analysis of one epilepsy self-help group. In this chapter we will integrate the results from these two studies in order to draw three sets of inferences concerning the *mere existence*, the *narrative form*, and the *instrumental content* of the communication in epilepsy self-help groups.

Research Studies

Because our inferences are based primarily on our work with epilepsy self-help groups, we need to describe briefly the two studies that form the bases for our understanding of the social support function in epilepsy self-help groups.

Self-help survey. Together with the Self-Help Center at the Center for Urban Affairs and Policy Research at Northwestern University and self-help group leaders, there was a three year collaborative investigation of epilepsy self-help groups. For two years an Epilepsy Self-Help Group Workshop was held in which 15 to 20 leaders of Chicago area self-help groups met with researchers on a monthly basis. The workshop brought in epilepsy self-help group leaders from other parts of the country for presentations and discussions. Researchers and group leaders were sent on site visits to epilepsy self-help groups in other states. From the information developed in the workshop and a clinic study of 157 people with epilepsy (Arntson & Montgomery, 1980), a 29-page questionnaire

154   CONTEXTS OF SUPPORTIVE COMMUNICATION

was put together, pilot tested with 27 Chicago group members, and then distributed nationally to epilepsy self-help group members and other people who had epilepsy. In total, 357 questionnaires were returned.[1] Approximately two-thirds of them were from self-help group members.

Chicago self-help group study. Several group members were approached at an Epilepsy Self-Help Group Workshop meeting and asked if an observer could begin attending their group meetings. They replied that the decision to allow an observer to attend must be made by the group. After the group voted its approval, attendance at group sessions and other events (e.g., social events at one member's home) continued for approximately eight months. Data collection began with the preparation of written summaries of each weekly session. After attending the first two sessions, however, the observer obtained permission to record group sessions on audiotape, subject to restrictions established by group members. Eight consecutive sessions were recorded.

This group met each Thursday evening from 6:30 until approximately 9:00. Many members went to a nearby restaurant after the meeting. (Those postmeeting gatherings could last until midnight.) Over the course of the eight recorded sessions, 33 people attended at least one meeting. Between 9 and 19 members were present at each session, with an average of 14 members per meeting. The group leader was a layperson with epilepsy. He was "assisted" by a core of 5 to 8 other members in leading the group. The general format for the group was a "round robin" procedure in which each member had a turn to discuss a problem or issue. See Droge (1983b) for a detailed description of this group.

These two studies plus our collaborative relationship with the Epilepsy Self-Help Workshop provide the bases for most of our generalizations concerning how communication functions in epilepsy self-help groups.

The Mere Existence of Communication

At the most basic level, communication functions in epilepsy self-help groups to give people a reason to be in each other's company. In other words, it hardly matters what is said, it only matters that people are talking to each other. We have two reasons for arriving at this somewhat strange conclusion.

The opportunity to talk. The self-help group meetings that we observed were often quite chaotic. Members would suddenly leave the meeting room for coffee, a cigarette, or a private conference in another part of the office complex; others would leave to go to a restroom on another floor of the building; some would engage in telephone conversations while in the meeting room; and other members would enter late and immediately take over the floor, interrupting any discussion in progress. Multiple conversations often occurred. At times the group leader had to shout for order. From our perspective, the discussions were often cliché laden and occasionally dysfunctional to the person being "helped" (see Droge, 1983b).

When members were asked after the meeting how the group had helped them, they often answered by saying that the group was willing to listen to what they had to say. The group provided an audience for the members to talk about themselves. At this level of analysis, we are echoing Silver and Wortman (1980) when they conclude that the opportunity to express one's feelings and concerns is in itself beneficial and is perceived as offering support.

Epilepsy self-help groups can provide a sanctioned time and place for people to talk about themselves and their social and physical conditions. Members do not have to worry that they are imposing on other people or apologize for complaining or bringing up the same thing over and over again. Nor is there a social service or professional meter running on members' talk time. At this first level of analysis, the existence of epilepsy self-help groups serves as a "refuge or sanctuary" from the patient role and other disabled role relationships (Caplan, 1972). Members have the freedom to bring up topics that may no longer be welcome in other contexts and the time to talk about them. The opportunity to talk to other people who are expecting to listen can be self-affirming.

The "restaurant effect." Besides providing people with an opportunity to talk about themselves during the meetings, the mere existence of the groups gave some members an excuse to meet socially after the meetings and during the week. In visiting a number of groups around the country, we noticed that most self-help groups would convene an informal postmeeting gathering at a restaurant near the group's formal meeting place. At these sessions, members would engage in informal conversations about topics introduced at the formal meetings or about sports, the weather, and other general topics of conversation. Based on our observations, we included in the national survey a question asking, "Do you attend informal activities with the group after the regular meeting? If YES, what do you do?" In total, 97 respondents indicated that they attended formal meetings only, and 99 respondents also attended informal activities; virtually all of those attending informal activities reported that these activities occurred at a restaurant.

In order to understand who attended the informal sessions, we compared the informal and formal only members on a number of quantitative and qualitative measures. Those attending informal sessions were more likely to rate social reasons for joining higher than were those who attended formal meetings only. Informal participants were significantly more likely to endorse all four leadership functions (emotional stimulation, caring, meaning attribution, and executive functions, see Lieberman et al., 1973) as being descriptive of their behavior, significantly more satisfied with the groups, and perceived the groups to be significantly more effective (summing Yalom's, 1975, curative factors) than did the formal members only. As one might expect, informal participants had attended more self-help group meetings than had formal-only members.

These quantitative and qualitative differences between informal and formal-only participants indicate that the existence of the groups provided a reason for approximately half of the members to expand their social networks. The informal participants reported that they were more active in the groups, attended more sessions, and were more satisfied with the groups than the members who attended only the formal meetings. Given that the informal participants had a greater opportunity to establish friendships in the group, all of these findings make sense.

Our observations of the Chicago self-help group confirmed the survey's findings. About half of the members went to a restaurant after the meeting was over. Often the informal sessions lasted longer than the regular meetings. These members also met in each others' homes and a few dated each other. The members that went to the restaurant tended not to have personal social networks outside the group. The opportunity to interact socially (outside of the structured group meeting) was an attractive experience for those who were more isolated socially.

Both the opportunity to talk and the existence of another social network are at the most basic level of explicating the functional aspects of communication in epilepsy self-help groups. The narrative form of the communication in these self-help groups has the potential to be another functional aspect of communication for the members.

The Narrative Form
of the Communication

Early on in our research we were struck by the amount of narrative activity that took place in the self-help groups we were observing (Arntson, 1980). Often we would hear the same stories repeated across meeting times. Some stories triggered no responses from group members. Other personal stories would engender a whole round of similar stories. And then some stories would be deconstructed, analyzed, and advice given. The question to be answered in this section concerns the possible functions that story-telling may serve in epilepsy self-help groups. Elsewhere we have argued that the key to understanding the considerable occurrence of narration in epilepsy self-help groups is to contrast the narrative and dialectical modes of communicating about one's health (Arntson, 1980; see also Bruner, 1986, for a recent discussion of two modes of cognitive functioning, the paradigmatic and the narrative, that closely parallels the distinctions being made in this essay).

While dialectical health communication can occur with family members, friends, and in self-help groups, it is in the practitioner-patient encounter that the dialectical mode is most intense and prevalent. At the content level, the scientific tasks of identifying symptoms, explaining test procedures, running them, discussing results, prescribing treatment, and explaining physiological processes may all take precedent over the development of a reciprocal social-emotional relationship and the exploration of a personal meaning system for the patient's condition. In the case of epilepsy, the encounters often center on EEGs, blood tests, blood levels, drug regimes, side effects of drugs, and so on. Practitioners are trained to sort through the patient's discourse to identify as early as possible the real physiological and/or psychological problems. The presenting problem is useful only to the extent that it helps the practitioner formulate a working hypothesis in language consistent with the practitioner's training. At that point, the practitioners' questions usually become much more leading and closed-ended. There is some evidence to suggest that the longer students have been in medical school, the fewer open-ended questions they ask, and the less they are concerned with the psychosocial aspects of the problem (Arntson, Zimmerman, Feinsod, & Speer, 1982; Helfer, 1970).

Nor is there time for extended non-task-oriented communication. For the practitioner, the health encounter is highly scripted, time limited, and repeated several times a day. Some neurologists at an epilepsy clinic would ask three questions while filling in the medical record: Have you had any seizures lately? Any problems with side effects? And when was the last time you had a blood-level test? Many encounters were finished in under a minute. For the epilepsy patients at the clinic, the encounter was usually very important, often anxiety inducing, and, it was hoped, occurred infrequently. Many epilepsy patients at the clinic were upset that they did not get to discuss other aspects of having epilepsy with the doctor. In one study, over 80% of the epilepsy patients indicated that their doctors only provided them with medical information (Arntson & Montgomery, 1980).

At the relational level, the practitioner-patient encounter contains a superordinate-subordinate role relationship (Friedson, 1971; Parsons, 1951; Waitzkin & Stoeckle, 1976). The interlocutor, through his or her questions, controls the interaction. No matter how benign the intentions of the professional, it is inevitable that the product of the professional-client relationship is always status inequality. John McKnight (1977) has argued that this hierarchical relationship can make the patient a passive recipient of knowledge and technical advice (see also Arntson & Philipsborn, 1982; Korsch & Negrete, 1972, for analyses of parent passivity in pediatric encounters). Through this hierarchical control of the patient, the practitioner can keep his or her professional distance in order to ensure objective treatment and avoid occupational burnout (Arntson et al., 1982). This professional distance, while functional for the practitioner, is not always what the patient is looking for in the relationship.

Unfortunately, for some patients with chronic disabilities like epilepsy, an ongoing hierarchical relationship with a professional expert or set of experts can magnify feelings of dependency, perceived loss of control, and even a sense of incompetence. People with epilepsy may rely on family doctors, neurologists, therapists, job counselors, and the like for definitions of their physical and psychological well-being, ability to drive, employment opportunities, insurability, and, of course, drugs. Ellen Langer (1979) has demonstrated how interacting with a highly competent person can create the illusion of incompetence in subjects. She has also suggested that doing something passive, such as waiting in an office, can cause a person to relinquish control further to a perceived expert.

It is in the language of the practitioner-patient interactions that we can see some of the most negative consequences of the hierarchical relationships in health care. Practitioners define patients' statuses when they categorize the physical and psychological characteristics of patients. This categorization has the power to stigmatize and legally sanction patients and their families (Edelman, 1977; Taylor & Harrison, 1976; Sontag, 1977; Scott, 1964). The label, "epilepsy," brings with its medical definition a host of legal restrictions and social reactions that can make patients with epilepsy feel a loss of personal control over their lives (Arntson et al., 1986).

Practitioner-patient interactions that decrease perceptions of control for people with epilepsy are adding to an already potentially serious problem. Given the unpredictable nature of most seizure activity, people with epilepsy may perceive that they no longer control their own bodies. The original cause of the seizures is not usually explainable in individualistic terms. Doctors cannot tell most people with epilepsy why they started having seizures while other people equally at risk did not. People are not comfortable with random events that can so profoundly affect their lives (Silver & Wortman, 1980). Dependency on drugs and the drugs' unpredictable side effects make the perception of control even more difficult. Yet the perception of control has both positive physiological and psychological effects in general (Garber & Seligman, 1980; Langer & Rodin, 1976; Schulz, 1980; Seligman, 1975; Silver & Wortman, 1980) and for people with epilepsy in particular (Arntson & Montgomery, 1980; Arntson et al., 1986).

In summary, the dialectical nature of practitioner-patient encounters has been characterized as often being hierarchical, ascribing potentially stigmatizing labels to patients, minimizing personal meanings while treating physiological aspects of the patient, and being very scripted for the practitioner and not necessarily for the patient. These characteristics ordinarily do not adversely affect people who occasionally see the doctor or other health care professionals. However, these characteristics can interact with the nature of chronic health conditions to heighten loss of control, the illusion of incompetence, and a sense of meaninglessness for people who are in a chronic patient mode.

Nothing that has been asserted here should be taken as questioning the good intentions of health care professionals. The dialectical mode may well be necessary for treating the body, if not the whole person (Cassell, 1985). Patient expectations and both economic and time constraints have imposed limits on practitioners' flexibility in the dialectical encounter. Nor is the dialectical mode of health communication confined to the practitioner-patient encounter. Some self-help group members indicated that family members and close friends would focus primarily on the physiological aspects of their epilepsy, medical treatment, and offer or prescribe "advice." They would ask how the member was doing, but would not necessarily want to know or respond to shared personal feelings. Maintaining the person with epilepsy in the patient role may be a way of minimizing or avoiding personally threatening and difficult topics of conversation. Some people with epilepsy clung to their patient roles, only dialectically discussing their condition, for the same reasons.

The reason for explicating some characteristics of the dialectical mode of health communication was in order to compare that mode with the narrative mode of communication that was often present in epilepsy self-help groups. The round robin format of most groups encouraged stories. Asking each member how his or her week went was an invitation to narrate about some problem or success that occurred. At times, the narration would trigger other stories on the same subject. This was especially true if the person invited to talk was new. There were other times when the story would be responded to dialectically with questions and advice. In understanding how the narrative form functions in epilepsy self-help groups we will take the perspective of first the narrator and second the auditor.

Narrator's perspective. There are four characteristics of the narrative form that help the narrator strengthen his or her perceived control.

First, the narrative form puts the "I" back into the person's understanding of his or her life at two levels. At one level, the narrator controls the story. The person decides what is in the story and what is left out. Members were heard to say, "Damn it, this is my story," when others attempted to modify the content or interrupt. An individual cannot rehearse a dialectical discussion of a problem. Stories can be polished for just the right effect. At another level, the story requires a subject, usually the narrator, that is treated as a whole person as opposed to being an object, or a collection of organs and symptoms. If the narrator believes that he or she is in control of the story, and is voluntarily telling it, then the self-attributions that are made in public can become a strong form of self-persuasion; especially if the story is affirmed by other members in the group (Antze, 1979, makes a similar point).

Second, the narrator, in telling the story, is required to sequence the events of the story temporally: "A" happens, then "B," then "C." These temporal associations may then well turn into cause-effect relationships. The story's "illusion of sequence" can impose order on a chaotic if not random set of events. Scientifically there may be no explanation for having epilepsy, recent seizure activity, or the occurrence of side effects. By placing these events within a narrative, they may no longer be so unpredictable for the narrator.

Third, the narrative mode of communication gives members the freedom to rebuild a personal meaning system for understanding their lives. These meaning systems are usually embedded in the stories or functional fictions that we have about ourselves. Narratives organize the relevant symbols in one's environment, making it possible for one to gain meaning from the past, give meaning to the present, and reduce uncertainty about the future. When telling a story one has the freedom to suspend literal truth claims about particulars in order to draw a higher-order truth about life. Both narrator and auditor have an implicit agreement not to quibble over slight exaggerations or distortions of individual facts. In the self-help groups, when a member would challenge some detail in a narration, that member would often be silenced so that the narrator could come to the point of his or her story. This agreed-upon suspension allows members to generate functional fictions for their lives. In the narrative mode, the point of the story organizes and shapes the particulars, perhaps even invents them. In the dialectical mode, the patient's facts are challenged and scrutinized in order for someone else to draw the appropriate inferences.

Clearly not all fictions are functional. Stories concerning God's punishment, blaming oneself or others, and having supernatural powers were all dysfunctional stories that we heard in the groups. However, for members whose old stories were no longer functional for their current disabling conditions, the necessity for creating new stories that answered two generic questions, "Why me?" and "What now?" seemed overwhelming.

Although "Why me?" narratives and discussions were not tolerated for long in some epilepsy self-help groups, it is interesting to note in our national survey that self-help members were significantly more likely to indicate that epilepsy had positive effects in their lives than did non-self-help group respondents (Droge, 1983a). One way to answer "Why me?" questions is to make positive attributions about the disabling occurrence. "What now?" questions generated a large number of narratives and discussions about employment opportunities and relationships with both employers and coworkers. Of the personal issues raised in the Chicago group, 25% were concerned with employment (Droge, 1983b). Seizure activity (16%) was a distant second.

The fourth characteristic of the story form that can strengthen the narrator's perceived control is that the narrative mode of communication can provide an opportunity for self-help members to develop a functional language for talking about themselves. In their book, *Life Sentences,* Taylor and Harrison (1976, p. 29) state, "People cannot be cured of what they are." Many members described themselves in stigmatizing and helpless words: epileptic, out of control, an embarrassment, depressed, unattractive, and so on. The Chicago self-help group that we observed and taped did not allow members to describe themselves as being epileptic. Victim narratives were also not well received after a while. The form of the narrative requires character development. The words used to build the characters can help construct a functional symbol system for talking and thinking about oneself.

The need for a narrator, a subject, a point to the story, and character development, together with the necessary time and freedom to create the story, can all contribute to the narrator's increased perception of control. Because in the narrative mode every narrator is also a recipient of other stories, we must add to the narrator's perspectives the auditor's perspective in order to understand fully how story-telling functions in self-help groups.

Auditor's perspective. The narrative mode of communicating about health problems can provide the auditors in self-help groups with an alternative to the patient role that is required of them in other contexts. From the auditor's perspective there are three characteristics of the narrative form that can help establish this alternative.

First, listening to a story about how someone else dealt with a particular health problem is a way of receiving advice nondidactically. The auditors have the freedom to select from the story whatever parts of it that are relevant to their own situations and reenact those parts in their lives. The narrative form requires that the action in the story is placed in a specific context. The auditors can compare their contexts to the story's context before accepting the point of the story. In the patient role, the members may have been in hierarchical relationships with practitioners, family, or friends where the members were given both chemical and verbal prescriptions. In self-help groups, members can listen to stories about how others have dealt with problems as well as receiving advice. Given the well-documented problems with patient compliance, advice and prescriptions are often not well received, even when coming from doctors. For some people who are reacting against the imposition of the patient role, listening to narratives may be more instructive for managing their lives than being told what to do.

Second, it is primarily in the narrative mode of communication that group members developed reciprocal social-emotional relationships in the group. When a member's narrative was responded to with other narratives on the same subject, one could see most clearly the reciprocity process at work. A story about employment discrimination would be followed by similar stories that would reveal the difficulties, feelings, and coping strategies of the narrators. In contrast, a dialectical response to the employment story would probably reveal little personal information or affect from the interlocutors.

The third characteristic of the narrative mode of communication in the Chicago group that can help the auditor was the development and continued refinement of an archetypal coping narrative. The person who founded the group and was its designated leader up until a few months before we started attending was the subject of this archetypal coping story. In recruiting new members he would tell them about himself: how he was an unemployed, depressed Vietnam veteran with epilepsy who turned himself around when he got involved in self-help groups. It was in the self-help group that he stopped feeling sorry for himself and started helping other people. It was through helping other people that he stopped blaming others for his problems, regained his self-esteem, and eventually found a job. This story not only recruited other members but, more important, was used in assessing and changing members' stories. In response to someone's story a member could say, "Like Jack" or "Feeling sorry for himself didn't help Jack any." Over time, the coping story changed to incorporate seizure activity and developing interpersonal relationships, two aspects of the leader's situation that were not so problematic. However, the essence of the coping story did not change: Being in the group and helping each other was what empowered each person to cope successfully. In Antze's terms (1979) this was the group's core ideology. It was through sharing a wide range of stories that members generated for themselves a coping narrative for their own lives.

Our analysis of how narrative communication functions in epilepsy self-help groups has not been supported with either self-report or behavioral evidence. Like Levy's work (1979), we have based our analysis almost totally on direct observation of the group's activities and informal discussions with individual members. However, the beneficial nature of dramatically talking about oneself was partially documented in our national survey of self-help group members. Norton's Dramatic Style Scale was the only measure in the survey of how much people perceived themselves talking about their epilepsy. In this sample, the reliability estimate for the scale was only .59. Even so, the Dramatic Style Scale was positively associated with self-esteem ($r = .40$, $p < .001$), life satisfaction ($r = .42$, $p < .001$), and internal control ($r = .15$, $p < .01$), and negatively associated with helplessness ($r = -.25$, $p < .001$), depression ($r = -.34$, $p < .001$), and anxiety ($r = -.17$, $p < .01$). While there is no causal argument in these data and the correlations are quite modest, it is important to note that people who are predisposed to communicate dramatically are also more likely to report being in control, satisfied with life, having higher self-esteem, and being less depressed and anxious. At present, the functionality of narrative communication in epilepsy self-help groups is an interesting but not yet proven idea.

The Instrumental Content
of the Communication

Up to this point we have treated the communication in epilepsy self-help groups as though it were content free. Yet there must be some instrumental tasks accomplished in order for the communication in the groups to exist, and the narratives must be about some instrumental activities in the members' lives. From our perspective, the core set of instrumental tasks that communication in epilepsy self-help groups must accomplish is to have members make controlling attributions about the contingent physical and social aspects of their lives. In Antze's terms, this instrumental task is counteracting a set of physiological, psychological, and social conditions experienced by some people with epilepsy that can lead to learned helplessness (Abramson, Garber, & Seligman, 1980). According to the reformulated learned helplessness model, people may become depressed and anxious and may lose self-esteem if the attributions of causality they make about noncontingent events in their lives generalize to other contingent events.

Earlier, researchers wondered if the unpredictability of seizure activity and drug side effects could lead to helplessness effects for some people with epilepsy (Arntson & Montgomery, 1980; Devellis, Devellis, Wallston, & Wallston, 1980; Silver & Wortman, 1980). We did find in our survey that people with epilepsy had higher levels of depression and anxiety than did a normative sample of people. We also found statistically significant interrelationships between measures of helplessness, depression, anxiety, and self-esteem. However, based on our data, the reasons for perceived helplessness may be more a function of the social restrictions and reactions to having epilepsy as measured by a stigma scale than the perceived seizure rate. The stigma scale was significantly related to helplessness, the perceived seizure rate was not. Further, in answering the open-ended questions, the respondents consistently identified economic and social restrictions, negative social reactions, and loss of personal control as distorting and disrupting their lives, and not primarily seizure activity. Therefore the instrumental tasks of communication in epilepsy self-help groups must counteract the internal, stable, and global attributions members may make about their seizure activity and the stigmatizing role attributions made by others; both of which can contribute to learned helplessness.

At the content level, communication in epilepsy self-help groups accomplishes these tasks by providing usable information for members and by giving members the opportunity to renegotiate their ascribed roles as "epileptic" patients. Both of these content functions can help group members increase their perceived control over their lives.

Usable information. One of the major ways that people can attempt to control their lives is through gathering relevant information. Lazarus and Launier (1978) have suggested that information seeking is an important coping strategy for reducing uncertainty and making people feel knowledgeable about their disorders. Thompson (1981) identified acquiring information as one way to control adverse events, although she was mostly looking at information prior to the event. Atkin (1972) probably best described the manner in which information seeking may increase perceptions of control for people with epilepsy. "If people cannot master their environment, at least they can attempt to attain an awareness and understanding of the latest developments that may affect their well-being" (p. 211).

In our survey, 87% of the respondents indicated that they had both looked for information in the past and that they were still interested in looking for new information about epilepsy. Three results in the survey related to information seeking may invite a learned helplessness explanation. The helplessness scale was curvilinearly related to looking for information. Respondents at the high and low ends of the scale were less likely to have looked for information than those in the middle of the scale. The life satisfaction scale was similarly related to having looked for information. The same type of curvilinear relationship existed between how severely the respondents perceived that epilepsy had affected their lives and whether or not they would look for new information (these results are only suggestive because of the small numbers in the not looking for information cells).

Group members in the survey rated all of the information reasons for joining epilepsy self-help groups higher than the social reasons. Nor did the importance of the information reasons decrease the longer respondents had been group members.

The kind of information that was shared in the groups can be seen from our analysis of the Chicago group's meetings. During the eight sessions, 167 personal issues were raised: 25% concerning employment, 16% with seizure activity, 14% with social service programs, 11% with family relationships, 7% with medical care, and then 5% each for education, transportation, police and paramedic problems, housing, and generally discussing the week's activities. The high occurrence of seizure activity is slightly misleading because each person was usually asked about their seizures. There was hardly ever a follow-up discussion about seizures after the initial question. The members were also asked about employment, however, this issue usually generated lengthy discussions.

The frequency of the issues raised by group members indicated both what difficulties the members were experiencing and the difficulties that the members thought the group had helpful information about. Outside of seizure activity reports, medical care issues were brought up only 7% of the time. Helplessness generating attributions concerning unpredictable seizures were often corrected as well as overdependency on doctors. Almost all of the other issues were concerned with restricted social opportunities and examples of how members had overcome those restrictions and had interacted with social service agencies, family members, police, and the like. For this group, the emphasis across all the issues was for each member to be as self-sustaining and independent as possible.

Renegotiating members' ascribed roles. A stigma is an "attribute which is deeply discrediting" in a social relationship (Goffman, 1963, p. 3). The negative social attributions of others can lead to helplessness, a diminished self-concept, depression, and social isolation. Unlike many traditional rehabilitation programs, self-help groups do not ignore the social causes of the problem while treating the psychological symptoms. Self-help groups attack the social origins of the stigma by giving members an opportunity to renegotiate their ascribed roles through helping other people. The emergence of "helping others" and "sharing thoughts and feelings" in the survey as being the two most highly rated curative factors and the caring function as the most highly rated leadership behavior all underscore that these groups act as reciprocal social support systems for members.

Group members' belief in their helpfulness can become self-fulfilling regardless of what happens in the group. Consider one session where a young man had written a poem indicating that his life would end soon. No one responded to the poem, but talked about him looking for a job. During the discussion one woman told him to "practice what you preach" three times. Some other advice he heard was "Keep a positive attitude," "You've got to crawl before you walk," "Instead of 'I can't do,' you know what you emphasize? 'I can do,'" "The best thing in the world you can build is you," "If you know you're a quitter you'll never win, and if you're a winner you'll never quit," and "We will kick him in the ass when need be and where need be." After this last comment was made, the person who had written the poem indicated that while they had given him encouragement, he was still feeling bad about himself. The episode ended by the leader commenting on how this was a good example of members helping each other.

The next week, the "poet" had found another job. He thanked the group in general and one individual in particular for helping him during the last session. He thanked him for suggesting that he "go to the Salvation Army." However, this statement did not appear in our transcript of the episode. Earlier, someone else had suggested that people with parental difficulties should attend the Salvation Army family counseling program. Both the source and the nature of the help were misattributed. What makes this particular episode even more interesting is that several members remarked later that it was one of the best examples of how group members help each other.

This perception of being helpful is the essential component of a social support system. Accepting help without being able to reciprocate can foster feelings of dependence, resentment at the imbalance in the relationship, and implies that one is socially incompetent because he or she has nothing of worth to offer other people. In the survey, members were asked, "What has been the single best experience for you in your self-help group?" The second most frequently mentioned response was some act of helping others (21%). Instead of being helpless, members are helpful in the eyes of other members, their families, and friends. Group members also become experts in life management: making presentations at schools, being on panels at social service conferences, inviting professionals to meetings to be educated, participating in health fairs, and conducting publicity and fund-raising campaigns. Again, members are seen as being successful and competent by their families, friends, each other, and themselves. By being given the opportunity to "act out" of their ascribed roles, the attributions of competence and control made by both others and themselves can change.

Although we do not know members' psychological states when they joined the groups, we are interested in examining if the length of time that they have been group members was related to their reported levels of helplessness, depression, anxiety, and self-esteem. The learned helplessness model predicts that these variables are affected by the kind of controlling attributions repeatedly made in the groups. We also looked at the relationship between how long people had been members and their employment situations because having a job was considered a mark of competently coping with one's epilepsy.

In the national survey we asked, "Overall, how many meetings have you attended?" Number of meetings attended was chosen as an index of length of membership because of the varying schedule of self-help group meetings (weekly, biweekly, and monthly). Because of the large number of members who had attended only one or two meetings, this variable was recoded into five categories of equivalent size. We found significant linear relationships between the number of meetings attended and satisfaction with the groups, self-perceptions of group leadership functions, endorsements of the curative factors, and the probability of identifying positive attributes of having epilepsy. However, we found only one significant relationship between number of meetings attended and any of the psychological indices. The more meetings a member had attended, the lower the member's level of reported anxiety. None of the other variables related to the learned helplessness model or the stigma scale were systematically related to the number of meetings that members had attended.

Members' employment situations were systematically related to the number of meetings attended. "New" members were less likely to indicate that they earned their own wages to support themselves. The proportion of members who supported themselves through their own wages increased as the reported number of meetings increased, but this proportion drops off for those who have attended a large number of meetings (over 57). Similarly, a larger proportion of new members say they have experienced job discrimination because of epilepsy. This proportion declines precipitously through about 15 sessions, then increases again. Indeed, a larger proportion of those who had attended the greatest number of sessions report experiencing discrimination on the job than any other group. Finally, the more sessions members had attended, the more likely they were to have tried to educate employers and coworkers about epilepsy.

Given the one-shot nature of the survey, it is impossible to assess the effects of length of group membership on the members' psychological states and employment conditions. Yet there are both some positive and problematic inferences that can be tentatively drawn from the survey data. Members who attended more meetings were less anxious, more willing to educate employers and coworkers, and more likely to identify positive attributes of having epilepsy. These findings are at least congruent with the instrumental tasks that we suggested were being accomplished in the group meetings. The employment situation of members who had attended the most meetings may mean that the groups act as long-term havens for members who experience the most discrimination. The findings related to employment may also mean that some long-term members substitute group activity for seriously attempting to obtain work and use employment discrimination as a rationalization for their present circumstances. These inferences must await longitudinal research for confirmation or rejection.

Summary

Throughout this chapter we have focused on how communication can function in epilepsy self-help groups to enhance the perceptions of control for group members. Unlike other researchers of self-help groups, we have attempted to reduce self-help group processes to one basic construct. Both Lieberman (1979) and Levy (1979) have warned against doing this. Yet their work tends to generate lists of change processes.

To this point in our research, we have primarily described how the mere existence, narrative form, and instrumental content of the communication can all work toward helping people with epilepsy feel more in control of their bodies and lives. Without longitudinal research that collects and analyzes the groups' processes and members' perceptions more systematically, we are not ready to generate a theory of how communication functions in epilepsy self-help groups.

While no two epilepsy groups are the same, much less groups that deal with different disorders, we believe that people who feel that they are a part of a reciprocal social support system in their self-help groups are more likely also to perceive themselves to be in control of their environment (Cobb, 1979). However, where the freedom to talk, tell stories, seek information, and "act out of role" are restricted, the social support network becomes a social control system and individuals' perceptions of control decrease. Perhaps it is the access to these freedoms in self-help groups that makes these groups such a growing phenomenon in our country at the present time.

NOTE

1. Most of the questions in the survey were open-ended. However, embedded in the survey were a number of scales. The psychological indices that will be reported here include *Stigma* (10 items reworded for epilepsy that were drawn from Lieberman & Borman, 1979), *Self-Esteem* (4 items taken from Coopersmith, 1967), *Life Satisfaction* (3 items taken from Robinson & Shaver, 1972), *Helplessness* (4 items that were reworded and taken from Lieberman & Borman, 1979), *Multidimensional Health Locus of Control Scale* (2 items from each dimension plus the inclusion of 2 items for an external family control dimension, from Wallston, Wallston, & Devellis, 1978), *Hopkins Health Checklist* (the anxiety, depression, and somatic symptoms subscales; Derogatis, Lipman, Rickels, Uhlenhuth, & Covi, 1974), and *Dramatic Style* (4 items from the Communicator Style Instrument; Norton, 1978). Four scales were employed to measure members' attitudes toward their self-help groups: 8 items measured members' *Reasons for Joining Self-Help Groups*, 5 bipolar pairs of adjectives formed a *Group Satisfaction Scale*, 4 *Leadership Functions* developed by Lieberman, Yalom, and Miles (1973), and a modified version of Yalom's (1975) *Curative Factors*. For a more complete description of the survey methodology, see Droge (1983a) and Arntson, Droge, Norton, and Murray (1986).

8

Supportive Relationships and Occupational Stress in the Workplace

EILEEN BERLIN RAY

On any unit where death threatens, no one can afford to remain aloof from other staff members. You have to share heavy emotional demands if you want to avoid emotional debilitation. (Blake, 1976, discussing intensive care nurses)

From the computer company competing to keep its cutting edge, to hospital nurses facing death and dying daily, to counselors at a spouse abuse center dealing with emotionally wrecked clients, irate spouses, and reduced funding, stress at work is unavoidable (Vredenburgh & Trinkaus, 1981). In both private industry and human service organizations, workers often face role conflict, role ambiguity, overload or underload, and a variety of other stressors (Kahn, Wolfe, Quinn, Snoek, & Rosenthal, 1964) due to the uncertain nature of their job or the external environment.

It is estimated that stress-related outcomes cost organizations between at least $20 and $30 billion a year (Niehouse & Massoni, 1979). And while the sources of these stressors may vary, the effects

AUTHOR'S NOTE: I would like to thank Terrance L. Albrecht, Mara Adelman, and George B. Ray for their helpful comments on previous drafts of this chapter.

are often negative for both the stressed individual and the organization. At the individual level, these effects include increases in coronary heart disease, cholesterol, heart rate, hypertension, ulcers, psychosomatic complaints, fatigue, depression, anxiety, and drug and alcohol abuse (Beehr, 1985; Kahn, 1981; Katz & Kahn, 1978; McLean, 1985). Costly effects at the organizational level include low productivity and morale, and high absenteeism. And workers are increasingly winning compensation lawsuits citing job stress as the source of physical or psychological disabilities (Ivancevich, Matteson, & Richards, 1985; McLean, 1985).

Given the serious consequences of job stress, it is important for organization members to keep the effects from becoming dysfunctional for all involved. This chapter focuses on the communication of support as one means for effectively reducing stress. Of particular interest is how supportive communication from significant others in the workplace provides workers with information that can reduce uncertainty.

The Importance of
Supportive Communication in Organizations

The importance of supportive communication with superiors and coworkers to the well-being of individual workers and the overall organization has been recognized since the Hawthorne studies (Cooper, 1981; Cooper & Payne, 1978, 1980; Gottlieb, 1983; Pines & Kafry, 1978). Social support best functions as a process for the discussion and venting of negative feelings about the job or self (Badura & Waltz, 1982; LaRocco, House, & French, 1980; McLean, 1985) and builds self-esteem (House, 1981). Supportive communication provides the worker with information from significant others that can reduce the uncertainty *causing* the stress.

Support is a process that develops and is maintained through the ongoing interactions of organization members (Wellman, 1981). The availability and accessibility of support is largely determined by the structure of ties organization members have with each other (Gottlieb, 1981). As House (1981, p. 29) observes, "Flows of social support occur primarily in the context of relatively stable social relationships rather than fleeting interactions among strangers."

Thus while internal or external functions and processes of the organization are in a state of continual flux, support results from the ongoing, stable relationships that develop as organization members work together and help each other through times of high uncertainty. These relationships may begin when a person enters the organization and are strengthened whenever they are effectively mobilized to help the organization member cope with stress.

Of particular importance is the recipient's perception of receiving support from significant others (House, 1981). As Beehr (1985, p. 36) observes, "It cannot be said that a subordinate is given true psychological support unless the subordinate *feels* supported." What becomes important, then, is how support is communicated by significant others (House, 1981; Katz & Kahn, 1978). Albrecht and Adelman (1984, p. 4) emphasize the communicative nature of support as "the way in which communication behaviors tie an individual to his or her social environment and function to enable the individual to positively relate to that environment." Only if support is effectively communicated will it be perceived and have the desirable effect of reducing uncertainty.[1]

It is important to remember that support may be only fully realized by those sharing the organizational context. As a worker at a day-care center said:

> When I try to tell my husband or friends what it's like at work, to deal with 15 screaming, fighting, attention-demanding kids for 8 hours straight, they don't really understand. The only people who really feel like I do are the people I work with. They're there and they know what I really mean.

Talking about stress with people who share the same organizational context can provide a valuable coping mechanism (Albrecht & Adelman, 1984) and help to alter members' perceptions of potentially stressful events (McLean, 1985). They share common organizational referents that nonmembers do not, enabling a shared code and value system (Katz & Kahn, 1978). The overt and subtle stresses in the workplace are known to members and unclear to nonmembers. As a result, supervisors and coworkers are probably in a better position to provide support than non-organization-members.

Selected Overview
of Empirical Research

Over the past decade it has become more common for organizational researchers from various disciplines to study the effects of support on job stress. While much of this research has not explicitly taken the approach of this chapter, some element of the communication process typically has been included. A review of this research reveals two general lines of inquiry. One has centered on the effects of available intra- and extraorganizational sources of support to worker health and job satisfaction. The issue of direct versus moderating effects of support on stress has been the emphasis of most of these studies.[2] The second line of research has examined the relationship of one's accessibility to support to job stress and burnout. Most of these studies have taken a network analysis orientation, examining the workers' location in the informal support network. Thus the focus of this research has been on either *available sources* of support or *accessibility* to support.

An overview of selected representative studies are discussed in Table 8.1 which includes the details of definitions of social support used in these studies, sample sizes, sources of support, outcome variables, and findings.

Available Sources of Support

This research has not examined the supportive communication process per se but has primarily investigated the effects of available sources of support in and outside the organization. The importance of differentiating sources of support has been substantiated by several studies.

LaRocco et al. (1980), for example, investigated the effect of perceived social support from supervisors, coworkers, and spouse, family, and friends on job stress, job strain, and physical and mental health among men in 23 occupations. They found support buffered job stress and mental health but not job dissatisfaction and boredom. While support from all sources was significant, coworker support appeared to be a stronger buffer against somatic complaints and depression. They also found direct effects for support and health from all sources. However, for Navy enlisted men,

TABLE 8.1
Selected Empirical Studies on Social Support and Job Stress

Study	Sample	Support	Stress	Outcome(s)	Results
		Available Sources of Support			
LaRocco, House, & French (1980)	men from 23 occupations, randomly stratified (N = 636)	emotional support from supervisors, coworkers, wife, family, and friends	quantitative workload, role conflict, job future ambiguity, underutilization of skills and abilities, participation, workload, role ambiguity, responsibility for persons, job complexity	job dissatisfaction, workload dissatisfaction, boredom, somatic complaints, depression, anxiety, and irritation	coworker and home support buffer general mental health symptoms, support for direct effect on health
House & Wells (1978)	men in tire and rubber manufacturing plant (N = 3725)	supervisors, coworkers, friends, and relatives	job conflict, role conflict, responsibility, concern for quality of work, quantitative workload, job satisfaction, work self-esteem, health measures		importance of support from supervisors as compared to coworkers, little evidence for buffering effect from coworkers
LaRocco & Jones (1978)	Navy enlistees (N = 3725)	supervisors, coworkers	role ambiguity and role conflict	job satisfaction, Navy satisfaction, intent to stay in Navy, self-esteem	no evidence for buffering of stress on strain, direct effects for leader and coworker support on stress and strain
Seers, McGee, Serey, & Graen (1983)	federal government agency (N = 104)	immediate supervisor, department manager, coworkers, family, friends	role ambiguity and role conflict	overall job satisfaction satisfaction with work, supervisor, pay, and promotion	support from different sources had direct effects on different aspects of satisfaction

Study	Sample	Support measure	Stressor	Outcome	Findings
Blau (1983)	bus drivers (N = 166)	perceived instrumental and/or socioemotional help from district superintendent, fellow operators, spouses, and friends	person-environment fit	job dissatisfaction, ineffective job performance	different stresses affected by different sources of support, significant relationship for support and job dissatisfaction but not job performance
Etzion (1984)	managers and human relations professionals (N = 657)	instrumental, emotional, informational, appraisal support from supervisors, coworkers, family and friends		burnout	supervisor and coworker support buffered stress for men; family and friend support buffered stress for women
Accessibility to Support					
Anderson & Gray-Toft (1982)	nurses in surgical unit (N = 42)	social networks	role ambiguity and role conflict	satisfaction with work, supervisors, coworkers, burnout, absenteeism	support buffered stress and burnout for day shift, supported had access to other burned out and not burned out nurses, importance of supervisor in determining access nurses have in support structure
Albrecht, Irey, & Mundy (1982)	child welfare workers (N = 96)	integration in organizational communication network		burnout (tedium)	integration in organizational communication network related to less burnout and greater satisfaction with supervisor

(continued)

TABLE 8.1 Continued

Study	Sample	Support	Stress	Outcome(s)	Results
		Accessibility to Support			
Ray (1983)	hospital nurses (N = 109)	integration in work unit communication network	identified through interviews with nurses	burnout	no support for integration in work unit communication network and burnout
Ray (1986)	public elementary school teachers (N = 60)	integration in organizational communication network	identified through interviews with teachers	burnout	dense support links were related to greater stress and burnout

LaRocco and Jones (1978) found superior support was more closely related to job satisfaction and coworker support more closely related to satisfaction with the organization (the Navy).

House and Wells (1978) found superior support reduced work stress and indirectly improved health among hourly male workers in a large tire, rubber, chemicals, and plastics manufacturing plant. They also found that support from superiors and spouses, but not coworkers, appeared to buffer health. Seers, McGee, Serey, and Graen (1983) examined the sources of immediate supervisor, departmental manager, coworkers, and family and friends, finding that support from the unit manager had a direct effect on satisfaction with supervision but not on other facets of job satisfaction. Support from family and friends was directly related to overall satisfaction while support from coworkers had a stronger relationship to satisfaction with work and supervision than family and friend support did. In general, supportive relationships appeared to provide a useful strategy for coping with, but not buffering, job stress.

In his study of job stress and social support among bus drivers, Blau (1981) examined social support received by the driver from the bus district superintendent, fellow operators, and significant off-the-job people (i.e., spouses, friends). He found superintendent support was negatively related to some stresses and coworker support negatively related to others. A significant relationship was found for support and job dissatisfaction but not for support and job performance.

A study by Etzion (1984) suggests the importance of examining sex differences in addition to sources of support. Examining the relationship of social support from superiors, coworkers, family, and friends with job and life stress and burnout among Israeli managers and human service professionals, she found different sources of support for men and women. For men, stress was buffered by supportive relationships within the organization (from superiors and coworkers). For women, life sources (family and friends) buffered work stress.

Accessibility to Support

This line of research has taken a more explicit communication orientation, focusing on workers' access to support based on their location in the informal communication network. The primary outcome variables have been job stress and burnout. Kanner, Kafry, and Pines (1978) note that job stress and burnout result from both the presence of negative and absence of positive conditions. If accessibility to support is a positive condition, organization members lacking this access should have higher job stress and burnout. The degree of access is determined by one's location in the communication network.

Anderson and Gray-Toft (1982) found nurses on the day shift with high stress and burnout were located in the center of the support network, while evening and night-shift nurses were not. Support buffered stress and burnout for day-shift nurses but not for evening and night. The accessibility of support depends upon the nurses' location in the social support network and the importance of the superior (head nurse) in creating ties throughout nurses' support structures. Without the buffering effect of social support, nurses under chronic, excessive stress tend to burn out.

The results of several network studies on burnout, connectedness, and integration have been mixed. Albrecht, Irey, and Mundy (1982) found that protective service workers who were group members in an organizational communication network reported less burnout and more satisfaction with their supervisor than those who were less connected in informal groups. Limiting the network to the work unit, Ray (1983) found no support for a relationship between network integration and job burnout among hospital nurses. However, Ray (1986) found a relationship between the structure of supportive communication links to stress and burnout for public elementary school teachers. Teachers with less dense, less connected supportive relationships reported less stress and burnout than teachers with dense, highly connected relationships. Less dense networks may be more supportive since they provide access to information from numerous diverse others (Albrecht & Adelman, 1984; Granovetter, 1973), while denser networks tend to consist of homophilous links (Rogers & Kincaid, 1981). In addition, high-density networks may be more stressful because maintaining the relationships requires much energy (Stokes, 1983).

With the exception of Ray (1983), these findings show that some characteristics of support networks mediate job stress and burnout. The operational definitions used in these studies may account for some of these differences. For example, Albrecht et al. (1982)

examined the dichotomous communication roles of group members and linkers within the entire organization. Ray (1986) operationalized organizational network integration as a continuous variable and included only reciprocal, multiplex links, while Ray (1983) limited the network to the work group.

Several limitations of the studies discussed above should be noted. First, there is a lack of guiding theoretic frameworks for this body of research (LaRocco et al., 1980; Thoits, 1982). Second, conceptual definitions of social support are vague and imprecise and operational definitions vary from study to study, making comparison between studies difficult (Beehr, 1985; Gottlieb, 1983). Third, none of these studies has longitudinally tracked the supportive communication process for more than two points in time.

Despite the limitations in these studies, they indicate that supportive relationships appear to reduce uncertainty, thereby increasing worker health and job satisfaction, or decreasing job stress and burnout. Different sources, both within and outside the organization, appear to affect different stresses and strains. However, researchers have not examined the content or frequency of the supportive messages, mode of communication, or perceived importance or satisfaction with the messages. Instead, they have generally focused on the effects of perceived support from different available sources on outcome variables. Finally, researchers have primarily examined chronic stress rather than acute events that may precipitate the need for support.

Critical Events for Support at Work

Numerous events occur at work that prompt the need for support. These experiences are stressful for organization participants because outcomes are highly uncertain. These kinds of events include the socialization process, performance evaluations, and organizational change. The extent to which supportive communication is available and accessible is determined by characteristics of the organization, such as the physical structure of the organization, the time available to get information, and the nature of the job. A discussion of each follows.

Socialization. Socialization is the process by which a newcomer to the organization "learns the ropes" (Schein, 1968, p. 2). It is typically a time of maximum uncertainty for the newcomer (Jablin, 1984), who experiences stress regarding expectations, attitudinal norms, roles, and goals (Katz, 1985).

> To the new hire, the supervisor *is* the organization. If he is good, the organization is usually viewed favorably. If he is ineffective in working with the newcomer, the organization itself is seen negatively. (Porter, Lawler, & Hackman, 1975)

The newcomer's supervisor is in a key position to ease this stress. Jablin (1984) found that newcomers to an organization appreciate receiving information and instructions during this time, although they wait for others to initiate these interactions. Supervisors and coworkers can thus provide support during this time by initiating these interactions. Inclusion in formal as well as informal activities can help newcomers become socialized more quickly. Perhaps the most important type of communication is that which provides guidance and reassurance regarding expectations (Graen, 1976). Uncertainty can be reduced as newcomers increase their ability to predict the outcomes of their behavior. Quarterly reviews and immediate positive and negative feedback provide workers with information about how well they are meeting organizational goals. Supervisors can further reduce newcomers' uncertainty by providing opportunities for them to observe and interact with others in the organization. In this way, they can make sense of their new settings by gaining an understanding and interpretation of reality within the work context.

Performance evaluations. Another critical event where organization members need support is performance evaluations. Given that these are often used to make decisions about pay, promotion, transfers, and layoffs, the anticipation can be extremely stressful.

An upcoming formal evaluation may evoke uncertainty if the worker is unsure of how his or her performance will be rated. Fairhurst, Green, and Snavely (1984, p. 273) observe, "As individuals define themselves in terms of how competently they perform their jobs, evaluations of that competency speak directly to the identity of the performer." If this identity is threatened, the subordinate is likely to respond defensively. While a positive review is less likely to be stressful, a mixed or negative review requires skillful handling by the supervisor to enable the employee to save face and avoid a defensive interaction. If face considerations are ignored, the employee's defensiveness will block the effectiveness of any positive feedback (Cummings & Schwab, 1973; Kay, Meyer, & French, 1965).

Thus it is particularly important for supervisors to provide a supportive climate for this meeting (Gibb, 1961), where they enhance their subordinates' feelings of personal worth and importance (Redding, 1972). Characteristics of this climate include supervisory behavior that is nonjudgmental, shows trust and respect for the subordinate, empathy (Gibb, 1961), open and candid communication, a willingness to listen, and sensitivity to subordinates' feelings and ego-defense needs (Jablin, 1979).

Allowing workers input to solve their own performance problems also sets a supportive climate. The superior who relinquishes some control provides workers with more autonomy to set their own role expectations. For workers with problem performances, greater autonomy has resulted in longer time periods between problem recurrence (Fairhurst et al., 1984). By having to meet their own expectations, workers have more control over the ultimate outcome and should experience less uncertainty linked to their performance evaluation.

Organizational change. From technological advances to cuts in funding, organizations regularly face change. During times of change, organization members have a strong need for information to reduce uncertainty. A lack of information invites distortion and anxiety and undermines the self-esteem of workers (McLean, 1985). This need for information is so strong that any information, positive or negative, is perceived as more helpful than no information at all (Miller & Monge, 1985).

In addition to having access to relevant information, uncertainty can be reduced if organization members have input on potential change relevant to them. One method to provide this access is through participation in the decision-making process. As McLean (1985, p. 90) notes, "The very basis of a supportive context is the unequivocal involvement of employees in both their own tasks and their occupational destiny." An organization's commitment to this involvement communicates its respect and value for its workers, enables employees to blend their individual goals with those of the organization, and increases workers' commitment to the change (McLean, 1985). Participation in decision making also increases productivity, employee satisfaction, morale (Kahn et al., 1964; Katz & Kahn, 1978; Likert, 1961, 1967), and worker self-esteem (McLean, 1985). Organization members feel they have a stake in the organization and are helping to shape it. Their uncertainty about the outcomes of change is lessened because of their increased information and input into the change process. By making workers feel valued, competent, and important to the organization, participation buffers job stress (Beehr, 1985).[3]

Because talking about new ideas or change can be risky, workers tend to share these ideas with those to whom they are closely tied (Albrecht & Ropp, 1984). As these ties develop and are strengthened through members' regular participation, perceptions of risk should decrease, and the generation of innovations should increase. As Cooper (1981, p. 289) observes, "Participation at work seems to provide the social support that innoculates people against stress; it's a kind of substitute family group."

Organizational Characteristics and Support

Physical structure. Relationships can develop only with those we come into contact with, and the more frequent that contact, the greater the chance for supportive relationships to develop (Homans, 1950). If supportive relationships are desired, workers must have physical and psychological access to their coworkers (House, 1981). However, there are physical characteristics of an organization that influence the development of supportive relationships. As Sommer (1974) observed, the architectural design of a building influences who interacts with whom. The pool of potentially supportive contacts can be structurally predetermined. Workers who share the same physical space share the same frame of reference, have a greater opportunity to interact on a regular basis, and, subsequently, have regular access to supportive communication from those around them. The "fish bowl" effect experienced in some settings provides this opportunity (Adelman, 1986).

We sort of work in a fish bowl, everybody is privy to what goes on and how we deal with babies. We have a good knowledge of how our co-workers operate and the kind of care they give because we see it. . . . If for some reason an M.D. is not pleased and upsets a nurse, the minute an M.D. leaves the room somebody is right there to say, "What's the matter with him?" or "I don't think that was an appropriate way to deal with it." That's helpful and it keeps us honest with how we deal with each other. (nurses in nursery work in close contact with and with open windows to the public)

Time availability. The amount of time available to spend developing these relationships is also an important factor. In the work context, these relationships probably develop at a slower rate than in nonwork contexts because of prescribed roles and the focus on job-related interaction (Altman & Taylor, 1973). Getting the job done must come first. If there is low job interdependence, there may be little time left over to spend on non-job-related talk. This was observed by a worker in a blood bank (Sypher & Ray, 1984):

We have a product [blood] to get out. If we have time for those other things [e.g., staff meetings, informal communication, participation in decision making, solving problems, etc.] after, it would be nice. (p. 783)

Obviously, jobs requiring high interdependence enable joint time for greater interaction than jobs with low interdependence. In a loosely coupled organization, such as an elementary school, teachers are more autonomous from their supervisor and colleagues in order to do their job (Weick, 1976). Their day is spent in the classroom, with short breaks between classes and one free period a day. Often this free period is spent writing lesson plans or copying materials rather than interacting with coworkers. In addition, the accessible coworkers are those who also happen to have a free period scheduled at the same time.

Nature of the job. The results of research on support show the importance of job structure and time available to interact with coworkers as potential impediments to the development of supportive relationships in the workplace (Ray, 1983, 1986). In addition, where there is limited access to coworker interaction, the relationship with the supervisor becomes more important (House, 1981). Some jobs are performed in relative isolation, often outside the organization structure. Blau (1981), for example, notes that for his sample of bus drivers, interaction among coworkers is limited by the nature of the job. There is little opportunity for the drivers to develop and maintain interpersonal relationships because the job is performed outside the organizational structure and interdependence among workers is not required in order for the job to be performed adequately. House and Wells (1978) also suggested differences in types of occupations as an explanation for why some research has found a relationship between superior support and job stress while others have found only evidence for coworker support. Anderson and Gray-Toft (1982) found significant differences in day, evening, and night shifts of nurses' support networks and job stress. Albrecht et al. (1982) studied protective service workers and found those integrated in a support network reported less burnout. As they note, protective service workers spend much of their time outside the organization. The supportive messages they receive from their supervisors and coworkers are critical to reduce the uncertainty experienced when they are out of the office.

When employees share the same physical space, their high social density promotes interaction. Szilagyi and Holland (1980) found that during organizational change, greater social density reduced stress and increased job feedback, satisfaction, and opportunities for friendships to develop. Thus in new situations where uncertainty is high, high density may be functional. Members sharing the organizational context are experiencing similar uncertainty and their dense ties provide redundancy necessary to address this uncertainty. It is not known, however, whether these dense ties remain functional over time.[4]

Organizational Support
and the Nonwork Domain

The preceding discussion emphasizes the importance of support within the organization to cope with high uncertainty. However, not all stress is due to the work experience or organizational characteristics. With the dramatic changes in the nature of the work force over the past 20 years (Kanter, 1983), issues external to the job or organization are raising workers' uncertainty levels, subsequently affecting their performance and health. For example, more than 50% of families have at least two wage earners (Kanter, 1983), with many of these being two-career couples. There are 52 million women now working ("Expectant Moms," 1986) and 54% have children under 18 at home (Terborg, 1985). Of these women, 80% are potential mothers ("Expectant Moms," 1986).

As a result of these changes, organizations must now provide support in the nonwork domain of their employees' lives. As discussed below, support resulting in flexible work arrangements, help with child care, and concerns of dual-career couples can reduce uncertainty by providing tangible help and emotional reassurance.

Flexible work arrangements. In most other industrialized nations, six months of paid maternity leave, with job protection, is typical ("Expectant Moms," 1986). However, despite the fact that there are 42 million potential mothers currently in the work force, there is no legal policy providing maternity leave in the United States. Many new mothers are faced with unpaid leaves and no guarantee of having a job to return to. For some, maternity leave is accrued from sick leave or taken under a short-term disability policy. While individual arrangements, such as flextime, may be made by women in senior positions ("Working Around Motherhood," 1982), the less skilled, lower-paid women are often unable to benefit from these arrangements.

Some U.S. organizations have recognized the need for liberal leaves. More than one-third of major companies allow unpaid maternity and paternity leaves ("Expectant Moms," 1986). Some organizations have instituted flexible working hours for new parents. Mothers or fathers may work a half day at the office and a half day at home or any variation on their working hours ("Working Around Motherhood," 1982). With the increase of women in the work force and fathers' increased participation in child raising, liberal parental-leave policies will enable organizations to recruit and retain employees needing this kind of support.

Child care. With 54% of women currently working having children under 18 at home (Terborg, 1985) and 80% of these women potential mothers ("Expectant Moms," 1986), the issue of child care is a salient one. Lack of adequate child care can cost the organization in many ways. Parents may have to miss work, arrive late, or leave early to accommodate their child-care arrangements, or spend much of their day at work worried about the care their children are getting (Dilks, 1984).

While other countries have provided nationalized day-care since World War II, on-site child care facilities in the United States are still relatively rare. However, some companies have started providing substantial assistance to employees with child-care needs. In these organizations, the benefits include higher morale, lower turnover, and workers arriving on time, concentrating on their work when there, and leaving on time (Dilks, 1984).

Dual-career couples. With the increase in dual-career couples has come an increase in stress. Careers, as opposed to jobs, can be characterized as a commitment to a work role and a developmental progression in that role (Gupta & Jenkins, 1985; McLean, 1985; Rapoport & Rapoport, 1971). Workers pursuing careers are expected to be willing to relocate and make the organization their top priority. In addition to their own career stresses, members of dual-career couples have the additional stress of coordinating their careers with those of their spouses. The stresses become even more intense if they are dual-career parents. Parents have the added stress of juggling the demands of two careers with the demands of child care.

A lack of organizational support for these couples will only add to their stress, lowering morale, productivity, and hurting recruitment and retention. Recognizing this, some organizations are providing support services. One service, spouse career counseling, is designed to help a spouse find a job when the other is relocated. Some organizations also offer flextime so that employees can fit work hours with those of their spouses and other responsibilities (Bralove, 1981). However, while organizations are beginning to show an appreciation for dual-career couples, they need to identify dual-career couples' special needs and provide appropriate support (Gupta & Jenkins, 1985).

Conclusion

Supportive interactions are those in which coworkers are able to vent feelings, clarify perceptions, and mutually define the work environment. In human service occupations, where goals are ambiguous and unclear, outcomes are intangible, and salaries are inadequate (Ray, 1983), talking about stress may provide workers with a sense of camaraderie and esprit de corps that adds value to the meaning of their work environment. Interpersonal relationships may function as intrinsic rewards compensating for the lack of extrinsic rewards.

It is also important that "complete" uncertainty reduction is not the goal of supportive communication and could actually be detrimental in the organizational context. One way uncertainty is eased is through self-disclosure. But more is not necessarily better. As Parks (1982) notes, an "ideology of intimacy" is problematic. Because of the power inherent in the supervisor's role, disclosure by subordinates can threaten upward mobility and retention with the organization. Employees who have high uncertainty and regularly communicate this to their supervisors may be perceived unfavorably. Organization newcomers initially need high levels of tangible and emotional support. It is expected that this need will decrease as the newcomer becomes socialized. If it does not decrease within a reasonable amount of time and the newcomer continues to disclose uncertain feelings, supervisors and coworkers may begin to doubt the worker's professional and/or emotional competence. Eisenberg (1984) suggests that the use of strategic ambiguity, rather than disclosure, allows workers to control what information they share without jeopardizing their organizational relationships.

Future Research Avenues

The research on sources of support indicates the importance of different intra- and extraorganizational support sources as buffers to different stresses. However, the content of these messages and workers' satisfaction with this support is not known. While some of this research has included spouses as a source of support, differences based on marital status are unclear. Do single people rely more on intraorganizational support? Do spouses provide more support than colleagues who share the work context? Can the potential sources of support be stressors? Intraorganizational support to attend evening meetings, work overtime, and/or work at home in the evenings or weekends may conflict with the expectations of the extraorganizational support source, the spouse. The stress of this conflict between support sources may be greater than the benefits of the support received. Another issue is if sources differ depending on whether the stress is chronic or acute. For example, coworkers and supervisors may be the preferred sources for chronic stress because they share the organizational context, while spouses may be preferred for coping with acute stress. The communication network research shares a general lack of correspondence between the conceptual and operational definitions of support. These studies have used frequency of communication as the primary indicator of supportiveness. However, supportive relationships also include positive (Fiore, Becker, & Coppel, 1983) and reciprocal communication (House, 1981). Conceptually, supportive links are implicitly assumed to be positive and reciprocal. Operationally, however, most have not included valence and, with the exception of Ray (1986), have not explicitly distinguished reciprocal from nonreciprocal links.

Finally, support can exist only to the extent that organizations are committed to a supportive climate and show this commitment symbolically and tangibly. McLean (1985) refers to this as "emotional climate control." This is a climate that allows people to cope successfully with the inevitable and constant changes in the workplace. The corporate philosophy that is either explicitly or implicitly communicated to workers sets the climate. One thing that excellent organizations share is a value and respect for their workers that is communicated by actively soliciting, using, and rewarding their input (Peters & Waterman, 1982). Symbolic and tangible support is communicated through a recognition that the new work force cannot separate their work life from their personal life and a commitment to both by organizations. They communicate this support by providing benefits such as child-care facilities, maternity and paternity leave, flexible work arrangements, and flexible benefits. When layoffs are necessary, these organizations may provide relocation services, job retraining, or skills evaluation. When one member of a dual-career couple is transferred, these organizations help place the spouse. Future research needs to examine how these tangible supports reduce uncertainty in the workplace.

Summary

What we know about the benefits of social support as a mediator of stress in the workplace is confounded by the lack of a guiding theoretic framework and problems with conceptual and operational definitions. The relationship of social support in the workplace to job stress is a complex one. What does appear evident is that supportive relationships help workers cope with uncertainty and reduce job stress. The development of these relationships is partly a function of uncertainty reduction, as well as the nature of the job and the structure of the organization. An examination of issues raised in this chapter can increase our understanding of the complexities of supportive communication in the workplace and build upon the strengths of existing research.

NOTES

1. Uncertainty reduction theory, as framed by Berger and Calabrese (1975), refers to the reduction of mutual uncertainty for development of the supportive relationship. As noted in Chapter 1, support also can *reduce the uncertainty* of the *individual* toward his or her work role and organizational environment. This aspect of uncertainty reduction was not covered under the original theory.

2. A major controversy in this research has been whether the relationship of social support to job stress is direct or moderating. Direct effects examine how support influences various strain variables while moderating effects examine how the relationship between job stress and various strains is affected by one's level of support.

3. Participation in decision making may, however, increase stress. For example, workers must process more information in order to make informed decisions. During times of high job activity, they may become concerned with spending too much time making decisions rather than doing their jobs. The resulting information overload and role conflict may increase stress levels. In addition, individual needs for participation vary. Some workers have no desire to be involved but may be forced to participate, resulting in more stress and decreased performance (Ivancevich, 1979). Finally, organizations may require members to participate in decision making but rarely use their input. Members are likely to become disillusioned and to question the organization's true commitment to the participatory decision-making process.

4. If the content of communication is negative, reverse buffering (Beehr, 1985), or the "contagion" effect (Adelman, 1986; Cherniss, 1980; Ray, 1983), may occur (see Chapter 11 in this volume). Instead of providing helpful support, the network may actually become another source of stress (Fiore et al., 1983; Stokes, 1983) by focusing on negative features of the job and/or organization. Spending every day at work talking with the same people about how bad things are can have only negative effects on both the individuals and the organization. As many have noted, accessibility to people outside the work group can provide important support by providing new information and fresh perspectives (Albrecht & Adelman, 1984; Anderson and Gray-Toft, 1982; Granovetter, 1973; Ray, 1986; Ray, Waldhart, & Seibert, 1985).

9

Facilitating Immigrant Adaptation:
The Role of Communication

YOUNG YUN KIM

> Successful communication with self and others implies correction by others as well as self-correction. In such a continuous process, up-to-date information about the self, the world, and the relationship of the self to the world leads to the acquisition of appropriate techniques, and eventually increases the individual's chances of mastery of life. Successful communication therefore becomes synonymous with adaptation and life. (Ruesch, 1951/1968, p. 18)

Life is a process of continuous change. From the moment of birth, we are exposed to various environmental challenges. And every challenge, desired or not, produces some degree of stress in us as we reorganize our internal state to accommodate the changing or changed reality. From the uncertainties in a new relationship to the helplessness in separation from a loved one, from the exciting anticipation of a new job to the reluctant departure from a home town, we adapt. In effect, the very meaning of human "growth" centers on this process of change, stress, and adaptation.[1]

Normally, we do not face change and the accompanying stress alone. We have people around us with whom we share our experiences of change. Often, they provide us with useful information and advice, and help us to feel stronger by showing their emotional support. Depending on the needs arising in a given situation, we may also seek from them concrete material or physical support.

Implicit or explicit in this interaction is an understanding that such support will be reciprocated when the situation is reversed. This exchange of social support makes the process of living meaningful and many of the stressful events bearable. For many people, however, securing a satisfying support system cannot be taken for granted. As the pace of social mobility and cultural change accelerates, a growing number of individuals find it difficult to develop and maintain stable relationships over an extended period of time. For varying reasons, they often find themselves separated from their familiar support network and in need of building a new one. Developing a solid support network, indeed, has become a special challenge in our contemporary world.

In this chapter I address the increasingly pervasive phenomenon of developing a support system as individuals go through various situations of "ecological transition" (Bennet, 1976). Specifically, the situations of immigrants and refugees who, voluntarily or involuntarily, have moved from one society to another is discussed.[2] The process of forming a new interpersonal system in this cross-cultural context is one of the most intense manifestations of the widespread problem of cultivating a functional support network. The situation of immigrant adaptation, unlike the situation of domestic migrants moving from one city or region to another, presents an added barrier of cultural differences to overcome. An immigrant must build a new social identity in the host society and make a living in much the same way as the native population. But developing such relationships is often a challenge in and of itself.

In this cross-cultural context, how do immigrants develop supportive interpersonal ties with the natives? What roles do ethnic individuals play in assisting their adaptation to a new environment? How do their support networks typically evolve? These issues are central to this theoretical essay, incorporating available empirical research when available. Exploring these questions will help us understand the situations of international migrants, as well as the situations of many others who, for one reason or another, find themselves having to adapt in an unfamiliar environment within a societal boundary. Although the situations of domestic migrants are typically less drastic, they nonetheless share with international migrants common experiences of change, stress, and adaptation.

The Process of Immigrant Adaptation

Through the process of socialization, individuals acquire the collective entity called "culture," enabling them to respond to various environmental messages. Internalized cultural attributes provide individuals in a given society with a common set of beliefs, values, norms, language, and verbal and nonverbal modes of communication. Although no two individuals in a given culture are identical, the basic commonality of their internalized culture enables them to communicate with one another with fidelity and to develop and maintain a multitude of interpersonal relationships.

Of the many relational ties that individuals maintain at a given time, ties with "significant others" play a particularly crucial role in providing social support. The term *personal network* refers to *an individual's social network that consists of close, supportive, relational ties with significant others.* This network generally includes family, relatives, and close friends who provide the individual with social support in some major ways. As Albrecht and Adelman (1984, p. 10) state, the personal network helps the individual "to reduce uncertainty through the process of social comparison, the exchange of information for problem solving, and to meet needs for affiliation and affection." Social support channeled through the personal network lessens stress by improving the "fit" between the person and the environment (Caplan, 1979; French, Rodgers, & Cobb, 1974).

The majority of new immigrants find themselves without an adequate support network, particularly during the initial stage of adaptation when they are confronted with the highly uncertain and stressful conditions of the host environment (Schuetz, 1944/1963; Zwingmann & Pfister-Ammende, 1973). Uprooted from their supportive ties in the home country, and accustomed to seeing and doing things in a manner different from that of the natives, many immigrants meet the challenges of the new environment almost single-handedly. Even if some members of the original personal network from the home country (such as family members) are still with them, the immigrants are faced with having to develop a new set of significant relationships with native members of the host environment.

Host Communication Competence
and Interpersonal Relationships

One of the most critical factors that promote or deter the immigrants' development of interpersonal relationships with the natives is host communication competence. Most immigrants "know" very well their inadequacies in communicating with the natives and their lack of ability to express, to be understood, and to develop meaningful interpersonal relationships with the natives. *Host communication competence, then, refers to an immigrant's overall capability to decode and encode messages effectively in interacting with the host environment.* It is the primary vehicle through which the immigrant is able to understand and respond adequately to various challenges of the host environment. This capability enables the immigrant to transform mental and behavioral resources into functional ways of dealing with inputs from the environment (Ruesch, 1951/1968).[3] As the immigrant becomes increasingly proficient in the host communication system, the effectiveness in managing his or her various life activities correspondingly increases.

This theoretical relationship also operates in the reverse direction, that is, the process of developing host communication competence is enhanced by participating in interpersonal relationships with the natives. One learns to communicate by communicating, so to speak, as one learns to swim by swimming. There is simply no better, more efficient way to acquire host communication competence than by engaging in communication activities with the natives. *Indeed, the development of host communication competence, and the cultivation of interpersonal relationships with the natives, occur side by side in the ongoing process of immigrant adaptation.* This mutual causation between host communication competence and relational development of immigrants should not necessarily be viewed pessimistically as a catch-22. Rather, the two interrelated activities should be viewed as both inseparable and mutually enhancing dimensions of the same process, that is, immigrants' second-cultural adaptation. In doing one, the other follows as well (see Figure 9.1).

This close association between the development of interpersonal ties with the natives and the development of host communication competence has been amply demonstrated in previous studies.

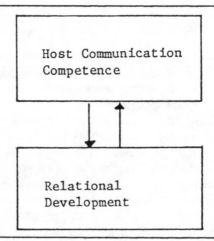

Figure 9.1   Mutual Facilitation of Host Communication Competence and Relational
Development

For instance, studies of Korean immigrants (Kim, 1977a, 1977b, 1978b, 1979b) and of Indochinese refugees (Kim, 1980b) have suggested that the indicators of psychological adaptation (e.g., alienation, social distance, and attitudes toward the host society) are clearly related to the extent that they have developed interpersonal ties with the natives. The better-adjusted immigrants are more involved with the natives in interpersonal relationships.

Dimensions of Host Communication Competence

The immigrant's host communication competence can be viewed as consisting of three interrelated dimensions: *cognitive, affective,* and *behavioral* (Gudykunst & Kim, 1984; Kim, 1979a, 1982). First, the immigrant must acquire cognitive information about codes and their meanings in the host communication system, particularly its language, verbal and nonverbal modes of expression, and rules of interaction. This knowledge will increase the immigrant's "perspective-taking" abilities (Fogel, 1979) and "coorientation" (Oshagan, 1981; Pearce & Stamm, 1973) with the natives. Second, the immigrant must acquire the motivational and attitudinal orientation that is compatible with that of the host culture. The emotional tendencies, aesthetic sensibilities, humor, and values of the host culture must be shared by the immigrant if he or she is to participate in meaningful relationships with the natives. Third, the immigrant must learn to perform in the various communication situations of the host society. This behavioral competence includes the ability (or skill) to speak, listen, read, and write the host language, to express and understand various nonverbal expressions in the manner acceptable to the natives, and to carry out social transactions in accordance with the appropriate interaction norms and rules of the host culture.

These three dimensions are organically interdependent. The way an immigrant communicates with native members of the host culture reflects the simultaneous interplay of his or her cognitive, affective, and behavioral capabilities. Together, the three dimensions of host communication competence contribute to the immigrant's overall effectiveness in dealing with the natives (see Figure 9.2).

Realistically, the average immigrant will not become fully competent in the host communication system to the extent that his or her communication modes are identical with those of the natives. The first-generation children of immigrants, however, are more fully adapted than their parents because they have been exposed to, and have acquired, host communication competence from early childhood.[4] Immigrants, on the other hand, make a workable adaptation as a result of their many trials and errors. They gradually become more capable of approaching the natives to elicit their responses, of responding to their approaches adequately, and of taking on various social roles they must perform. All of these adaptive changes help the immigrants to enhance their chances of achieving personal goals and aspirations.

Host Communication Competence,
Relational Development, and Adaptation

Adaptation, then, can be viewed as occurring through a process of individual transformation toward an increasing level of host communication competence and of relational development with natives.[5] Generally, the process of change is sufficiently subtle so that the person may hardly recognize it. Adaptive changes in immigrants occur even when they actively resist. Adherence to an ideology, such as cultural separatism or pluralism, that emphasizes deliber-

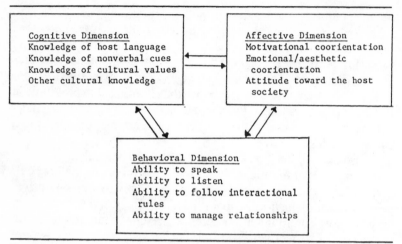

Figure 9.2   Interrelated Dimensions of Host Communication Competence

ate resistance against losing the original cultural identity, may minimize adaptive changes. Nevertheless, existing evidence clearly demonstrates that immigrants do transform themselves in the direction of increased similarity to host cultural characteristics and of greater integration into the host social structure (Alba, 1976; Crispino, 1977).

Thus adaptation occurs *naturally* regardless of the intentions of immigrants as long as they are functionally dependent on, and interacting with, the host sociocultural system for survival and self-fulfillment. It is similar to the case of family members who, as a result of an extensive exposure to each other and of sharing common life experiences, manifest many similar attributes with or without their conscious awareness.

Not all immigrants, of course, begin the process of adaptation with the same degree of preparedness and receptivity. Previous studies have identified a number of background characteristics that tend to prepare the immigrants with greater adaptive potential (Kim, 1977a, 1980b; Snyder, 1976). These background factors include the similarity between the original culture and the host culture, a higher educational level, and younger age at the time of immigration. Also, such personal qualities as tolerance for ambiguity and risk taking (Fiske & Maddi, 1961), internal locus of control (Johnson & Sarason, 1978), gregariousness (Bradburn, 1969), and hardy or resilient personality (Quisumbing, 1982) have been found to facilitate an immigrant's cross-cultural adaptation (see Figure 9.3).

As such, individual immigrants begin the process of adapting at different starting points and with varying personal dispositions. All immigrants, however, face a common challenge—a challenge to maximize their life chances in the new environment by increasing their communication effectiveness and developing supportive ties with natives.

Ethnic Support Systems

How, then, does the ethnic social support system influence the immigrant's overall adaptation process? Commonly, an immigrant today has access not only to native members of the host society but also to individuals of their national or ethnic origin. In the United States and other countries that have received a large number of immigrants, many immigrant communities provide some form of "mutual aid" or "self-help" activities. These community organizations render valuable services to those immigrants in need of material, informational, emotional, and other forms of social support (see DeCocq, 1976; University of Toronto, 1980; Weber & Cohen, 1982). The Vietnamese Association of Illinois, for example, assists with many of its members' needs by providing translation services, housing information, transportation, and counseling. Such community services are of particular importance to new arrivals who are lacking in host communication competence and other resources required for self-reliance. They also organize religious services and holiday festivities to promote a sense of ethnic identity and pride among its members. Frequently informal friendship networks also develop as immigrants continue participating in various organized ethnic community activities.

Ethnic Community and Initial Adaptation

In fact, many immigrants do have some ethnic ties (other than ties with members of their household) at arrival in the host society. In their initial migration into the host society, most immigrants find a place in which they have at least some access to an ethnic support system through family, relatives, friends, or visible community

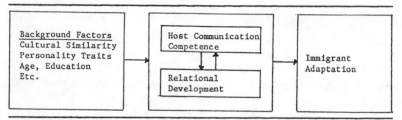

Figure 9.3   **Background Factors Facilitating Adaptation**

organizations. Snyder (1976) reported that a sizable personal network at arrival existed for most immigrants in five ethnic neighborhoods (blacks, Chicanos, whites, Arabs, and American Indians) in Los Angeles. (See also Smith, 1976, for a similar observation.)

It appears, then, that *new immigrants are naturally inclined to seek support among fellow immigrants within their ethnic community.* While interacting with natives involves a great deal of unfamiliarity and stress, ethnic relations are based on preacquired repertoires and, thus, are least stressful. The extensive reliance on other immigrants within the ethnic community for support has been frequently observed in previous studies. Valdez (1979), in a study of the relational patterns of Puerto Ricans in an industrialized city, reported the immigrants' high integration into ethnically homogeneous networks of family, friends, and coworkers. Le (1979, in Deusen, 1982, p. 238) also reported that the personal networks of Vietnamese refugees in Los Angeles consisted predominantly of other Vietnamese, and that they serve as a primary source of help for mental health problems. (See also Y. Kim, 1977b, 1978a, 1978b; King, 1984; Krause, 1978; Silverman, 1979; Yum, 1983, for similar findings.)

The natural inclination for immigrants to affiliate with fellow immigrants in their ethnic community is consistent with the view of Albrecht and Adelman (1984) on support-seeking behavior. Based on the uncertainty reduction theory, they hypothesized that individuals are likely to seek support from those with whom they perceive less relational uncertainty, and that those who share a stressful context will be perceived as more helpful than those who do not share the context (p. 20). Rather than taking the risk of performing inadequately in the unfamiliar modes of the host communication system, immigrants tend to prefer to seek social support from fellow immigrants.

The reliance of immigrants on fellow immigrants for social support has also been observed to be influenced by at least two additional factors: the immigrant's marital status and the "institutional completeness" of the ethnic community. Alba and Chamlin (1983) argued that those who are "in-married," that is, married to members of the same ethnic group, are likely to be more involved with other ethnic individuals for social support. A similar finding was reported by J. Kim (1980) in his study of Korean immigrants in the Chicago area. Institutional completeness of an ethnic community refers to the degree that the community is established in religious, media, welfare, business, political, and other organizations (Breton, 1964). Inglis and Gudykunst (1982) replicated Y. Kim's (1976) study of Korean immigrants in the Chicago area and among Korean immigrants in Hartford, Connecticut, and reported a significant difference between the two groups in the overall size of ethnic relational ties. The degree of ethnic involvement of the immigrants in Hartford, an area with less institutional completeness, was found significantly lower than that of the immigrants in Chicago, an area with greater institutional completeness.

**Ethnic Community
and Long-Term Adaptation**

Although an ethnic support network clearly plays a vital role in providing social support to immigrants, it is generally regarded as either insignificant or dysfunctional to adaptation in the long run. Broom and Kitsuse (1955, p. 45) argue, "A large part of the acculturation experience of the members of an ethnic group may be circumscribed by the ethnic community." Similarly, Shibutani and Kwan (1965, p. 982) state: "To the extent that . . . a minority group participates in different sets of communication channels, they develop different perspectives and have difficulty in understanding each other."

Supporting this view, Y. Kim's (1980) study found a negative influence of ethnic communication on both early and later stages of the cultural adaptation of Korean immigrants. The variance in the immigrants' acculturation level explained by their participation in relationships with natives was two times the variance explained by the ethnic communication. Also, no statistically significant association was observed in Y. Kim's (1976) study of Korean immigrants between the degree of ethnic involvement and indices of adaptation to the American cultural environment. This and other empirical evidence suggests that, *in the long run, an immigrant's participation in ethnic communication activities does not substantially facilitate, and in some cases may even hinder, the adaptation process.* This tentative generalization, of course, recognizes that ethnic ties with highly adapted individuals can be greatly beneficial to the immigrant's learning not only during the initial phase, but throughout the adaptation process.

Adaptive Changes in Personal Networks

In spite of the supportive role played by ethnic ties at the beginning, it is ultimately from the native members that much of immigrants' adaptive capacities are acquired. The natives, knowingly or unknowingly, present feedback to immigrants as to whether they are in tune with the host communication modes. Often such feedback is given in the form of subtle nonverbal expressions of understanding or puzzlement, comfort or discomfort, and approval or disapproval. Based on such feedback, immigrants examine their own cognitive, affective, and behavioral tendencies and modify what they can.

As immigrants become increasingly proficient in communicating with the natives, they are better able to cultivate and maintain interpersonal relationships with them. In time, they incorporate natives into their personal network of supportive relationships in more meaningful ways. This means that, by examining their personal network patterns, we can understand the degree of their host communication competence. Indeed, the relational ties that an immigrant has developed at a given time is one of the most frequently used indicators of his or her overall adaptation (see Y. Kim, 1976, 1979a; Nagata, 1969; Yum, 1983).

Of many possible aspects of the nature of the' immigrant's personal network, three are suggested here as reflecting, as well as facilitating, their host communication competence and adaptation most characteristically. The three aspects are network heterogeneity, strength of ties with natives, and the centrality of natives in the immigrant's network. (A fuller discussion of these network characteristics is presented in Y. Kim, 1986b.)

Heterogeneity. The network *heterogeneity* generally refers to *the degree that nonethnic members of the host society are included in an immigrant's personal network.* It has been observed by identifying the size and the ratio of relational ties with outgroup members to the total number of ties in the immigrant's personal network. For example, Yum (1982), in her study of Korean immigrants in Hawaii, measured network heterogeneity by the degree of nonethnic members included in the personal network. In this study, "communication diversity," or the level of integration of Americans in the immigrants' information sources, was significantly influential in their acquiring the information necessary for their functioning in the United States. Y. Kim (1977b, 1978a, 1978b, 1980b) also reported an increasing number of natives in the interpersonal networks of Korean and Indochinese immigrants during the initial years.

Findings such as these are reinforced by the positive association between a greater network heterogeneity and the "cosmopolitan" (as opposed to local or provincial) psychological orientation proposed in nonimmigrant settings (Craven & Wellman, 1973; Fischer, 1982; Rogers & Kincaid, 1982). A higher-level inclusion of nonethnic individuals in an immigrant's personal network indicates a higher-level host communication competence. Conversely, someone whose personal network consists primarily of fellow ethnic individuals is likely to be less competent in communicating with the natives and less adapted to the host environment. Further, composition of a primarily ethnic personal network is indicative of the lack of facilitative influence on the immigrant's future interaction and relationship development with natives.

Tie strength. Once the heterogeneity of the personal network is determined, we may proceed to examine the content of each relational tie. One relational content relevant to the immigrant's host communication competence is "tie strength" (Granovetter, 1973; Marsden & Campbell, 1983). The term refers to *the level of "bondedness" or intimacy between individuals in a relationship.* It implies an overall level of interdependency between the involved persons, that is, the relative degree of difficulty to break the relationship. Altman and Taylor (1973) described such an attribute as indicating a high degree of "social penetration" in the relationship development. For the present analysis, individuals in a stronger relational tie are considered to exchange a greater amount of social support than those in a weaker relational tie.

Strength of ties with nonethnic persons can be assessed in a number of ways. One may focus on the amount (or rate) of interaction between the immigrant and each member of the personal network for a given period of time (e.g., daily, weekly, monthly). This is based on the assumption that, on the whole, intimacy is reflected in the amount of communication. Tie strength can also be assessed by the intensity of positive or favorable feelings that the individual attributes to a given relationship. Often this is done by asking the respondent to assess the strength of relational ties in a rank order, or in terms of a number of "intimacy zones" such as "acquaintances," "casual friends," and "intimate friends" (Alba, 1978; Y. Kim, 1976, 1978a, 1980b). If we were to focus only on the personal network of intimate friends, we could further differentiate the degree of tie strengths by assessing both the overall volume of communication and the ratings of perceived intimacy.

Research findings have shown the close association between the strength of ties with natives and the degree of an immigrant's host communication competence. Y. Kim (1977a, 1978a, 1980), for example, has consistently found that, as the immigrant becomes better adapted to the host environment, his or her interpersonal ties with natives tend to become more intimate. An increase in the immigrant's intimate American friends was significantly associated with indicators of English proficiency as well as the level of "cognitive complexity" (i.e., understanding of the American cultural system).

Centrality. Another content attribute of relevance to immigrant adaptation is the degree of the "centrality" of natives in the immigrant's personal network. In network terms, *centrality refers to the degree that a person has a short distance to others in a personal network.* It represents the person's accessibility to other persons in the network, and thus the degree of information and influence within the network (Mariolis, 1979; Yum, 1984). This means that the higher a native's centrality in an immigrant's personal network, the higher the person's significance to the immigrant.

Even though few immigrant studies have used this centrality concept, *it is considered a potentially useful indicator of the extent that natives are integrated into the immigrant's personal support system.* As the centrality of ties with natives approaches or exceeds that of fellow ethnic ties in an immigrant's personal network, the immigrant's host communication competence and adaptation is considered to have increased as well. Together with the two other network characteristics (network heterogeneity and the strength of native ties), the centrality of native ties appears to serve as a useful framework in which an immigrant's host communication competence and adaptation can be understood.

Research Needs

So far, the process of second-culture adaptation has been discussed emphasizing the development of host communication competence and personal network patterns. Based on the premise that personal networks serve vital functions in facilitating the adaptation process, the present approach has explicated the relationship between the immigrant's host communication competence and network ties (both within and outside the ethnic community). Key ideas presented above can be summarized as follows:

(1) Adaptation is a natural process of individual transformation in line with all environmental changes. The adaptation of immigrants, in particular, occurs as a result of a changed cultural environment that presents both extensive uncertainty and support. In this cross-cultural context, the task of developing a support network is of paramount importance.

(2) Immigrants' ability to develop and maintain supportive relationships with natives is closely associated with their host communication competence. The immigrants must acquire the necessary cognitive, affective, and behavioral orientation compatible to that of the host culture.

(3) Immigrants are naturally inclined to seek social support from fellow immigrants in their ethnic communities because of the low degree of stress and threat involved in communicating with them. As immigrants acquire an increasing level of fidelity in the host communication system, they tend to become less reliant on ethnic ties, and more on native ties. In the long run, ties with natives, not with fellow immigrants, facilitate adaptation to the host environment, although ethnic ties provide vital support in the initial stage of the adaptation process.

(4) The degree to which natives are incorporated into the immigrant's personal network, the degree to which native ties are strong, and the degree to which they are central in network position, are considered to reflect, as well as facilitate, the immigrant's host communication competence and adaptation.

Existing studies have been reviewed to provide empirical support for these generalizations. They generally fall into two groups based on their purpose and research orientation. The first group includes relatively recent studies in which the primary research purpose is to develop a theoretical framework to explain immigrant adaptation employing various communication concepts as central to adaptation (e.g., studies by J. Kim, Y. Kim, and Yum). The second group consists of descriptive studies that ascertain the patterns of ethnic support networks in relation to mental health in specific ethnic communities (e.g., studies by Alba, Cobb, Deusen, and Snyder). These studies are more "applied": Few of them have dealt explicitly with the theoretical linkages between support networks, communication patterns, and long-term adaptation. In spite of the different research orientations, findings from these two groups of studies often reinforce or complement one another and collectively provide tentative support for the present conceptualization.

Future research must test the general observations made in this chapter in a more systematic and comprehensive manner. Accurate and full descriptions of the nature of adaptive changes in immigrants, their communication patterns, and the development of their supportive network system need to be made. Although immigrants have long been an important object of scientific investigations, researchers have only begun to address these important communication-relational dimensions. A combination of the communication perspective and the network analysis, as proposed in this chapter, promises to be fruitful in understanding the dynamic process of second-culture adaptation. For a continued effort to extend the current understanding of immigrant support networks, the following issues are presented.

Clarification of network concepts. We need to understand in depth how the different patterns of an immigrant's personal network operate in the reality of second-culture adaptation. The three network concepts presented earlier (heterogeneity, tie strength, and tie centrality) need to be closely examined to refine the theoretical ideas and to develop ways to assess them realistically and efficiently. Of the three concepts, network heterogeneity is the only concept that has been extensively investigated. Typically, it has been assessed simply by counting the number of ethnic and nonethnic ties in a personal network, and by computing the ratio between the two relational categories. *No systematic attempt has been made, for instance, to determine if nonethnic ties need to be limited to natives only without including nonnatives outside an immigrant's ethnic community. Nor is it clear whether nonethnic ties need not necessarily include members of any dominant or majority group in the host society* (e.g., white Anglo-Saxon Protestants in the case of the United States). Also, as noted by Alba (1976), *we do not know if an immigrant's personal network includes others from many different backgrounds, or if they may all be from one group, so long as it is different from the immigrant's ethnic group.*

Clarification of these issues is vitally important to assess the immigrant's network patterns accurately and to widen the consensus among researchers on such assessments. To do so, future studies must go beyond the use of a simple in-group (ethnic) and out-group (nonethnic) distinction and ascertain the specific composition of group membership in the immigrant's personal network.

Elaboration of communication activities over time. We need to uncover detailed and specific communication activities within the personal networks of immigrants. In addition to simply measuring the overall characteristics of relational ties, we need to elicit in detail what actually occurs during encounters. *Selected relational ties in an immigrant's personal network can be investigated in-depth for specific communication activities and accompanying psychological orientations.* Through intensive interviews and observational methods, the relational ties can be closely examined to understand, for example, the differences and similarities in the immigrant's support seeking from natives and from fellow ethnic friends.

Efforts must also be made to observe such communication activities over an extended period of time. By doing so, we are able to identify consistent or changing communication problems encountered in developing supportive relationships with fellow immigrants and natives. Such longitudinal studies allow us to examine the aspect of host communication competence that are critical in developing supportive relationships with natives. Also, the developmental pattern of native ties can be compared to that of ethnic ties. These and other related research questions will help us to understand the dynamic communication process between immigrants and their relational counterparts. Such information cannot be adequately obtained through studies conducted on a one-time basis.

Facilitating Immigrant Adaptation

Many more questions need to be asked, indeed, if we are to enhance our present understanding of the process of immigrant adaptation. Yet the information presented in this chapter suggests a number of insights into the support network development in immigrant adaptation and of ways to help facilitate the process.

Either-or dilemma. The interrelatedness of the immigrant's host communication competence and their involvement in ethnic and native ties presents a potential conflict in philosophical views concerning the goal of adaptation. Must immigrants give up their involvement in personal relationships with other fellow immigrants to maximize their chances of successful adaptation in the host society? Or must they maintain ties within the ethnic community to maintain their cultural identity even if such ethnic affiliation may hinder adaptation in the larger environment?

This apparent dilemma is based on a rather simplistic ideological basis that demands an "either-or" choice between ethnic and nonethnic communication activities of immigrants. *In the reality of the adaptation process, most immigrants do maintain ties both within and outside the ethnic community.* As they develop an increasing level of host communication competence, their association with natives increases both in quantity and quality. This tentative generalization does not necessarily mean that close ties with ethnic friends must end as well. Supportive relationships, once developed, can be maintained with little relevance to the adaptive goal, but simply based on an emotional bond and a positive regard for each other.

The issue facing the immigrants, then, is not having to choose either native friends or ethnic friends, but having to prevent ethnic ties from interfering with the adaptive process. If, for example, an immigrant's personal network consists primarily of ethnic friends for a prolonged period of time, this (almost) exclusive reliance on an ethnic support system tends to impede the immigrant's effective integration into the larger society. An immigrant's ethnic identity can be maintained without impeding effective functioning in the host society, if a sufficient level of host communication competence is developed to manage new roles in the host society. This observation resembles the common wisdom that one must not become overly dependent on floating devices if one wants to become

Facilitating Immigrant Adaptation

a competent swimmer. Similarly, an excessive or exclusive reliance on an ethnic support system, in the long run, is likely to deter the immigrant's functioning in the host society and hinder his or her capacity to overcome communication barriers and to adapt.

Mainstreaming social services. Recently, a number of researchers who have participated in studies of various social service programs for immigrants have pointed out the importance of "mainstreaming" (rather than segregating) immigrants' service needs from the host environment in general. As Herberg (1980), as well as Keefe, Padilla, and Carlos (1978), pointed out, *many public and community services (e.g., services related to physical and mental health) need to be closely linked to the natural ethnic support system.*[6]

Consistent with this view, some innovative mechanisms have been implemented to rework the patterns of service within and between agencies to include more effective use of ethnic resources. Cohon (1978, in Deusen, 1982, p. 239), for example, utilized Southeast Asian paraprofessional trainees working under the clinical supervision of a native psychologist in providing mental health services in a special San Francisco area project. The project's emphasis on linking native professional and ethnic paraprofessional personnel was proved to be useful in crisis prevention in the community (Deusen, 1982, p. 239).

This emphasis on combined ethnic and host team social service delivery recognizes the interactive nature of the process of immigrant adaptation. The merging of ethnic and host team social service delivery is an approach sensitive to the cultural and communication barriers that the immigrants experience, as well as facilitative of their adaptation by enhancing the "interaction potential," or accessibility, of the host social environment (Kim, 1979a; Coombs, 1978/1979).

Host acceptance. Social agencies, however, are only a part of the larger host environment. Every person an immigrant encounters in the course of daily life activities contributes to the process of adaptation in some way. *The natives can express their support for immigrants, motivate them to acquire host communication competence, and encourage them to participate in the development of supportive relationships.* Although much of the adaptation task must be carried out by the immigrants themselves, their efforts alone cannot be realized successfully unless the host environment presents them with receptivity and acceptance (see Berry & Kalin, 1979). Individuals in the host society must realize that it is in their collective interest to accept immigrants as fellow members of society rather than regard them as "foreigners." Without genuine acceptance of, and regard for, immigrants, the natives are likely to send out subtle, nonverbal messages of apathy and denial, if not outright hostility. These negative messages can be a critical source of discouragement to those immigrants who are already experiencing a great deal of stress in trying to overcome communication barriers.

Ultimately, it is a matter of the individual immigrant's conscious or unconscious decision that influences the extent to which they should strive to adapt to the host environment. If immigrants hope to become functional members of the host society, they must participate as actively as possible in interpersonal relationships with natives. The longer they wait, the longer will it take for them to become competent in the host communication system, and the slower will be the process of becoming fully functional. Self-determination in overcoming the various psychological, social, and cultural barriers is crucial to maximizing their chances for successful living in the host society.

The history of the United States is filled with stories of successful immigrants who have willingly and courageously overcome the challenges of the new environment and who have "made it." Such cases are concrete evidence for the enormity of human resilience and adaptability. With determination, learning, and participation in the communication processes of the host society, many more immigrants will be creating their own success stories. The personal triumphs of our immigrants present invaluable lessons to all of us who strive to secure a warm corner of social support in this world "on the move."

NOTES

1. A detailed discussion of adaptation and the human growth process is presented by Kim (1986a) from a communication approach. Atwater (1983) presented a psychological process of adjustment in relation to personal growth. Adaptation has been discussed frequently in other psychiatric or psychological literature (for example, see Geyer, 1980; Moos, 1976; Ruesch, 1951/1968). The

primary emphasis in existing discussions of adaptation is placed on "mental illness" (or lack of adaptation), rather than the growth process itself.

2. The term *immigrants* will be used throughout this chapter in an inclusive manner to refer to all international migrants, such as refugees and missionaries, who have been socialized in one society before moving to another on a more or less permanent basis. International students, short-term visitors, and tourists are not included in this definition, although the nature of their adaptive experiences is similar to immigrants' experiences during the initial phase. Various sources of statistical information on international migration are available including *World Refugee Survey, Annual Report of the United States Immigration and Naturalization Service,* and *United Nations Statistical Yearbook.*

3. Communication competence has been a topic of much research and academic debate in recent years. Earlier presentation of the concept was made by Ruesch in conceptualizing mental health/illness. More recently, Geyer (1980) integrated various social psychological theories of alienation using a general systems approach, and presented a comprehensive conceptualization of alienation. Geyer viewed alienation as essentially a result of the lack of competence in an individual's information-processing capacities. In the field of communication, Spitzberg and Cupach (1984) present a comprehensive review of diverse approaches to communication competence, along with their own model of interpersonal competence. See also Parks (1985) and Bostrom (1984) for articles that conceptualize and describe communication competence in a number of social settings.

4. Many studies have examined the adaptation patterns across generations of immigrants. See, for example, Allen and Lambert (1972), Alba (1976), Chan (1978), and Conner (1977).

5. The term *adaptation* has been used (see Berry, 1980; Brody, 1970) along with other similar terms such as *acculturation* (see Broom & Kitsuse, 1955; Kim, 1982; Nagata, 1969; Padilla, 1980), *adjustment* (see Coelho, 1958; Deutsch & Wong, 1963), and *assimilation* (see Crispino, 1977; Decroos, 1979; Gordon, 1964). While these terms vary somewhat in their respective emphasis and focus of analysis, they all refer to the common process of change in immigrants in relation to the host environment. In this chapter, the term *adaptation* is used in the broadest sense of its meaning, encompassing the meanings of other terms.

6. Similar arguments have been made concerning the practices of bilingual education for immigrant children. Donahue (1982) and Lum (1982), for example, propose a broadened perspective on bilingual education emphasizing the integration of multicultural education into the mainstream educational practices of the entire society rather than treating it as a separate and isolated service program for immigrant children only.

10

The Diffusion
of Supportive Information

VICKI S. FREIMUTH

I have to have an explanation. I just could not live with it any other way. I can live with anything I can understand. (cancer patient, quoted in Skipper & Leonard, 1965)

Any health threat, whether the discovery of a suspicious lump or the symptoms of a cold, creates uncertainty. What is wrong with me? Should I see a doctor? Will I get better? What kind of treatment will I need? Can I afford the treatment? Will I be unable to work? These uncertainties frequently cause anxiety and fear. Usually we attempt to reduce these uncertainties and the anxieties they spawn by seeking information. We believe that information may give us more mastery or personal control over our environment. In that sense, information itself is a form of social support. Eyres and MacElveen-Hoehn (1983, p. 3) define support as "information and resources from others in the environment . . . that minimize the perception of threat, maximize actual and perceived mastery and facilitate direct action and anticipatory modes of coping."

The purpose of this chapter is to examine the process of disseminating supportive information to the individuals who are experiencing uncertainty in the face of a health threat. In this chapter I will examine this process from two perspectives. First, I will look at individuals as consumers of information, that is, where they seek information, what they expect to find, and how they might use the results. Second, I will examine the process from the information disseminator's point of view and describe two theoretical models of the dissemination process—diffusion of innovations and social marketing—and describe some examples of information campaigns using these models.

Information Consumers

As already stated, an individual faced with the uncertainty of a health threat turns to information to relieve anxiety. Dervin (1976), however, has found that awareness and use of potential information sources, especially professional and nonprofit institutions, is low except among the educated elite. This apparent inconsistency between information needs and use may result from different meanings associated with the term *information*. Information is usually defined as "thing," that is, as objective data that describe reality. Dervin (1976), however, asserts that information should be defined as "construction," that individuals take external information and organize it within their own already collected internal information in order to make "sense out of their world." Therefore the individual actually "creates" his or her own information. Dervin (1976) considers that although the input of others has some utility and although individuals seek external information to close gaps in their understanding, ultimately information has value only insofar as it helps the individual to make his or her sense out of reality.

Leventhal, Safer, and Panagis's (1983) explanation of health behavior reinforces the information-as-construction idea because it suggests that health information is understood, organized, and remembered in terms of the individual's underlying beliefs. According to these authors, people construct a representation of their illness and a plan to cope with it. These naive or commonsense models of illness appear to be based on the integration of current symptom experience with ideas from past illness episodes and information from medical practitioners, friends, relatives, and media. Comaroff and Maguire (1981) found the same phenomenon in their study of childhood leukemia: "Parents . . . typically tried to bring the stunning diagnosis of leukemia into relation with perceived medical facts, the experience of others and their own biographies and world-view" (p. 119).

Three broad sources of health information contribute to the models of illness that patients construct: intrapersonal, interpersonal, and mass media sources.

Intrapersonal Sources

Intrapersonal sources of health information consist of all the previous knowledge, beliefs, and attitudes about the illness that might have been developed from interactions with family, friends, and health practitioners, and from health messages on the media. The public's perception of cancer, for example, is frequently confused and skeptical. In a 1983 National Cancer Institute (NCI) survey of the public's perceptions of cancer, about half the respondents believed that everything causes cancer and that there was not much a person can do to prevent cancer. The respondents were able to identify tobacco, sunshine, and X-rays as cancer risks. But almost half said bumps and bruises could increase the chances of getting cancer. Other frequent misconceptions were that cancer was contagious, hereditary, and spread by surgery.

Concrete body sensations, such as symptoms, as well as memories of past body sensations also are intrapersonal sources of health information. The importance of these body sensations is demonstrated in a study reported by Leventhal et al. (1983), in which 80% of a sample of hypertensives agreed that "people can't tell when their blood pressure is up." The frequently heard medical message that hypertension has no symptoms is remembered and repeated. But nearly all of the respondents believed *they* could tell when their own pressure was elevated with such body sensations as headaches, flushed faces, and nervousness.

Interpersonal Sources

The second source of health information comes from interpersonal communication. People turn to others for information about their health problem. Not all interpersonal sources are equal information resources, however. Health professionals, especially doctors, usually enjoy the most credibility and influence, but are the most difficult to use because of unavailability, status differences, and tendency to use technical jargon. In a 1983 survey of the public's attitudes, beliefs, and behavior about cancer (NCI, 1984) physicians were cited as one of the most reliable and credible sources of information. However, when asked if they ever had talked to a physician about ways to reduce their chances of getting cancer, nearly 86% of the respondents said no, and only 14% said yes (NCI, 1984). Many patients may have questions for their physicians but are hesitant to ask them because they are afraid to reveal their ignorance, are reluctant to take up too much of the physician's time, or are afraid to question a strong authority figure.

Waitzkin's (1985) report of 336 encounters between 34 doctors and 314 of their patients illustrates some of these difficulties in patient/physician communication. He found that in an average encounter of 16 minutes, the doctor spent 1.3 minutes or 9% of the time giving information yet the doctors perceived that they had spent almost seven times that long providing information. Patients averaged eight seconds asking questions or 1% of the encounter. The patients asked 2.8 questions in a typical interaction and the doctor provided 7.1 explanations, 29% of which were in response to questions and 71% of which were spontaneous explanations. In 28% of these question/answer exchanges, there were discrepancies between the technical level of the question and its answer. Waitzkin (1985) also discovered some reasons for the variation in information giving in the medical encounter. More information was given the poorer the prognosis was, the longer the doctor had known the patient, the higher the socioeconomic level of the doctor and of the patient, and the less busy the doctor was.

Doctors are not the only health professionals who are used by patients as information sources. Nurses are often more accessible to patients and sometimes will share information even when told to withhold it (McIntosh, 1974). However, nurses also use strategies to discourage information seeking. They may, for example, feign busyness in order to make themselves unavailable to answer questions. They also may view questions as complaints and communicate subtly to patients that they should not be asked (McIntosh, 1974).

Another interpersonal source of information that is often overlooked is the fellow patient. McIntosh (1974) cites evidence that TB patients and even child polio patients discuss their diseases among themselves and compare themselves with other patients to judge their own conditions. Self-help and volunteer patient groups, such as Reach to Recovery, Make Today Count, and I Can

Cope, are proof of the need cancer patients have to communicate with each other. This need for communication with similar others may vary with stages of the illness. For example, Comaroff and Maguire (1981) found that leukemia patients and families had an intense need to identify with others who had the same affliction at times of crisis, such as initial diagnosis, relapse, and death. But when definitions of the illness had reached relative stability, and hence the search for meaning was satisfied, referencing decreased and other patients were avoided as possible sources of disorienting information.

Other interpersonal sources of information as support are those individuals seen on a regular basis but who are only superficial acquaintances or weak links.[1] These sources have been called "community gatekeepers" or "urban agents" and might include teachers, bartenders, hairdressers, and grocery checkers. These weak links are particularly rich sources of new information.

Finally, the most familiar interpersonal sources are family and close friends. From these interpersonal sources patients might compare symptoms, borrow remedies, refer one another for treatment, and comment on one another's appearance. Miller (1973) studied this kind of lay consultation by interviewing 139 head and neck cancer patients about the advice they sought when they first suspected a problem. Of these individuals, 62% first discussed the problem with medically uninformed sources, 26% consulted with medically informed persons, and only 12% went directly to health professionals. Miller (1973) concluded that this use of lay consultation did not delay patients from seeking professional care but was a positive force in encouraging them to seek appropriate care.

Mass Media Sources

The third type of informational resource is mass media. People credit the mass media as the source of most of their information. In 1978, the American Cancer Society (Lieberman, 1979) found that the most often mentioned source of cancer information was mass media. Of those surveyed, 82% reported that they heard about cancer on television, 65% through newspapers, 61% through magazines, and 42% through radio. The 1983 NCI survey asked about sources of cancer prevention information and found that the most frequently reported sources of information were magazines (64%), newspapers (60%), and television (58%).

Mass media may disseminate health information both deliberately, through campaigns designed specifically to have this impact, and incidentally, through programming that contains health-related information. Studies of mass media effects over the last several decades have moved from simplistic descriptions of a "hypodermic needle" effect, a direct and universal response to the media, to the two-step flow model, where messages flow from the media to opinion leaders who then disseminate them to others, to more recently, the multistep flow model, where messages can reach audiences directly and/or through many layers of interpersonal contacts.

Relationship between mass media and interpersonal communication. There is considerable agreement that the primary function of the mass media is to create awareness and reinforce existing behavior, whereas interpersonal sources can influence change. Chaffee's (1972) reference to the "interpersonal context of mass communication" perhaps best describes the complex, transactional interplay of media and interpersonal sources in the diffusion of information. Chaffee (1972) strengthens the case against a unidirectional flow of information and for a dynamic exchange among senders and receivers by citing evidence that individuals' choices of media are often related to their social contacts, that individuals' use of media can be motivated by "communicatory utility"—that is, individuals selectively retaining information they believe to be congruent with the views of those with whom they expect to communicate at some future time—that nonleaders engage not only in actively seeking information but also in "opinion-sharing" with leaders. Butler and Paisley (1977, p. 9) describe this complex network in the following way:

> From the time the information is born as a concept within the communication program to the time it modifies a person's image in such a way as to produce desired outcomes, the message may have traveled over several networks and through many phases of transformation, some of them external to the person, others internal.

Slaughter, Napolitano, and Freimuth (1985) studied information sources used by mothers to decide whether to get their infants immunized with DPT. They found support for the transactional interplay of media and interpersonal sources. Mass media represented a majority of first sources of the DPT controversy but quickly declined as a source for subsequent communication, thus reinforcing mass media's role as a vehicle for creating awareness and stimulating public discussion. Further support for these functions derives from the fact that the influence of the media on subjects' decisions was only moderate (3.7 out of a possible 7) and that the primary effect of mass media sources was to raise uncertainty rather than to strengthen existing beliefs about the vaccine. Conversely, interpersonal sources and health professionals occurred less frequently as first sources but increased in frequency as subsequent sources.

Problems in mass media coverage of health. There are several problems inherent in the type of health information the mass media can provide. First, tensions exist among scientists, science reporters, and editors as to what is appropriate health information to cover. Because the mass media deal in fragments of air time and print space, information must be tightly packaged by writers and editors, which often results in oversimplification. Scientific research is a slow process in which knowledge is built incrementally. Yet media like to cover sensational, fast-breaking events. Finally, many health issues, such as cancer, are emotional issues and subject to highly personalized interpretations.

Newspapers. Studies of newspaper coverage of cancer in 1977, 1980, and 1984 (Greenberg, 1986) provide evidence of some of these problems. In general, the newspaper coverage in all three years did not include much helpful information for the cancer patient. The articles emphasized dying rather than coping. Less than 5% in any of the studies mentioned resources for coping. In fact, human interest stories constituted only 7% of each sample. Even the health columns analyzed included very little information on coping with cancer and resources available. Thus very little direct emotional support or even information on where to find emotional support was available through the newspapers.

Patient education materials. Some of these limitations of the news media coverage of health are overcome in the specialized media information sources known as patient education materials. These materials usually consist of pamphlets, booklets, and audiovisual programs that can be targeted more specifically and can present more detailed information about the health problem. Even these materials, however, must present information that will meet the typical patient's needs and cannot respond uniquely to each patient. We know that patients need different kinds of information depending on timing, whether they have just been diagnosed or are recovering. Yet Evans and Clarke (1986) report that most information on cancer given to patients is cognitive in nature and is given within 24 to 48 hours after diagnosis. Patients are also more receptive to different sources at different points in the treatment process. At some points, a physician may be the best source; at others, a successful former patient, someone in the same stage of treatment, or a significant other may be best. Situations also differ, for example, certainty of treatment outcome, length of regimen, and unpleasantness of side effects of treatment.

New media. One suggestion for meeting this enormous array of information needs has been to vary delivery means as well as content. The new interactive media, in which the computer acts as a message control device, has been offered as one solution (Evans & Clarke, 1983). A variety of media for informational display can be used on this type of system, such as audiotape, frames on conventional television monitors, and segments stored on videodiscs. It is anticipated that the process of using interactive media may begin to confer self-confidence and a sense of control. Patients can choose a segment, pause when necessary, replay a segment, and take self-administered tests. Unfortunately, these innovative information disseminating systems are unavailable to most patients.

Television-public service announcements. Several forms of broadcast media are used for health information. We are familiar with public service announcements (PSAs) on both radio and television. "Fight cancer with a check-up and a check" and "Do it for the loved ones in your life" are two well-known slogans from PSAs. PSAs, however, have some serious limitations. Because the air time is donated, not purchased, PSAs often are aired in the wee hours of the morning, when the number of viewers is quite low. Moreover, PSAs must be very brief messages, usually no more than 30 seconds. And PSAs have to compete with slickly produced commercial advertisements both for air time and for audience attention.

Television-health programs. There are only a few regular health programs on television and several programs such as *Sixty Minutes,* the network morning news shows, and women's shows that regularly discuss health topics. Occasionally, there are special programs devoted to health issues. These programs are more frequently aired on PBS than on commercial television. One of these PBS specials was *Joan Robinson: One Woman's Story*, a documentary of a middle-aged woman from Massachusetts who was dying from cancer. Through this program, Robinson allowed the audience an intimate look at the physical and emotional trauma she faced. Another PBS special, *Why Me?* featured eight women who had surgery for breast cancer openly discussing their personal experiences. Nationwide surveys discovered that the majority of women who had viewed the program had favorable responses and found it helpful. One woman summed it up, "Now I know what breast cancer is all about, and I think I could handle it if it struck me personally."

Television-entertainment programs. Television also communicates health information incidentally in the plots of entertainment programs. Long (1978) reports a study that asked respondents about health information learned from dramatic shows and found that 48% of those who watched them reported getting some useful information from them. A recent study (Turow & Coe, 1985) in which the treatment of illness on all three networks was examined over a two-week period demonstrates that few models of effective coping behavior were available in these television programs. Of 723 illness episodes analyzed, only 10% involved psychosocial coping. Only 2 of the 248 commercials referred to psychosocial coping and only 18% of the noncommercial illness episodes depicted psychological aspects of coping with the problem. One of the few models of coping available in the televised illness episodes was a heart patient on *St. Elsewhere* who listened to classical music to keep her mind off her upcoming transplant.

Sometimes health issues are handled accurately and sensitively, such as the episode about breast cancer on *Cagney and Lacey,* a series about two policewomen. One of the most controversial current medical entertainment programs is *St. Elsewhere,* a weekly, hour-long drama that attracts an estimated audience of 18 million people. Some of the show's major themes include the fallibility of doctors, strained relations among staff or between doctors and patients, the daily mingling of humor and tragedy, and the ethical dilemmas inherent in the practice of medicine.[2] Patients may react to these programs differently than the general public. One former fan of *St. Elsewhere* has been unable to watch since she had lung surgery. She says her hospital experience "was amazingly similar. It was the pitch, the fever pitch. . . . It's recreating something I really choose to forget" (Okie, 1986). For the general public, a program such as *St. Elsewhere* may provide an image of what a hospital experience is like and hence reduce some of their uncertainty and fear associated with hospitals. For this particular patient, however, the program was so realistic that, instead of being supportive, it was disturbing because it recreated an experience she wished to forget.

Radio. Much less is known about the use of radio as a health information source. Generally, when asked on surveys, people do not credit radio as an important source of health information. Tony Schwartz, the well-known media consultant, has a different interpretation of what he calls the "most invisible and emotional of all media" ("Media's Muscleman," 1977, p. 64):

> People don't remember radio as a source of information because they don't consciously listen to it. Rather, they bathe in it and sit in it. Just as we are not conscious of breathing, we are not actively aware of radio-mediated sound in our environment. Yet we are deeply involved with radio, and we are strongly affected by radio programming that allows us to participate. ("Media's Muscleman," 1977, p. 65)

The coverage of health on radio is similar to that of television except that radio has far more talk or interview programs where a guest expert may discuss a health topic and then listeners can call in and ask questions of that expert. Little research has been done on use of this format for information seeking.

Telephone. Another source of health information is an interesting cross between a mass medium and an interpersonal source—the telephone. Altman (1984, p. 21) suggests that the "advantages of health telephone programs is that they combine some of the positive components of mass media—high exposure, convenience, cost-effectiveness, user anonymity—with some of the positive components of face-to-face interactions—personalized attention." A CIS caller expressed the advantages of the telephone quite well when she said, "I cannot discuss personal matters with friends and relatives; I can with strangers, on the phone" (Altman, 1984, p. 319).

The most common use of the telephone for health information is to call the doctor to discuss symptoms. This traditional use of the telephone has been expanded to include hotlines that offer counseling, such as suicide prevention services; dial access services, such as Tel-Med, which allow callers to request the playing of any of 250 prerecorded messages on such health subjects as smoking cessation, venereal disease, and arthritis; and information/referral services, such as the Cancer Information Service (CIS) and related regional services such as the Cancer Lifeline in Seattle, where trained staff answer questions and refer callers to local resources.

An analysis of nearly one million calls made to the CIS between January 1983 and July 1985 revealed several interesting observations about information seeking as a form of social support. Over twice as many calls to the CIS were made by family and friends of cancer patients than by cancer patients themselves. Seeking information appears to be a tangible form of social support that can be offered to the cancer patient. It has also been suggested that family/friends act as agents for cancer patients who may be too ill or anxious to engage in much information-seeking behavior themselves.

Women callers outnumber men by about three to one. This finding is consistent with the role of the woman as caretaker of the family's health, which emerges from most research on sex differences and health behavior. Cancer patient callers are more likely to be older (58% are 50+), while family/friends of patient callers tend to cluster in the age range of 20-40 (43%). Similar results were reported for an evaluation of Tel-Med, a dial access telephone information service (Diseker, Michielutte, & Morrison, 1980). Respondents over the age of 50 were somewhat more likely to have called the service about personal health problems than were adults ages 21 to 49. These differences are of course due to the higher prevalence of cancer in older people but suggest also that information seeking as social support may be more likely to come from children of older patients than from their contemporaries.

Information Disseminators

This section of the chapter focuses on information dissemination—how supportive information is diffused to those who need it. What if, for example, you were on the staff of the Alzheimer Disease and Related Disorder Association and wanted to develop some print materials to help family members cope with the disease. How would you determine the messages to include in the print materials? How would you get those materials into the hands of the appropriate people? Two theoretical models—diffusion of innovations and social marketing—will be presented to guide this dissemination process. The first theoretical model examined—diffusion of innovations—has been developed primarily from sociology and contributed to by many researchers across the social sciences.

Diffusion Theory

Diffusion (Rogers, 1983) is a multidisciplinary theory of planned social change, change that is brought about by the spread of new ideas or new technologies throughout a social system. Communication between a change agency and the client system and further communication within that system result in individuals or groups deciding to adopt or to reject the innovation. It is assumed that a decision to adopt reflects an anticipation that adoption will bring desirable consequences for the clients. Diffusion theory includes the following key concepts: innovations, communication channels, time, social system, and change agents and opinion leaders. Each concept will be explained in the sections below.

Innovations. An innovation is an idea or behavior perceived as new by the individual (Rogers, 1983). Although in the health area there are some technological innovations (e.g., new drug to treat cancer), most innovations are health behaviors that, while perhaps known to the individual, are not currently being practiced by him or her (e.g., exercise). Diffusion of health information is concerned primarily with "preventive" innovations. According to Rogers and Adhikarya (1979, p. 71), "Preventive innovation is a new idea, x, that is adopted 'now' in order to avoid the possible loss of desired value, y, in the future." For example, Kellogg and NCI encourage us to add more fiber to our diet now to prevent colon cancer later. Preventive innovations minimize loss, and their adoption is often motivated by a "cue-to-action," an event that changes an attitude into behavior. For example, a cue-to-action to motivate the use of family planning is often provided by an unwanted pregnancy or a pregnancy scare. A cue-to-action for the smoker may be the heart attack of a contemporary who smokes. Little is known about preventive innovation decisions, except that the adoption rate is usually slower than the adoption rate for other innovations (Rogers & Adhikarya, 1979).

Innovations can be classified according to five characteristics: (1) relative advantage, (2) compatibility, (3) complexity, (4) trialability, and (5) observability (Rogers, 1983). High levels of complexity of an innovation can impede diffusion; high levels of relative advantage, compatibility, trialability, and observability can facilitate diffusion. Medication for high blood pressure (HBP) may have few relative advantages—it is expensive, it may be difficult to remember to take, and it may cause some side effects. Clearly, taking medicine is an advantageous alternative to the consequences of uncontrolled HBP, stroke, and heart attack, but these consequences are not immediate. The compatibility of taking medicine daily with an individual's life-style depends on the individual's orientation to medicine in general. If the individual must take several pills and watch his or her diet, the behavior becomes quite complex. Trialability is possible with HBP medications, but the treatment is lifelong. Finally, the most serious liability is the observability characteristic; since HBP has no symptoms, taking the medicine produces no observable rewards.

Communication channels. Communication channels are the means by which a message travels from a source to a receiver. Mass media channels are most effective in creating an awareness of the new idea, while interpersonal channels are most effective in persuading people to adopt the new idea (Rogers, 1983). In communicating about a coping resource, the public service announcement often is the vehicle used by the mass media to create awareness of the new resource. Health professionals are frequently used as the interpersonal channels to diffuse health information, as are families, neighbors, and friends.

Time. Time is involved in the diffusion process in three ways: (1) the innovation-decision process, (2) innovativeness, and (3) an innovation's rate of adoption. The innovation-decision process is the mental process through which an individual passes from knowledge of a health behavior to a decision to adopt or reject and, later, to confirmation of this decision (Rogers, 1983). A smoker who wants to stop, for example, first learns of a smoking cessation program and is persuaded that this program can help him or her stop smoking. He or she next makes the decision to enroll in the program and may then seek reinforcement of that decision.

Innovativeness is the degree to which an individual is early in adopting new ideas compared to other members of his or her social system. Five adopter categories are discussed in the classical diffusion model: (1) innovators, (2) early adopters, (3) early majority, (4) late majority, and (5) laggards (Rogers, 1983). Rate of adoption is the relative speed with which an innovation is adopted by members of a social system. Some innovations are diffused much more rapidly than others. Modern math, for example, reached 100% adoption by public schools in five years, while kindergartens took 50 years (Rogers, 1983).

Social systems. A social system is a collection of units that are functionally differentiated and participate in joint problem solving to reach a common goal. Social systems can vary considerably in size. A family is a social system, as is a rural community in Alabama, and the entire population of the United States. Some social systems facilitate change, while others impede it. Frequently, the process of diffusion may even change the structure of the social system (Rogers, 1983).

Change agents and opinion leaders. Rogers (1983) discusses two important roles that an individual might play in the diffusion process. Opinion leaders are individuals who can spread support and/or information to members of their networks. Opinion leadership is an informal position in the social system, but it is earned and maintained by technical competence, social accessibility, and conformity to the system's norms.

A change agent is a professional who disseminates information and/or support that is deemed desirable by a change agency. A change agent has an official position in the sense that dissemination is a part of his or her job. Professional health educators and public health administrators or health care providers are prime examples of change agents.

Pohl and Freimuth (1983) have identified a third role that lies conceptually somewhere between change agent and opinion leader. Individuals who fulfill this role are called co-change agents. A co-change agent is an opinion leader who has become actively involved in diffusion efforts. He or she may have been recruited by a change agent to assist in planning and/or implementing diffusion strategies. A co-change agent might be a minister of a black church who is quite influential in his community and who assumes the role of coordinator of a community smoking cessation program.

Centralized Versus Decentralized Diffusion Systems

Most of the previous research on diffusion has assumed a centralized focus, that is, the information originates from some expert source and is diffused as a uniform package to potential adopters who accept or reject it. This emphasis on centralized systems probably developed because of the success of the agricultural extension service and the fact that the diffusion paradigm grew out of the Ryan and Gross (1943) hybrid corn study. Agricultural diffusion in this country was relatively centralized in that a few expert officials made most of the key decisions about what, how, and when to diffuse innovations.

Recently, the classical diffusion model has been heavily criticized for this centralized focus and more attention has been given to decentralized diffusion. In general, the centralized diffusion system is based on a linear one-way model of communication. Decentralized diffusion systems more closely follow a convergence model of communication (Rogers & Kincaid, 1981) in which participants create and share information with one another in order to arrive at a mutual understanding.

Decentralized diffusion systems have several advantages. The information that decentralized diffusion systems develop is likely to be quite compatible with the users' needs and problems. Users feel more of a sense of control over decentralized diffusion systems. They make their own decisions about which problems have priority, what information might best solve those problems, how to seek information and from what sources, and how to modify and adapt the information to meet their own needs. Great differences between change agents and clients no longer exist. Decentralized diffusion systems are usually more cost-efficient. Such systems encourage user self-reliance and are generally quite popular with users.

These decentralized diffusion systems also have certain disadvantages. Frequently technical expertise is not available, which may allow "bad information" to slip through the system and be diffused. For example, laetrile might be considered "bad information" that diffused through decentralized networks of cancer patients. In addition, decentralized systems often lack the necessary coordinating role and make it difficult to see the big picture.

Duplication of effort and ignorance of available resources may result. If a national government wants an innovation diffused that the people do not feel they need, a decentralized diffusion system will prevent its dissemination.

Rogers (1983) recommends that the decentralized diffusion system is most useful with information that does not involve a high level of technical expertise among a set of users with relatively heterogeneous conditions. He also suggests that elements of both centralized and decentralized diffusion systems can be combined to form a diffusion system that uniquely meets a particular situation.

Three examples of systems to diffuse supportive information will be described in the following section. The first, the Coping with Cancer Program from the National Cancer Institute, is an example of a relatively centralized diffusion system. The second, the women's health movement, is an example of a relatively decentralized diffusion system. The third, the Chemical People, represents a hybrid system that combines elements of both centralized and decentralized diffusion systems (see Figure 10.1).[3]

A centralized diffusion system: coping with cancer. In 1976, the Office of Cancer Communications, National Cancer Institute, identified a problem in answering inquiries from the public related to the psychological and social aspects of cancer. These questions addressed such issues as depression, fear, changing relationships with family and friends, and school attendance for young people with cancer. This need motivated the initiation of the Coping with Cancer program.

Blumberg (1982) reports that the first step was to decide what NCI should say to the cancer patient and family as well as to those to whom the patient and family go for information and support concerning how to cope with the disease. After researching the relevant literature and discussing the topic with researchers, program planners, and cancer patients, the following four messages were selected.

(1) Cancer is not necessarily fatal. More individuals than ever before are living with the disease.
(2) However, living with cancer creates certain pressures and problems with which patients and their families must cope in order to maintain decent qualities to their lives.

**CENTRALIZED DIFFUSION
SYSTEM**

Change Agent

Opinion Leaders or Intermediaries

Individual Receivers

**DECENTRALIZED DIFFUSION
SYSTEM**

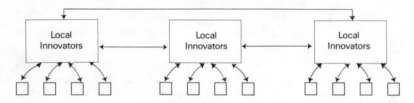

| Local Innovators | Local Innovators | Local Innovators |

HYBRID DIFFUSION SYSTEM

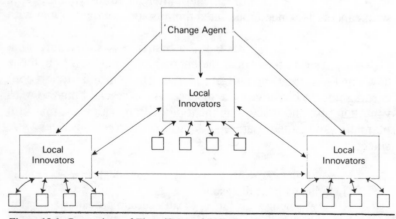

Change Agent

Local Innovators

Local Innovators

Local Innovators

Figure 10.1 Comparison of Three Types of Diffusion Systems

(3) There are useful coping behaviors that can be learned to help patients and their families improve (or retain) the quality of their lives.

(4) Often, problems inherent in coping with cancer (and other chronic diseases) are not unique but rather are common to many patients and families. However, the applicability of a particular coping approach depends on the individual patient and his or her circumstances (Blumberg, 1982, p. 85).

Target audiences were selected on two bases: (1) the developmental age, particularly who and what are important to the patient at different ages, and (2) stage of the disease. Primary audiences include young patients, their siblings, peers, and parents; adolescent patients and their siblings, peers, and parents; and adult patients and their appropriate family members and peers. The secondary audience is made up of those to whom the patient and family go for care, information, and support. Members of secondary audiences would include physicians, nurses, occupational therapists, social workers, work colleagues, community leaders, and others.

The general objective of the Coping with Cancer program is to provide a variety of skills that will help patients deal with their illness and gain some sense of control over their lives. Coping materials were sought and developed, if necessary, to meet the needs of the target audiences while communicating the four basic messages. The following are examples of some of the materials available:

- "Taking Time—Support for People with Cancer and the People Who Care about Them" is a booklet for persons with cancer and their families, addressing the feelings and concerns of others in similar situations and how they have learned to cope.
- A cassette tape and booklet for adolescents with cancer that focuses on the special concerns of the adolescent, including relationships with parents, peers, and health professionals, school attendance, and body image.
- "Financial Aspects of Coping with Cancer: A Primer for the Patient and Family" is a booklet that addresses financially related aspects of the disease.

It is obvious that the Coping with Cancer program is a centralized effort by the National Cancer Institute to disseminate supportive information to cancer patients and their families and the health professionals who work with them. The decisions concerning the nature of the information and the appropriate target audiences were made at the federal government level. The program is an example of a top-down diffusion from experts to local users of the information. The format of the materials discourages local adaptation and reinvention as it diffuses among users.

Decentralized diffusion: the women's health movement. [4] The evolution of the women's health movement in the 1970s began with consciousness-raising groups during the 1960s women's movement. Health was often an unavoidable topic of discussion. One group that began meeting in Boston in 1969 was history making.

The Boston Women's Health Book Collective (BWHBC) was both a model and a motivator for others. It began in a small discussion group on "women and their bodies" as part of a women's conference, which was one of the first gatherings of women meeting specifically to talk with other women.

> I began to talk with other women about the kind of care doctors gave us and also about our bodies, the quality of our sex lives. I'd thought I was the only one to have questions and problems about birth control and childbirth. But it turned out that many other women were concerned with the same things. Our personal discussions began in our living rooms and kitchens. They then blossomed into many kinds of health groups and projects. We all moved easily back and forth between expressions of needs and ideas and political action. (BWHBC, 1984, p. 598)

From their early searchings through medical libraries, textbooks, and journals, the women finally assembled enough material for the first edition of the now classic *Our Bodies, Ourselves.* Courses then began to spring up throughout the country, and a nationwide educational effort began (Lipnack, 1980).

The first two women's health centers providing routine gynecological care were opened in 1970—the Emma Goldman Women's Health Center in Chicago and the Elizabeth Blackwell Women's Health Center in Minneapolis. In 1971, more than 800 women gathered in New York for the first National Women's Health Conference.

According to sociologist Cheryl Ruzek (1978), by 1973 there

were 35 ongoing women's health projects in the United States and 116 women's centers. By the following year, the number had grown astronomically and the New York Women's Health Forum had identified more than 1,200 groups providing some form of health information and advocacy. The number of women estimated to belong to women's health organizations was judged to be in the tens of thousands.

The mid-seventies saw the formation of the first national lobbying and advocacy organizations for women's health. The National Women's Health Network, the Women and Health Roundtable, and the Coalition for the Medical Rights of Women were all born out of a need to have a voice at the national level with regard to women and health. Monitoring health policy, testifying at regulatory hearings, and presenting position papers and congressional briefings were all activities taken on by groups such as these.

By the mid-seventies, the movement also had attracted the attention of the media. "With nearly 2000 feminist journals and newspapers publishing regularly, a nationwide communications network was firmly in place, reaching enough people to attract 2500 participants to the 1975 Conference on Women and Health in Boston" (Lipnack, 1980, p. 50). Sponsored by such diverse groups as Planned Parenthood and the New England Chapter of the American Medical Women's Association, the conference spawned a number of significant projects that focused on particular issues such as DES, abortion, childbirth, cancer, and sterilization. The academic community began to take note and, in 1976, a new journal, *Women and Health,* began publication (Lipnack, 1980). This event marked the first time that women activists were joined by academics and the medical establishment in disseminating information on women's health.

This example of the women's health movement shows the characteristics of a decentralized diffusion system. The power and control is widely shared among the members of the diffusion system. There is peer diffusion of the information through horizontal networks. The information comes from local experimentation by nonexperts, who often are users. Moreover, there is a high degree of local adaptation and reinvention of the information as it diffuses among adopters.

A hybrid diffusion system: the Chemical People. The Chemical People (Kaiser, 1983), a project to combat school-age drug and alcohol abuse, was developed by WQED, a public broadcasting station in Pittsburgh, Pennsylvania. The Chemical People model has two major components: media, both electronic and print, and outreach, grass-roots intervention and organization. There were two national Chemical People television programs. The first program, aired on November 2, 1981, revealed the facts of "The Chemical Society." The second program, on November 9, described how task forces work and what they can do. It was called *Community Answers.*

A great deal of community organization occurred prior to the broadcast of these two programs. A few days prior to the first program, *An Appeal to All Americans* was aired. It was hosted by Michael Landon and contained an appeal from Nancy Reagan for viewers to attend town meetings in their communities on November 2 and 9. There were four regional reports outlining state by state how many town meetings would be held in each. The amazing national total was 10,675.

The outreach efforts extended from a core (for example, drug and alcohol agencies, parent groups) to penetrate the community and help develop a local group. The groups could then respond to their own community needs. Outreach was used to develop a task force in each community to provide a structure for the energies aroused by the shows and to funnel those energies into positive action. The result of this project was more than 50,000 volunteers creating nearly 11,000 task forces (Kaiser, 1983).

The Chemical People project represents an interesting hybrid diffusion system. The initial effort in broadcasting the two special programs and organizing the town meetings was a centralized diffusion effort, but the task forces that developed and attacked the problem at the community level represented a decentralized diffusion system.

This hybrid diffusion effort deserves more attention because of serious liabilities of both of the other models. The centralized diffusion paradigm has been attacked for being too linear, laying blame for its failures on individuals rather than social systems, and increasing rather than decreasing the gap between the "haves" and "have-nots" in a social system. On the other hand, the decentralized diffusion paradigm is too disorganized and unpredictable to be managed effectively by a change agency. The hybrid approach appears to be an effective combination of the strengths of the other two models.

Social Marketing

Social marketing is a relatively recent concept. It can be traced to an article by Kotler and Levy (1969), who argue that the principles of marketing that have been applied to profit-making organizations can be applied to nonbusiness settings. In his 1982 book, Kotler defines social marketing in the following way:

> Social marketing is the design, implementation, and control of programs seeking to increase the acceptability of a social idea or cause in a target group(s). It utilizes concepts of market segregation, consumer research, concept development, communication, facilitation, incentives, and exchange theory to maximize target group responses. (p. 490)

The basic components of social marketing, as of marketing, are the four Ps: product, promotion, place, and price. The product should be developed by analyzing the needs of target audiences and designing products and services that are responsive to those needs. These products must then be "packaged" in attractive and useful ways.

Communication and persuasion are at the heart of promotion. The product has to be presented in a way that is acceptable and desirable to potential users. Typical marketing techniques include advertising, personal selling, publicity, and sales promotion. The social marketer must analyze the target audiences and the resources available and then decide what mix of these techniques to use.

Place refers to the contact points where exchange relationships actually occur. The social field does not have retail outlets as the business world does. Attention must be given to offering action outlets. For example, in a campaign to get people to join smoking cessation groups, individuals must know where and how to sign up.

The final marketing component is price. In commercial marketing, price is a central issue because profit is so important. In social marketing, however, monetary price is generally not a major issue, but other types of price become important, for example, energy costs, psychic costs, and opportunity costs. The user must be convinced that the "product" is worth the risk, inconvenience, or effort involved in trying it.

Although it is possible to identify the similarities between marketing in the business and social areas, there are hurdles to transferring the technology from the business to the social realm. Fox and Kotler (1980) identify several of these hurdles. It is more difficult to analyze the social market because there are fewer quality data about consumers. It is more difficult to segment the market because there is often pressure to serve the entire market in an equitable and simultaneous manner. The pricing variable is less flexible. Distribution channels are unavailable or difficult to control. Social organizations often do not have sophisticated marketing or management skills.

The marketing process. Novelli (1984) describes the marketing process as circular, or iterative, with the final stage of six stages feeding back into the first in a continuous cycle of replanning and improvement. The six stages, in sequence, are: (1) analysis, (2) planning, (3) development, testing, and refining of the plan elements, (4) implementation, (5) assessment of in-market effectiveness, and (6) feedback to stage 1. This six-stage marketing process is designed to take into account consumer wants, needs, expectations, and satisfactions/dissatisfactions; to formulate program objectives; to utilize an integrated marketing approach and marketing mix (product, price, communication, distribution); and to track consumer and market response continuously (Novelli, 1984).

A smoking treatment program in a hospital setting. Martin and Prue (1984) provide an example of using the social marketing process to "sell" a smoking cessation program in a VA hospital. Their market analysis revealed that in that particular hospital, roughly 90% of their in-patients and a large number of staff were smokers. The *product,* smoking treatment, was positioned as a research program to evaluate alternative methods of assessing and treating smoking behavior and overall health risk due to smoking. The target audience was both patients and staff. The *place* was a clinic, consisting of a three-room suite off the fourth-floor elevator lobby, a location that was visible and had moderate traffic. The *price* was free, at least in monetary terms, but the psychic costs were very high. In addition to the psychological and physical pain of withdrawal from tobacco, the time and energy costs of attending assessment and treatment sessions, completing self-monitoring tasks, and engaging in intensive behavior modification techniques were considerable. These costs had to compete with the hospital canteen store that sold cigarettes below retail prices.

The following eight different marketing/*promotional* interventions were employed in the next 14 months to get referrals to the clinic:

(1) clinic announcements
(2) memoranda to all physicians and wards
(3) ward visits
(4) posters
(5) staff newspaper advertisements
(6) nurse posters plus general hospital posters
(7) the Check-Your-Smoking-Health-Risk display booth
(8) nurse posters only

During the marketing process, it became clear that the *product*, the assessment and treatment program, had to be modified. Over 75% of those accepted for treatment dropped out before the treatment program was completed. Various changes were made to make the *product* less costly to the participant. For example, the initial screening and assessment were reduced from a three-hour assessment and a one-week self-monitoring period to a single, thirty-minute session (Martin & Prue, 1984).

By using a systematic marketing process, this hospital was able to try several different techniques to promote its *product*, assess the results of these efforts, and make changes during the course of the program in order to increase overall effectiveness.

While the diffusion school has been developed by sociologists and psychologists and the social marketing school has grown from the field of business, the two fields have many similarities. Their objectives and many of their methods overlap. Both are concerned with the dissemination and use of innovations—new products, techniques, ideas, and programs. The difference is that the diffusion people approach their subject from a humanistic or nonprofit point of view, while the social marketing writers draw upon profit-making motivations.

Suggestions for Practical Applications

Many human services and nonprofit organizations have low budgets and will not be able to wage expensive information campaigns. These models can be helpful, however, even when one brochure needs to be disseminated to an audience. The following are some important guidelines for any information dissemination effort.

(1) Determine clear, measurable goals for the dissemination effort.
(2) Segment your audience into specific target groups and set priorities regarding the importance of reaching each target group.
(3) Study the knowledge, attitudes, and behaviors of those target groups.
(4) Develop information to meet the needs of the target audiences.
(5) Pretest, informally if necessary, to gauge the audience's reactions to all materials used in the dissemination effort.
(6) Produce materials as professionally as possible.
(7) Work with gatekeepers to ensure exposure of your materials.
(8) Obtain feedback continuously so that corrections can be made as needed.
(9) Recycle what has been learned in this experience into the next dissemination effort.

Summary

We attempt to reduce the uncertainties and anxieties from health threats by seeking information. Since information can give us more personal control, it functions as a form of social support. This chapter examined this form of social support from two perspectives—individuals as consumers of health information and professional change agents as information disseminators.

Individuals turn to three broad sources of information to help them understand the health problem and develop a plan to cope with it: intrapersonal, interpersonal, and mass communication. Intrapersonal communication includes body sensations experienced as well as the individual's image of reality developed from previous knowledge, beliefs, and attitudes. Interpersonal includes health professionals, self-help groups, and family/friends. Mass media sources include printed materials such as newspapers and patient education materials; television, encompassing public service announcements, health programs, and entertainment programs; and radio, telephone, and new communication media.

Information from all of these sources can be supportive by helping the individual reduce uncertainty, and hence anxiety, and plan methods of coping. Mass media and interpersonal sources, particularly self-help groups, can offer the additional supportive function of providing models of coping behavior. In addition, most mass media sources allow the information seeker to remain anonymous, so there is little interpersonal risk associated with requests for information.

Two theoretical models—diffusion theory and social marketing—were offered to information disseminators to guide their efforts to get this supportive information distributed to the appropriate audiences. Extended examples of campaigns using each of these frameworks were given. Suggestions derived from both of these models were offered to practitioners.

NOTES

1. See Chapter 6 in this volume.
2. While a medical show such as *St. Elsewhere* is likely to have its own medical adviser, the Hospital Advisory Council and the Physicians Advisory Committee on Radio, T.V., and Motion Pictures help writers and producers involved in the creation and production of shows that occasionally cover medical issues to keep the information and scenes presented factual and accurate.
3. David Crosson designed the graphics for Figure 10.1.
4. I would like to express my appreciation to Elayne Clift for the preparation of the material on the women's health movement.

PART III

Dilemmas, Applications, and New Directions for Research

11

Dilemmas of
Supportive Communication

TERRANCE L. ALBRECHT
MARA B. ADELMAN

Most cancer patients find themselves in an uncomfortable situation, a "catch-22": either they can express their feelings and be themselves, thereby incurring others' avoidance and rejection, or they can enact a charade, pretending that everything is fine, and at least obtain some support from others. Because neither of these alternatives is satisfactory, the patient may vacillate . . . sometimes putting on a good face, and sometimes confronting others with their pain and anxiety. This vacillation, of course, pollutes the social environment . . . and makes it even more difficult for friends and relatives to know how to respond to the patient. (Wortman & Dunkel-Schetter, 1979, pp. 142-143)

With all its virtues, supportive communication has many unfulfilled promises. Examples of problematic outcomes abound, not only for those seeking support but also for those giving it. While our focus in the preceding chapters has been on the positive ways supportive communication reduces uncertainty for healthful effects, in this chapter we review some of the very real dilemmas confronting those involved in such interactions.

Coverage of this counterside of the support process is important for several reasons. First, the natural appeal of the topic to the etiology of disease and psychosis has led to a research stampede. Unfortunately, the area is increasingly suffering from a gap where empirical findings are outdistancing theoretical development.[1] Unless attention is paid to the difficulties present in those interactions, we lack a basis for setting scope conditions in theory-building efforts. Theoretical prediction, explanation, and control will continue to be hampered until these issues are woven into mainstream thinking in the area.

Further, blinding assumptions about the positive effects of support seriously hinder rigorous scientific investigation. Uniform thinking that fails to consider the potentially toxic character of supportive relationships (e.g., learned helplessness, stress contagion) can lead to an "ideology" about the process.[2] This is inevitable if researchers and commentators are driven by the belief that support is wholly "good" and compatible with cultural values of helping, relational stability, and altruism. Alternately, recent thought and investigations (e.g., Adelman, 1986; Chesler & Barbarin, 1984; McLeroy, DeVellis, DeVellis, Kaplan, & Toole, 1984; Rook, 1984; Wortman & Lehman, 1985) have begun to show the debilitating side of social support, a factor that should discourage ideological commitment to the phenomenon.

The following are a select set of the dilemmas or tensions that can occur in the reduction of uncertainty and the development of control for supportive purposes. As this is a relatively new direction for research, our overarching goal is to stimulate thought and avenues for future studies. The review includes problems encountered by recipients in *seeking* support and those of providers in *giving* support.

Problems in Seeking Support

The need for support, for another to reduce one's sense of uncertainty, can be a two-edged sword. When a provider gives us a perspective for coping during a time of life stress, we essentially come to share in that person's life view. While meaning is ultimately the individual's creation, binds arise from the perception that another person has or will help to create that meaning and from the transaction of the message exchange. For the receiver, these problems include difficulties with impression and identity management, learned helplessness, incurred relational costs, and the balancing of sometimes incompatible strong and weak relationships.

Impression Management

Needing and actively pursuing support from others may sabotage the important "impression management" process (Goffman, 1959). Obtaining support from others may prove costly to an individual's self-esteem, particularly to his or her sense of personal control and self-worth. Essentially, one is caught in a bind. Enlisting a supporter to help reduce one's uncertainty by clarifying solutions to a problem may help immediate circumstances, but if the provider forms an opinion of the receiver as "weak," "unknowledgeable," or lacking good reasoning ability under stress (as in the case of nurses working in critical care units) the long-term effects can be harmful for the recipient and the relationship.

The root of this problem lies in the risk of rejection and negative judgments by those acting as supporters (Coates, Wortman, & Abbey, 1979). Estimates that such negative attributions will be made increase the receiver's "evaluation apprehension" (Wills, 1983), stemming from fears of stigmatization, negative judgments of competence, attractiveness to the supporter, or threats to the stability of the provider-recipient relationship. Chesler and Barbarin (1984, p. 125) report that parents of children with cancer felt stigmatized by their friends' treatment of them as "needy" or "abnormal." Nadler, Shapira, and Ben-Itzhak (1982) found that sex and attractiveness of the helper prompted concerns for face saving on the part of the help-seeker. DePaulo (1982) noted that people will refrain from seeking help if they think others will like them less. And some types of people may be simply less likely to feel better as a result of venting their feelings to others (e.g., males are sometimes less desirous of support than females) because they think others may be unreceptive and judgmental toward their emotional displays (Silver & Wortman, 1980). Indeed, there is at least some initial empirical evidence for such fears. In an experimental study with college students, Hammen and Peters (1978) found that depressed persons were rejected more intensely than nondepressed persons, particularly by those of the opposite sex.

Uncertainty toward the interaction and others. Undergirding much of the anxiety associated with impression management as a "stress" of social support is the uncertainty of what will occur during the interaction itself. The impression-related consequences of disclosing or venting to others may be unclear. Disclosure of private information can produce uncomfortable feelings of uncertainty because an individual may not know what change may come about affecting his or her self-concept and/or the relationship with the other (Miller & Steinberg, 1975). Even a slight suspicion that others' reactions might be negative (or have longer-term repercussions) can be stressful.

If uncertainty toward providers is too high, it may be more functional *not* to engage in some supportive interactions, resulting in what Kessel (1964) termed an "armour of loneliness." Henderson (1980) applied this disengagement strategy to the plight of the schizophrenic, saying that some individuals needed to withdraw and isolate themselves as a protective mechanism, given their inabilities to handle difficult or complex social stimuli.

Receiver expectations. Seeking support may also pose difficulties in impression management if the receiver is put in the position of having to act in accordance with others' (potential supporters) expectations and situational definitions. To obtain support, the seeker/recipient may feel pressured to mask true feelings and respond to the stressful situation in ways others expect. Wortman and Dunkel-Schetter (1979) illustrated this with cancer patients (see quote at the beginning of this chapter), who are often unable to express their fears and pain without social costs of rejection by others. Indeed, some cancer patients have had to reexamine some of their closest relationships to determine those to whom they could "safely" self-disclose. Many friends and kin have strong expectations against any discussion of the illness (Peters-Golden, 1982; Wortman & Dunkel-Schetter, 1979).[3]

This is also apparent in some situations, particularly organizations, where strong social expectations exist for the behavior of those in certain roles. Abdel-Halim (1982) called support a "mixed blessing" in the organization; any benefits accrued usually come at a price (e.g., anxiety over possible negative evaluations and indebtedness resulting from such interactions). The management of relationships in competitive contexts is complicated by the need for support (i.e., to acquire information and reassurances) from others while maintaining the appearance of competence, cool judgment under pressure, and independent professionalism. Nurses especially run the risk of being labeled "weak" and undependable in emergency situations if they seek help from coworkers or supervisors in coping with the stress of the job (Albrecht & Ropp, 1982).

And clergy are often bereft of sources of personal support given that many parishioners expect them to have clear views and answers to life's problems and perplexities. Admission by the clergyman or clergywoman of insecurity, loneliness, or uncertain fears could be professional suicide if it shook the beliefs of followers or caused them to lose faith in the individual's competence. Knowing this, the minister, priest, or rabbi may not have someone other than a spouse or family member to turn to for support and ventilation.

Identity Management

Disclosure of personal weakness or lack of knowledge may make one more vulnerable and dependent on others—a particularly threatening experience to one's self-identity in competitive environments. Such interactions may serve to legitimize the supporter's assertion of superior ability, position, or power (DePaulo, 1982). And disclosure of uncertainty may reveal "that one is not as competent as one has in some sense claimed to be" (p. 270), thus endangering the individual's sense of face or credibility in the long term. This situation is especially tense for new hires in the organization. Although they need to project the capability and confidence asserted during the selection phase, at the same time they need information from organizational veterans to cope with the experience of high uncertainty, surprise, and cognitive overload (Louis, 1980).

Outside the organizational context, fears of being open or vulnerable to help may come from sex-role images. Fathers of children with cancer, for example, may withdraw from interaction with friends to avoid undercutting their roles as strong leaders during a family crisis and creating dependence on others (see Chesler & Barbarin, 1984, p. 127).

Finally, in contrast to fears of negative evaluations by supporters, dilemmas are created when receivers fear that engaging in supportive interactions will result in negative self-evaluations. Concerns over personal identity are often at stake in seeking support. Not having the answers, feeling uncertain, and needing the wisdom of others can be threatening to the individual's self-esteem and sense of confidence for independent achievement (DePaulo, 1982; Williams & Williams, 1983). Drawing from Blau (1955) and Homans (1961), DePaulo (1982, p. 269) argues that reluctance in help-seeking stems from the fear of having to confront one's own sense of inadequacy personally. The self-perception of being helpless and lacking control and vision can be personally debilitating for many people.

Learned Helplessness

Learned helplessness is associated with an individual's awareness that he or she cannot control some undesirable life event or outcome. When the individual attributes the failure to control to an internal, stable, and global cause (i.e., incompetence, lack of self-discipline) helplessness and hopelessness can occur, impairing future performance (Abramson, Seligman, & Teasdale, 1978; Miller & Norman, 1979; Parks, 1985). For example, poor performance can confirm a self-fulfilling prophecy of an internal attribution of failure, setting up future expectations of inadequacy (Parks, 1985). Similarly, long-term dependence on others for care may set up habitual patterns of incapacity and help-dependent relational cycles. McLeroy et al. (1984) found that instrumental assistance had a significantly negative effect on the physical recovery of stroke patients ($n = 393$). Patients who are physically incapable of caring for themselves may be slower to achieve independent control because the supportive assistance makes it mentally easier to accept the physical infirmity as stable and global.

Supportive messages based on cognitive restructuring of the attributional process (e.g., Dweck, 1975; Parks, 1985; Raps, Reinhard, & Seligman, 1980) can be most helpful in thwarting this effect. Redirecting the attribution of poor performance from an internal, stable, and global cause to an external, unstable, and specific source frees one from the bondage of negative self-evaluation. Widows who were encouraged to be self-sufficient and not focus on their grief were better adjusted to their new life situation (Bankoff, 1981).

Relational Costs

Partners in relationships often have rather strong expectations for social equity and reciprocity to avoid overburdening any one individual. Equity theorists argue that partners strive to receive equal relative gain from their relationship, where inputs and outputs are perceived as justly distributed or in balance (Walster, Walster, & Berscheid, 1978). If the relationship is seen as inequitable, one person often feels unfairly treated or exploited, resulting in distress and conflict in the relationship (Walster et al., 1978). Indeed, perceptions of inequity tend to undermine the satisfaction and stability of many intimate relationships (Hatfield, Utne, & Traupmann, 1979).

Several studies on support have found that reciprocity is also a necessary condition for supportive relationships to endure (Clark, 1983; Pattison & Pattison, 1981; Politser, 1980). Reciprocity is the extent to which supportive messages are exchanged on an equal basis by both parties to the relationship. Antonucci and Depner (1982, p. 243) even define a support network as a system of *mutual* obligations, noting that networks "not only provide support, but demand it as well."

The demand for equity and reciprocity may constrain the support-seeking process for many troubled individuals. Knowledge that one may be unable to reciprocate supportive communication in the present or future may cause an individual to withdraw altogether from a supportive relationship (see Greenberg & Shapiro, 1971; Morris & Rosen, 1973). If one does seek and receive support, a sense of indebtedness may arise (Greenberg, 1980) further overwhelming and burdening the stressed individual (DePaulo, 1982; DiMatteo & Hays, 1981).

Equity theorists argue that the perception of equity will vary depending on the degree of intimacy shared in the relationship (Hatfield et al., 1979). As relationships become more intimate, a "tolerance for inequity" will likely increase (Hatfield et al., 1979). When people consider sources of support they are more likely to think of their close relationships (House, 1981). They likely feel freer to seek and accept help from intimates because such persons are known entities and future obligations toward such relationships are usually clear. And intimates may not be as sensitive to demands for immediate reciprocity as nonintimates (DePaulo, 1982). Recipients counting on delayed equity may find intimates more understanding and accommodating without threat to face and the relationship.

However, there are limits on the drawing power of intimate relationships. Although it is unclear what the threshold levels are for tolerances of inequity, even greater reciprocation may be expected in the future. Cunningham and Antill (1981, p. 33) drawing from Hatfield and Traupmann (1981), note:

> It is unlikely that love will survive a chronic, complete moratorium of rewards received from the partner. More likely is the prospect that love can be self-sacrificing to a degree or for a time, *but that more will be expected in return the longer this continues.* (emphasis added)

In short, a bind is created for the help-seeker: Not only will equity be demanded by the partner, but the help-seeker will have to reconcile a larger debt than was originally framed in the initial transaction.

Management of Strong and Weak Ties

Research on network density has made it tempting to advocate low dense structures as optimal for maximizing supportive opportunities (see Chapter 3 in this volume). However, such conclusions are premature and overly simplistic when one considers the bind produced in attempting to balance strong and weak ties. The addition of weak links to new acquaintances, groups, or colleagues may be costly to the individual if they disrupt existing strong ties to family and friends. The difficulty arises in contexts where loyalty and dependency are tightly woven into strong ties (such as the family or organization). These issues constrain the development of functional weak ties because of obligations owed to strong ties.

Management of strong and weak ties is particularly difficult when the basis for strong, supportive ties is born out of economic need. Groups such as single mothers are most vulnerable (Henderson, 1980). While low-density structures are beneficial in their search for new identities, these women are often in need of *practical* assistance (i.e., child care and material necessities) in order to manage and control their lives. Yet tangible support is most likely to come from densely integrated, kin-dominant ties (see Henderson, 1980). Family members may disapprove of the single mother's new relationships and exercise veto power over her affiliative activities. She is left with few options other than severing her new ties or jeopardizing her valuable strong relationships (on whom she and her children are resource-dependent). Even in situations where the single mother reciprocates in the best way she can by providing love and nurturing to family members, her help is often undervalued or at least not perceived as equivalent to the help provided to her (Belle, 1982a).[4]

A similar problem occurs in organizational contexts where issues of loyalty and dependency on powerful others can hamper desires to form weak ties outside of primary circles. Mentors may discourage protégés from developing relationships with those in competing units or groups if they view those ties as potentially threatening. Communication with outsiders may be seen as acts of disloyalty, especially in competitive, politically charged environments.

It is empirically unclear how people resolve the tensions created in attempts to balance incompatible strong and weak links, or whether they simply tolerate a deficit of ties to outsiders. In some cases, such as in the organization, the dilemma may be resolved through information control, where individuals resort to secrecy or ambiguity about their range of contacts. However, the extent to which these strategies are functional for trust building and teamwork is an open question.

In short, further empirical work is needed to determine the role played in relationship development by strong links. It may be that whether the individual is "freed" and even assisted (e.g., with child care or money) in forming weak ties is largely determined by the actions and encouragement of the primary network of relations with powerful kin and close associates.

Problems in Support Giving

Providing support—whether for reasons of pure altruism, personal satisfaction, or social manipulation—can also promote difficult outcomes. Providers may incur difficulties including drainage of personal resources, social contagion, and uncertainty over whether supportive attempts will incite conflict with the recipient.[5]

Drainage of Personal Resources

Clearly, providing social support is often accompanied by a satisfying feeling of caring and concern for others; yet, time, energy, goods, and emotional nurturance involved in the uncertainty reduction for another are also valuable resources for the provider. These are costly for the provider if depleted, resulting in emotional exhaustion and relational strain. Individuals possess a "fund of sociability" that can be drained if the demand for support is excessive (Nelson, 1966; Weiss, 1974). Family members faced with caring for the chronically ill, for example, are taxed by having to cope with a new change in family relationships and by the length of time needed to provide support (DiMatteo & Hays, 1981). Friends of parents with children suffering from cancer reported hard-hitting emotional impacts from hearing of the diagnosis, resulting in exhaustion from helping and listening to the parents, sometimes continuing over a period of years (Chesler & Barbarin, 1984). Belle (1982a) argues that women are particularly subject to the stress of caregiving given that much of their support goes unrecognized and unreciprocated. The ongoing, consistent demands for attention are stressful for the caregiver and drain the energy normally devoted to other relationships (and possibly precipitating marital breakups or increased isolation from friend and community contacts).

The fund of resourcefulness is particularly stretched among the economically disadvantaged. Social ties are stressful for impoverished persons because they enforce dependence on others. People who already have little to give are burdened by others who have even less, thus depleting their limited storehouse (Belle, 1982b). The problem is also doubleheaded in that these relationships further entrap both the provider and recipient by limiting mobility (Belle, 1982b), thus cutting off the possibility of opportunities for breaking out of poor housing arrangements and welfare.

Social Contagion Effects

Providing emotional nurturance to a disheartened or stressed person is risky in another way; one can also become stressed, producing a "contagion effect" (Cherniss, 1980; Hammen & Peters, 1978; Mechanic, 1962). While the term *contagion effect* probably works best as a general metaphor for social stress (or the stress incurred by supporting distressed others; see Adelman, 1986), it is a powerful and apt image nonetheless. Coyne (1976) and Hammen and Peters (1978) found that normal individuals were significantly more depressed and anxious following a conversation with depressed individuals than normals who conversed with nondepressed persons. And communication about some issues (such as cancer, death, rape, or grief) may evoke in the provider feelings of his or her own emotional distress, insecurity, or uncertainty (Chesler & Barbarin, 1984; Coates et al., 1979; Wortman & Dunkel-Schetter, 1979; Wortman & Lehman, 1985). Mechanic (1962) argues that students preparing for an exam may withdraw from their colleagues as a way to decrease their test anxieties. Attempting to help others cope with the exam may result in increased uncertainty and anxiety for one's own situation, even if the perception was not initially troubling. This strains and decreases the amount and quality of support a provider can give. Finally, if the problem cannot be resolved satisfactorily, the nature of the receiver's problem may have a contagion effect on the source. The inadequate support giving may further depress the supporter, making him or her feel unworthy or inadequate in the caregiving role (DePaulo, 1982; Wortman & Lehman, 1985).

Since contagion is a response to stress, members in a network already undergoing stress may be more vulnerable to experiencing the stress of others (Adelman, 1986). The spread of contagion throughout the network can place the *system* at risk, affecting everyone's morale and motivation (Albrecht, Irey, & Mundy, 1982). Eckenrode and Gore (1981) hypothesize that increased network stress decreases the probability of receiving adequate support from those systems. In their study of hysterical contagion, Kerckhoff, Back, and Miller (1965) found that network integration facilitated uniform response patterns. Thus the impact of contagion may be intensified in cloistered networks lacking in sufficient linkages to outsiders. Social stress renders the network ineffective as a reliable structure of support channels. While satisfactory data are lacking on this notion of network-based contagion, whatever stress-producing problem is ventilated to others in the system needs to be resolved—for both the recipient and provider—in order that the stressful uncertainty does not become exponentially multiplied in the system.

Unfortunately, discussion of some issues (e.g., death and dying) may provoke many feelings in a provider, no matter how much support is given or received (see Wortman & Lehman, 1985). These can disturb the provider by evoking emotional distress, insecurity, or uncertainty. The experienced nurse who counsels a young recent graduate nurse who has just lost her first cancer patient, a child, may find that old unsettled feelings about the meaning of death begin to stir. For these reasons, Wortman and Lehman (1985) argue that supporters may be less open or may become "scripted" in their supportive communication, which may seem as though they are disregarding or minimizing the receiver's problems (p. 468). More research is needed to sort out the topics that are involved most readily in the problem of contagion, the ways providers and receivers cope with its occurrence, and the effects on the nature of those communication relationships over time.

Uncertainty over Causing Possible Relational Conflict

A final category of interaction dilemmas for the source is uncertainty over whether or not to support a recipient when it is possible that the interaction will produce relational conflict. A source may know that the supportive interaction could be unhelpful to a receiver, particularly if his or her privacy is invaded or the source's message invalidates the receiver's emotional feeling (even though the source thinks the feeling is unfounded).

Privacy invasion. Providers may feel reluctant to offer help to a receiver if they feel their actions will be interpreted as intrusive. Lacking clear cues from the receiver and possibly experiencing their own emotional distress over the plight of the friend can further compound uncertainty and hesitancy in attempts to aid.

The issue is compounded under times of real crisis for the recipient (as in the diagnosis of cancer or bereavement, or the like). Under such circumstances, the source is uncertain, not only out of concern for the receiver's personal privacy, but because of the often swift, unanticipated change in the relationship from a social friendship to one of need and help orientation. Chesler and Barbarin (1984, p. 124) note that such concerns reflect concrete problems of "discomfort or confusion about the new boundaries involved as peers create a helper-helpee relationship."

Invalidating receiver perceptions. At times inexperience in dealing with someone coping with a crisis can leave a supporter unsure about what to say or ignorant about the recipient's needs (Wortman & Lehman, 1985). As a result of misconceptions about the crisis or coping responses, a provider may unintentionally discount or undermine the recipients' interpretation and emotional response to the critical situation. Peters-Golden (1982, p. 490) points out the misplaced concerns of providers responding to patients recovering from mastectomies:

> The tendency of the lay population to overemphasize the loss of a breast, and not the fact that the woman has cancer, is an overwhelming complaint voiced by the patient population. They feel that cancer is generally regarded as a devastating physical illness, while breast cancer is simply viewed as losing a breast. Patients were surprised that family and friends did not understand that mastectomy was "a small price to pay" for arresting their cancer. The fact that the cancer was in their breast seemed to serve as a diversion to others, clouding the issue at hand, and interfering with their interactions with family and friends.

Premature attempts to reframe negative perceptions, point out fallacious thinking, and redirect outlook may create resentment toward the source if receivers feel their judgments are correct. Brickman et al. (1982) argue that incongruent assumptions between the helper and recipient about responsibility for the problem identified and the solution can result in a "secondary victimization" for the afflicted individual (i.e., victimization to the initial crisis as well as to people's misunderstandings regarding their situations).

At risk in these situations is the possibility of invalidating the recipient's self-concept by denying his or her sense-making abilities. Offering a counterperspective may offend and cause the receiver to feel foolish or rejected. While the supportive message may be well intentioned, and may reflect an honest effort to help the recipient restructure a negative interpretation, such encounters may clearly make the receiver defensive. Both partners are thus put in a relational bind. The provider may feel frustrated or hurt that the attempt to recast the situation positively for the receiver was rejected, and feel that future efforts with this person will be similarly unproductive. The receiver may be left justifying his or her negative perceptions to the source, feeling defensive that his or her own interpretation was refuted. Such polarization solidifies the receiver's negative meanings, making the experience more painful and harder to change. In effect, the process of experiencing rejection and denial by *both* the source and receiver fuels relational conflict and hinders future supportive exchanges.

Summary and Implications

Treating supportive relationships as wellsprings of altruism perpetuates a myth of unlimited human resources. This is clearly not the case for most ties. As shown earlier, the lack of attention to how these relationships are constrained presents a critical gap in our knowledge about the process of communicating support. As Hammer (1981, p. 47) notes:

> Support may be one function of a set of social connections. As such, it may prove misleading if we are not alert to the complementary impact of restraint, opposition, demandingness, mere presence, range of access, and whatever-else-may-matter, within these sets of social connections.

The dilemmas of support for both receivers and providers stem from personal debilitating consequences as well as concerns over costs to the other and the relationship.

Communication scholars can add much to this growing area of research. By approaching dilemmas that arise as interaction based, one sees that many of these problems are best addressed relationally and not at an individual/psychological level. Providers and recipients are acutely aware of their own needs and distress as well as one another's difficulties (Chesler & Barbarin, 1984). The problems that arise are best reflected at an empirical level in the messages exchanged and the meanings created together in the midst of their uncertainties. In addition, a perspective that includes a larger frame than just immediate parties may enable us to break out of dysfunctional relational cycles by introducing weaker ties as mediators and others who can add to the pool of support resources.

Dilemmas of supportive interactions are social realities, but are resolvable realities. As we begin to close the gaps in understanding the rewards and costs of communicating support, we must tackle the applied implications of these binds and formulate interventions that are accountable to the empirical research findings as well as the critical needs of individuals.

NOTES

1. For example, Fiore, Becker, and Coppel (1983) empirically demonstrated the need to separate conceptually perceived *helpfulness* from perceived *inadequacy* of support, given differences in the relative explained variance in depression with inadequacy accounting for more variance, $R^2 = 34.1\%$. Similarly, Rook (1984) found that negative social interactions had more serious effects on well-being than positive social exchanges.

2. Our point here is similar to the criticism made by Parks (1982) about the value-driven literature in interpersonal communication. In much of the writing in that area, intimacy has been seen as unquestionably desirable in all relationships, despite empirical evidence to the contrary.

3. Indeed, the patient is sometimes placed in the role of "supporter to supporters." For example, a cancer patient may have to comfort a family member or friend who is unable to cope with the fact the patient has cancer. The patient must refrain from disclosing personal feelings of anguish and uncertainty for fear of "upsetting" the other.

4. A further problem for single mothers is their limited time and money for moving out and forming ties to new social circles. They may be unsure how to cultivate satisfying relationships with attractive others. It is unclear how they resolve the uncertainty or the extent to which they simply tolerate the lack of ties to unconnected social groups.

5. Some of the classic work in psychology and social psychology has fostered additional recent research and commentary on problems incurred in the individual's attempts to be helpful. Taking a traditional psychological arousal perspective, Coke, Batson, and McDavis (1978) proposed a two-stage model for helping that begins with the arousal of a person's empathic emotional response when sensing another's distress. This in turn leads to behavior directed toward reducing the other's discomfort. Cognitive and emotional responses that cannot be sufficiently resolved through support provision may result in social withdrawal and negative outcomes for the provider. In addition, social psychological studies generally have shown that the size of a group audience inhibits bystander rescue behavior. In their review of these studies, Latane and Nida (1981) point out that helpers may feel a sense of duty yet fear public embarrassment if their interpretations of the situation are erroneous (particularly in cases where others have not made a seemingly obvious first move to help).

12

Intervention Strategies for Building Support

MARA B. ADELMAN
TERRANCE L. ALBRECHT

I think you begin to have an ear after a while for something that someone says. Especially if they have said "I'm uncomfortable with this. I'm afraid of cancer . . . " You begin to have clues, and there are ways you can feed those clues back to the client. Because very often when they first say something, it's almost as if they don't hear it. It's in their head and it comes out, but they're not really examining what it is . . . finding a way to feed it back to them without being really obvious. Very often you can almost just repeat it . . . switch it around, maybe add something on, a little question or whatever. It begins to draw them out. They begin to take what it is they're saying and start to examine it themselves. (volunteer, cancer telephone hotline)

Knowing how to support another is not always easy. "Beginning to have an ear" is a powerful image for the difficult process of learning to help others make sense of themselves, their actions, and their situations during crises. Supportive communication helps people to construct some semblance of useful meaning out of their feelings of distress and the chaos around them. For volunteer helpers, it is a process that emerges from training and experience, from translating theory into practice, and from personal self-reflection.

Much of the motivation for social support research is for discovery and design of new approaches to mental health care. Research findings are being translated into policy recommendations at federal, state, and local agency levels (Brownell & Shumaker, 1985). Certainly interventions and practice tailored to enhancing the informal support in people's lives have been used by human service professionals (Froland, Pancoast, Chapman, & Kimboko, 1981; Gottlieb, 1983).[1] This chapter was written with the practitioner in mind, either the lay provider or the professional who is concerned with the network, symbolic, and interactional processes of social support in everyday life. Because our concerns for helping others can sometimes blind us to potential questions, we begin with key ethical issues and limits on intervention. We then turn to selected literature on network approaches to social support that demonstrate innovative interventions for assessment, mediation, therapy, and training. We also present a rhetorical perspective on managing symbols for influencing others. The effectiveness of social programs designed to introduce or augment support systems are tied to the meanings recipients have for these interventions. Finally, we cover selected problems encountered by untrained providers and overview two training programs for lay personnel as representative models for developing verbal helping skills.

Ethical Concerns
and Limits on Intervention

We begin with a note of caution. Our intention is to broaden the scope and sensitivity of practitioners in considering intervention agendas. Brownell and Shumaker (1984) identify several important ethical issues associated with supportive behavior. They note that the ideological assumptions of advocates of social support may lead to inappropriate alterations of receivers' values. Intensely supportive actions by sources may impose on receivers' self-perceptions, countering views they may hold of themselves as autonomous decision makers. Supportive acts that invade feelings of privacy and independence may cause relational conflict, and undermine self-confidence and control. As Kessel (1964, p. 140) illustrates about the satisfied, self-protecting isolate:

> Their ways have to be solitary. The attentions of outsiders are unwelcome. Society should not try to force its concern upon them. Let

them alone. Charity and common sense demand they should be allowed to live their strange lives apart.

Practitioners and researchers also need to be vigilant about interventions that inadvertently promote "adaptation to adversity" (Brownell & Shumaker, 1985, p. 113; Rook & Dooley, 1985). Support groups for highly stressed employees may serve to co-opt individuals simply to tolerate higher thresholds of stress. Such an influence process subverts potential political action by diffusing tensions. It can be a mechanism for ignoring organizational stressors that should be directly addressed.[2]

As a final note, the ethical implications of mass media messages that encourage high-risk behaviors should be considered (e.g., advertisements that portray the glamour of smoking, "junk food" commercials, or even televised violence that shows such acts as the "ideal" means for conflict resolution). Without an understanding of these types of larger societal influences, the practitioner runs a risk of targeting change efforts toward the individual to the exclusion of attempts to reshape macro-level entrapments (Brownell & Shumaker, 1985).

Given concerns with congruency, co-option, and negative media influences, we turn now to consider prime directions for research applications of supportive communication: in the management of networks, symbols, and interactions.[3]

Managing Communication Networks

General approaches to network interventions have included enhancement of existing network relations and the training of non-primary group members (Rook & Dooley, 1985). The former approach has included the reinforcement of existing ties to family and friends and artificially grafted supports to self-help groups and third parties. The latter approach has emphasized the training of weak links, i.e. "natural helpers," within the larger social environment including the "urban agents" who provide nonprofessional support to their clients in the community (see Chapter 6).

Several goals have been identified for fostering helping networks. Froland et al. (1981) suggest that increasing network size, changing the content of interactions, network restructuring, strengthening of existing ties, and the creation of ties between formal and informal sources of support are all actions that directly benefit a target individual.[4]

Such useful goals are compatible with several current and innovative approaches to managing the support networks of specialized groups and the general population. These include network assessment strategies, third party mediators, network therapy, and network training.

Network assessments. These are baseline evaluations of support network activity that are used to advise structural changes in relationships. Strengths and weaknesses of an individual's social arrangement (e.g., an elderly widow with physical limitations, the support system of an occupationally stressed nurse) are diagnosed using network properties similar to the ones discussed in Chapter 2 in this volume (see also Mitchell, 1982; Pattison & Pattison, 1981).

Network assessments have been conducted for clinical, residential, and community-level interventions (see Froland, Brodsky, Olson, & Stewart, 1979). For example, Garrison and Podell (1981) designed a Community Support Systems Assessment (CSSA) instrument that has been used in clinical and psychiatric intake interviews. The format is used to elicit information about the individual's reference groups, the degree of subcultural variation in the network, the availability and interaction with network members, and the potential for extending these supports. The instrument includes a social network diagram (which the authors argue may be inaccurate but is a beginning point for understanding the patient's view of his or her "social world," p. 103), a "reconstructed week" of clients' descriptions of their contacts that may or may not be congruent with the social diagrams, and an "open-history" of help-seeking to gain insight into the patient's health belief model for treatment and recovery.

Network analysis has also been applied for assessing the communication patterns of special residential groups. Cohen and Adler (1984) used the Network Analysis Profile (NAP; see Sokolovsky & Cohen, 1981) for generating normative data on the residents of single-room occupancy (SRO) hotels. Several interactional properties (frequency, duration, intensity, and direction of aid) were examined for six relationships, including tenant contact with other tenants, nontenants, kin, hotel staff, agency staff, and social institution personnel (e.g., social workers). These assessments were helpful to practitioners for deciding whether an individual's network held capabilities for instrumental support, and a potential for help from second-order linkages (people indirectly connected to the focal individual through a network member). Circumstances when support from formal services could be more helpful than informal contacts were also determined.

Finally network assessments have been drawn of community group patterns. Warren (1982) used structured interviews to evaluate "problem-anchored helping networks" (PAHNS). He developed a typology of helping networks in various communities based on the effective integration of informal and formal sources of support used by individuals in those communities (see Chapter 2 for additional information on this research). Although this kind of work can lead to highly generalized conclusions (which should not be drawn to the exclusion of individual-level assessments), such typologies of community patterns are useful for designing prevention, treatment, and after-care service programs.

Network assessments of supportive interaction patterns should include the target individuals' and helpers' receptiveness and resistance to help. Subjective measures of the recipients' support nets can help uncover personal meanings that people attach to their supportive relationships. These guide the choices of the types of interventions that can be used to enhance rather than subvert individuals' perceptions of control. Subjective measures of recipients' relational perceptions can serve to reveal the amount of congruity or incongruity between recipient needs and program goals. Alternatively, more objective measures (such as contact records, family size, and proximity) may be used to identify the availability and motivation of informal providers as well as to detect problematic and negatively reinforcing relationships. Given that negative social interactions can seriously outweigh the effects of positive social ties (Rook, 1984), practitioners need to exercise caution in restructuring network systems and consider potentially toxic strains on both recipients and providers.

Third-party interventions. A "communication broker" is an intermediary between the focal individual and his or her informal support system who facilitates interaction between the parties. As noted in Chapter 11, providers can be overwhelmed and feel vulnerable in situations when they are unprepared or incapable of responding appropriately to a distressed individual. Recipients may be confused or unable to communicate their needs for help effectively. Cancer patients often react to their treatment of the disease (such as radiation therapy) with anxiety and depression (Peck, 1972). Yet as the cancer progresses toward later stages, communication becomes increasingly limited with family members (Krant & Johnston, 1977-1978). In this case, uncertainty may be high for both parties in simply not knowing how to manage interactions effectively.

A third-party mediator can assist in structuring expectations and reducing uncertainty for communication encounters. They may be specially trained as communication facilitators or emerge naturally in the setting due to their social skills and familiarity with the problems of the interactants. A workplace supervisor may assist a worker experiencing job stress in having more contact with experienced, energetic, and healthy personnel. Some nurses, due to their experience and backgrounds, can help family members cope with dying relatives by helping children talk about their feelings and help the patients develop realistic expectations of their families. These nurses can facilitate family rituals at the moment of death that enable members to grieve and provide mutual support.

Highly unfamiliar, volatile, and sensitive situations also trigger feelings of helplessness and loss of control for both recipient and provider. The presence of an experienced, reassuring guide can help frame the episode, context, and interaction so that members are able to reduce uncertainty about how much and what to expect during encounters. In some cases (e.g., after a patient's death or loss of a job) the third party can help structure the individual's interpretation of the situation to provide a sense of control over a potentially incomprehensible and profound loss. The temporal immediacy of this support may be critical to long-term coping once the individual is removed from the stressful situation.

Certainly professionals such as social workers, clergy, and counselors are appropriate mediators for many network interventions. But lack of accessibility to such persons or perhaps the stigma associated with needing their help may preclude the use of their services. Alternatively, lay providers who receive training in support counseling and network assessment techniques and who are familiar with community resources may be suitable mediators who can also bridge informal and formal support systems for individuals. A director of a volunteer, 24-hour telephone hotline for persons with cancer-related needs informed us that home visits are occasionally requested. Families of cancer patients sometimes need a forum to talk about their feelings. The volunteer can structure discussions of emotion-laden issues that would otherwise strain family relationships. (Unfortunately, the effectiveness of these practices by lay providers remains speculative due to a dearth of evaluation research.)

Network therapy. The premise of this work at the applied level is that in order to treat the individual, one must also work with the social web of relationships. Prominent examples of this approach have included networks of kin and friends coping with a member suffering from alcohol, drug abuse or mental illness (Rueveni, 1979; Schoenfeld, 1984; Schoenfeld, Halevy-Martini, Hemley-Van DerVelden, & Ruhf, 1985). Speck and Attneave (1973) proposed that treatment of psychiatric disorders needed to involve complete social systems surrounding the patient including family, friends, neighbors, coworkers, and acquaintances.

Network therapy is generally designed as a brief, high-impact intervention designed to bring the patient's social network together as a functioning, integrated system. Members are expected to be capable of supporting each other and the patient (Schoenfeld et al., 1985). According to Schoenfeld et al., three therapeutic processes must occur in order for the therapy to be effective. First, family members must personally contact network members and ask for a meeting to help in the crisis situation. "The very act of gathering the 'tribe' for such a purpose often has an immediate 'healing effect'" (p. 282). Second, outside facilitators should encourage network members to engage in open and frank communication about the patient, and their feelings, problems, and solutions to the crisis. Finally, members must identify a key problem related to the patient (e.g., finding an apartment or extended care facility) and work together to accomplish this objective. Network therapy can be a powerful strategy when recipients are surrounded by a visible web of caring others whose presence symbolizes their emotional support and whose concrete assistance enhances control.

Network training. Assisting individuals in self-understanding of the functional and dysfunctional features of their networks can aid them in gaining positive control of their social environments. Personal network mapping is a way for target persons to learn how their networks operate during times of work or life stress.

A typical strategy is to have individuals identify their network

members and identify the various resources exchanged and interactions shared with each individual. Network members are then
placed on a grid with judgments made about the extent of interconnection existing among the set of contacts. Individuals are instructed
in how to assess properties of their networks (multiplexity, density,
size, heterogeneity, and so on—see Chapter 2).

Such patterns can be heuristic for individuals in thinking about
their relational environments. When seen visually, these network
maps often stimulate participants to consider how their network
ties constrain and promote supportive outcomes (e.g., a sense of
belonging or need for privacy). For example, we have used this
technique in social support workshops for human service professionals experiencing occupational stress. In one case, a workshop
participant mapped her support network and afterwards realized
her entrenchment within an insulating and highly dense set of work-
related ties. She then understood why she experienced relief with
her more superficial social contacts. Network training can provide
a macrorelational perspective for life stress management by helping normal and recovering individuals to evaluate realistically the
human communication webs that provide pathways or entangle-
ments for healthy living.

Managing Symbols

The language of social support carries a rhetorical dimension
important for those concerned with effectively helping others. The
rhetorical dimension of language deals with the ways meaning is
used to influence others to achieve some desired effect. The language and symbols used in supportive transactions will have consequences for the individuals involved, their relationships, and the
programs designed to promote social support.

Certain symbols carry both denotative (content-laden meaning)
and connotative (affect-laden meaning) levels of interpretation (Bettinghaus, 1980; Osgood, Tannenbaum, & Suci, 1957). Terms
associated with social support processes, populations, and stressful events can connote for individuals meanings that influence how
they make sense of themselves and the situation. For example, the
words used to refer to the recipients of support (helpees, patients,
clients, and so on), providers (helpers, caregivers, supporters, and

so on), target populations (terminally diseased, abused spouses, "the afflicted," and so on), or personal disorders (obesity, cancer, substance addiction, unemployment) can invoke negative or positive affective responses depending on the nature of the audience. Careful attention then should be paid to selecting language that will help create desired effects. In a vivid example, Bart (1985, p. 406) details her search for an appropriate term to describe women who had been assaulted by a rapist but had avoided being raped:

> I changed the language three times in labeling these women. I first called them "victims and non-victims" but after some time I realized that the term "non-victim" was inappropriate. It implied that all women could be described in terms of victimization. It further suggested that women who avoided being raped were not victims. In some sense they had transcended victimization, but, indeed, because someone had tried to assault them, they may have felt victimized. I decided to call them "avoiders." . . . A Chicago feminist who worked with women who had been raped told me she preferred the term "survivors" because it emphasized the positive aspects of the experience, i.e., the women's strengths in coping with the assault. Calling the woman a "survivor" rather than a "victim" might help her to internalize this more positive label and thus this change in terminology could function as a self-fulfilling prophecy. In light of this information I changed the terms to "survivors" and "avoiders." . . . I may decide to make still further changes in my forthcoming book (e.g., "raped" and "not-raped" women).

Bart's reflections illustrate that language usage has central consequences for how attributions are assigned for the event, the perpetuation of self-fulfilling prophecies, or the reframing of the incident as a redeeming strength. Attempts to support those who avoided the rape will be successful to the extent the provider uses terms that describe the personal strengths of the women rather than those that reinforce the sense of helplessness and vulnerability to the violent acts.

Planners also need to be careful in how they phrase their services during publicity phases. In some cases, audience response to labels for services will depend on messages that do not arouse fear or carry stigmas. The leaders of a nonprofit self-help group that provides informational and emotional support to "people touched by infertility" (phrasing in the organization's brochure) found they had difficulty attracting men to an upcoming lecture they were sponsoring on this topic. The lecture was entitled "Male Infertility" and they suspected that male attendance had been inhibited by the social stigma attached to the topic. A similar problem faced trainers who had designed a workshop on developing support skills for managers of employees with life-threatening illnesses. Because discussion about life-threatening illness can invoke fear and anxiety, the planners decided on "Living Through It . . . " as their program title.[5]

Managing Interactions

Learning how to manage supportive interactions has usually focused on communication skills for helping. Models for teaching helping skills (e.g., Carkhuff, 1973; Danish, D'Augelli, & Hauer, 1980; Egan, 1982) for a diversity of training for informal caregivers have included programs for community members (Ehrlich, D'Augelli, & Conter, 1981; Wiesenfeld & Weis, 1979), paraprofessionals (D'Augelli & Levy, 1978), and hotline volunteers (LaFayette & Wooldridge, 1982). In this section we focus on models for helping lay providers of social support better anticipate interaction patterns and to develop fuller repertoires of helping communication behaviors.

Research background. A lack of adequate social interaction management skills may mean that attempts to help people in distress will not function to reduce uncertainty or enhance control, even when the assistance is motivated by good intentions. Research on the verbal behavior of untrained providers in initial helping interactions showed that helpers were more likely than trained volunteers to use advice giving, directive statements, and strategies that discouraged recipient disclosure and control over interactions. Knowles (1979) found that the predominant response mode of untrained applicants ($n = 350$) in simulated crisis-line calls was advice giving (which constituted 70%-90% of helpers' responses across two problem situations). Response strategies of reflection, interpretation, self-disclosure, or questioning were used significantly less than more directive responses. Similarly, D'Augelli,

Danish, and Brock (1976) found that untrained paraprofessionals used more directive and leading responses than responses that encouraged recipient self-disclosure or initiative in solving his or her own problems. These authors concluded that advice giving and highly directive statements in initial helping interactions may interfere with the receiver's sense of competence, level of self-disclosure, and perceived trust in the helping relationship. These studies examined helping behavior in dyads where both participants were strangers. It remains empirically unclear whether directive strategies in the initial phase of a helping encounter between parties with a developed relational history would permit more directive responses.

Prior work on crisis coping has emphasized the importance of allowing the receiver to ventilate his or her concerns (Silver & Wortman, 1980). In the initial phase of the interaction, highly directive approaches to recipient problems can function to increase uncertainty in several ways. From a relational perspective, unfamiliar providers may not have achieved sufficient credibility through rapport building and trust to warrant control over the exchange. Efforts to offer advice or control the interaction too quickly without allowing client self-expression may be perceived as manipulation or scripted attempts to invalidate the recipients' situation. Sense making by the recipient can occur through talk, sometimes necessitating several tangents and reiterations of feelings and ideas. But a trained, empathic listener can help the recipient formulate an emerging cause-effect pattern in their considerations of stressful experiences, contingencies often obscured by pent up feelings. Moreover, recipient perceptions of mutual understanding and trust in their relationships with listener/providers may increase their openness to more directive approaches and receptivity to advice or information to better handle their situations.

The following are two training models representative of basic helping skills that can be used by natural helpers. The importance of early rapport building is emphasized through the use of non-directive, person-centered messages that convey concern for the recipient and encourage self-disclosure.

Training crisis hotline volunteers. In an effort to provide systematic, short-term training for volunteers of a cancer hotline, LaFayette and Wooldridge (1982) designed a processual training model for client interaction. The easily remembered acronym "TCAP" is used to describe the four steps of the helping process: talk, clarify, assess, and plan (see Table 12.1).

Much of the training in this program is oriented toward the TCAP model, including a rationale for each of the steps, general types of strategies, and examples of key phrases. Specific responses are provided as guidance rather than rules to avoid overly scripted response patterns and to help volunteers overcome uncertainty about what to say to clients.

In a recent study we observed several advantages of this training program for short-term, specialized support situations (Albrecht et al., 1986). First, TCAP provides terminology enabling trainees to discuss specific steps in the interaction and identify areas of difficulty. Second, the model is a framework for volunteers to visualize and mentally rehearse a process that can encompass a whole episode from initial interaction to disengagement. The coherence in the structure helps the volunteer to reduce uncertainty about managing the interaction, to assess personal competence, and to ensure feelings of closure about the call. Although data on client perceptions are not available, presumably the very process of moving from a state of ventilation to one of clarification would help clients obtain a perceived schema for their feelings and situation. Volunteers reported that clients often sought validation for their emotions. Given the absence of social comparisons for coping with their distressful situations, response to the question, "How am I doing?" became critical for reducing uncertainty. Once clients feel understood and affirmed by the provider, they may be more open to taking steps toward further self-help (e.g., to seek a community referral or to make assertive attempts at self-management of pain).

Training community helpers. Shifting from the faceless context of telephone hotlines, training programs for natural helpers in the community also exist. Ehrlich et al. (1981) designed the Community Helpers Project (CHP) for developing informal helping skills of rural caregivers. The purpose of the CHP was to create an ongoing self-sustaining training system where trained volunteers could extend their experiences and knowledge in a pyramid style to other rural helpers.

The program adapted the work of Danish et al. (1980) on helping skills based on a learning skills model. The following steps were taught sequentially: (1) effective nonverbal behavior, (2) con-

TABLE 12.1

Using Communication Skills to Structure a Call (TCAP)

Structure	Purpose	Phrases That Work
Talk freely	• let the caller talk freely, set priorities • make no assumptions • allow caller to vent and build trust • listen for the feelings	• "Tell me more about . . ." • "How did it feel when . . ." • "Help me understand the situation better . . ."
Clarify	• use active listening, paraphrasing, open-ended questions, check perceptions to help clarify • help caller define own concerns—define "it," work in small steps	• "You sound (tired, frustrated, like you're giving lots of support to, etc. . . .)" • "This sounds like a difficult time, situation . . ." • "If I understood, you've said . . ." • "I'm not sure I understand your question . . ."
Assess and focus	• prioritize caller's concerns • decide which need referral to other community resources • help caller explore his own resources (family, neighborhood, church, etc.)	• "What's the (hardest, easiest, scariest, etc.) thing about this (situation, time)?" • "What would be most helpful if you could have anything?" • "We aren't trained or have resources to deal with that particular need. We can help you find some resources."
Plan	• find information for referrals • discuss resources, options, and decide how to use them • keep focus on caller's way of deciding, coping. • watch out for helping traps (don't band aid) • offer ongoing support by outreach volunteer	• "I have _____ . Would that be helpful to you?" • "Would you be comfortable trying this idea with your (mother, husband, doctor, etc.)?" • "What questions and concerns does your doctor need to understand in order for you to feel satisfaction on your next visit?" • "Let's review what we've spoken about . . ."

SOURCE: Reprinted with permission by P. LaFayette, Director of Cancer Lifeline in Seattle, and J. Wooldridge, Program Manager of Washington State Cancer Information Service (CIS). This version of TCAP is currently used in training phone counselors in both agencies. The Washington State CIS is part of a national network sponsored by the National Cancer Institute.

tinuing/reflecting responses (statements that address both content and relational concerns of receivers), (3) leading/directive responses (including closed and open questions and statements designed to influence or advise), and (4) self-referent responses (statements from providers showing personal involvement or self-disclosure toward recipients). Each skill was rationalized and defined in behavioral terms with models provided of effective and ineffective examples.

The authors found that training the initial trainers resulted in significant changes toward more nondirective response styles. However, the diffusion of the training in a tiered progression from trained volunteers to other trainee volunteers throughout the community was less effective (especially in changing those trainees whose response patterns tended to be highly directive). Danish et al. (1980) conclude that "slippage in dissemination" (p. 330) resulted in second-order trainees attaining lower skill competency levels (though the ranges varied in specific groups and types of skills).

Concluding Note

It has been clear from our review of the social support literature that theory and empirical research remain grounded in concerns for the management of social problems. The interweave between conceptual thinking and application is evident both in broad theoretical treatments of areas such as family systems, stress, and coping, and helping behaviors toward middle-range theories for specific populations (e.g., rape victims, people undergoing life-threatening illness, and life transitions). Creative efforts to link research and intervention are evident in the ways measurements of network indices become assessments for clinical and nonclinical intervention while simultaneously being used as forms for data collection, contributing to a growing body of knowledge.

A likely direction in the application of social support will be toward expanded efforts of health care practitioners to foster collaborative programs with natural helpers. Such efforts are critical in light of the economic, political, and social changes that are rapidly altering health care delivery in this country, shifting sources of caregiving from formal to informal systems. Social support among family, friends, and weak ties is no longer a preference; it has become a health care reality. As Ehrlich et al. (1981, p. 334) note, "For many people, such informal helping is and will remain their only help."

NOTES

1. The pragmatics of funding and mobilizing human energy have consequences for program planners. Interventionists need to consider both efficacy and efficiency when designing and implementing programs. Froland et al. (1981) detail the costs and outcomes of human service programs. Populations targeted by formal services designed to reinforce informal systems have included the elderly, children, families, the developmentally and physically disabled, and mental health care clients.

2. We acknowledge Professor William Scott (School of Business, University of Washington) for his insight on this point.

3. Ideally, the selection of specific intervention strategies will be guided by conceptual and practical understanding for intended outcomes. Rook and Dooley (1985) identify three topics relevant to considerations of appropriate interventions: (1) populations targeted for intervention, including the needs of the general public or specific high-risk groups; (2) the unit of analysis for intervention from the individual to the group or community level; and (3) the nature of social support deficiencies, including the quantity, quality, and utilization of support.

4. See Chapman and Pancoast (1985) for an application of these five goals to strengthen the support systems of the elderly.

5. This example was provided by Pam LaFayette, Director of Cancer Lifeline of Family Services (Seattle, WA) and Jean Wooldridge, Program Manager, Washington State Cancer Information Service.

Epilogue:
New Directions
for Communication Research

TERRANCE L. ALBRECHT
MARA B. ADELMAN

We end with a look to the future. Our goal in this book has been to describe a research agenda for supportive communication processes, functions, and structures. Building on the implicit questions raised in each of the chapters in this volume, the following is a set of general topics that we view as important for the next generation of studies.

Expansion of initial theoretical framework. Further systematic testing is needed of the ideas presented in Part I. Of particular concern will be to determine the conditions under which social support processes lead to the empowerment of the individual rather than undue dependence on supporters. This will be one avenue for longitudinal work where the changing nature of supportive interactions and the structural density of support networks can be interwoven to understand better the functional consequences of the changing nature of support (for example, in the case of significant life transitions such as divorce or the widowhood experience).

In addition, we emphasize a focus not only on support effects but on the nature of these relationships and their cycles of development and dissolution. Clearly beginnings are apparent with studies on the role of reciprocity and strong/weak tie engagements. More work should incorporate uncertainty reduction models for relationship development (Berger & Calabrese, 1975; Parks & Adelman, 1983) in understanding supportive ties. The dynamics of the relationship should be contrasted with the effects on the individual.

Explication of supportive messages. There should be continued emphasis on the interplay between verbal and nonverbal messages of support. The attention to nonverbal communication should include studying the effects of silence, touch, and the effects on comforting when cues are restricted (as in the case of limited channel access, that is, telephone hotlines and so on). Certainly expectations for supportive nonverbal behavior will vary with the type of relationship existing between supporter and provider; these should be sorted out more clearly at the empirical level. Violations of expected behavior should also be assessed to understand better the possible effects on relational development.

More work is needed on complex message strategies that help recipients clarify uncertainties, focus attention, and reshape attributions for personal control perceptions. While simple strategies of advice giving, empathic listening, and the like have been catalogued, interactions are often more developed with use of multiple behaviors. More work should assess the efficacy of strategies used to persuade recipients to shift their cognitive frames initially in order to reap the effects of the overall support strategies.

Finally, much research emphasis has been given to those experiencing uncertainty and anxiety from stressful or negative life events. We suggest that interesting contrasts could be drawn if research populations included those who were experiencing uncertainty and lack of experienced control from seemingly positive conditions. What are the message behaviors used to support those undergoing life transition from positive events (i.e., marriage, job promotion, lottery wins)? How do the support systems of such people change and what do recipients find they can no longer expect in the way of support from others to help them cope with changed circumstances in their lives?

Explication of network structures. Certainly much research has been devoted to studying the properties of support networks. However, a broader range of support network indices should be incorporated in future designs for more cross-level analysis. Most studies have been limited (often by time and money) to individual-level perceptions of structure. This has been a reasonable move in the past given that one's perceptions of one's support environment count as legitimate data (House, 1981; see also Richards, 1985). However, efforts should be undertaken to conduct smaller scale but highly descriptive studies of network patterns incorporating points of view of network members as well as the focal individual. Network capabilities for resource provision could be better assessed and communication dilemmas of overly dense or enjoined systems could be more fully documented.

Research is also needed to clarify the interplay between support systems. For example, what are the effects of connections (or lack thereof) between work and outside-work nets? How do these enable the individual to resolve job-related uncertainty, particularly under times of greatest disruption to work networks (such as early organizational entry phases or job promotions/demotions)?

Given the amount of information we have already gained from studies of support networks, steps should be taken to create better outlines of prototype support systems that show optimal balances between strong and weak ties. This is important not only for understanding the position of the focal individual but also for learning the kinds of structural arrangements that best enable supporters to provide assistance. Demonstrating the social architecture of functional systems will be critical for training and intervention.

Research and social commentary. Research findings have far-reaching implications for formulating local, state, and federal policies for health care delivery. As such, researchers must remain responsive to the social, political, and economic undercurrents that have consequences for empowerment or co-optation of people within the larger society. Social commentary or criticism of these systems is needed to alert us to the ever-changing ethical issues that accompany our work. Critiques of ideologies at the organizational (e.g., Scott & Hart, 1979) and cultural levels (e.g., Bellah, Madsen, Sullivan, Swidler, & Tipton, 1985) reveal value systems that have profound consequences for societal functioning. Taken-for-granted assumptions about relationships and societal arrangements should be examined systematically in future work to provide a regulating mechanism for challenging personal and professional worldviews.

Evaluation research. Finally, more studies of extant support programs will be helpful for mobilizing organized, but informal, volunteer sources of support assistance. Evaluations of documentation data can be conducted readily using existing data banks of nonprofit agencies (such as hotline or counseling services). Such research is not only useful for understanding support seeking but also assists the organization in program planning, budgeting, and grant funding.

Projections toward demographic shifts. Current research should account for projected trends in the population. Specific groups such as single parents and the elderly (particularly single elderly women, one in three; Fuchs, 1983, p. 175) will continue to draw significant interest, given their increasing percentage rates of growth and economic dependence on society. Additional groups in need of specialized support and services will be increasing numbers of working mothers, displaced homemakers, early male retirees (who often lack close personal ties outside of family), and dependent children (of unwed mothers and divorced families) (Fuchs, 1983). Studies of members of these groups who are managing well would inform future work on the needs and concerns best addressed by supportive ties. Alternatively, these are groups where studies of the binds and dilemmas of supportive relationships will be particularly crucial.

**   **   **   **   **   **   **

Understanding the communication of support will be critical not only for projected populations but for all of us. While the standard of living has improved for many people, well-being is also intertwined with the nature of social environment. Writing from an economic perspective on future trends, Fuchs (1983, p. 241) cautions:

> The fruits of the market system—science, technology, urbanization, affluence—are undermining the institutions that are the foundations of the social order. Human beings need more than an abundance of material goods. They need a sense of purpose in life—secure relationships with other human beings—something or someone to believe in. With the decline of the family and religion, the inability of the market system to meet such needs becomes obvious, and government rushes in to fill the vacuum, but does so imperfectly and at great cost.

We conclude this book by bringing home the theme of social support. Pilisuk (1980, p. 29) notes that we are unlikely to influence others if we as researchers cannot derive benefits of social support for ourselves. Continued efforts to contribute to this important area of study will undoubtedly affect the quality of professional and personal life for all of us.

References

Abdel-Halim, A. A. (1982). Social support and managerial affective responses to job stress. *Journal of Occupational Behavior, 3,* 281-295.

Abramson, L. Y., & Alloy, L. B. (1980). Judgment of contingency: Errors and their implications. In A. Baum & J. E. Singer (Eds.), *Advances in environmental psychology: Vol. 2. Applications of personal control* (pp. 111-130). Hillsdale, NJ: Lawrence Erlbaum.

Abramson, L. Y., Garber, J., & Seligman, M. (1980). Learned helplessness in humans: An attributional analysis. In J. Garber & M. E. Seligman (Eds.), *Human helplessness* (pp. 3-35). New York: Academic Press.

Abramson, L. Y., Seligman, M., & Teasdale, J. D. (1978). Learned helplessness in humans: Critique and reformulation. *Journal of Abnormal Psychology, 87,* 49-74.

Adelman, M. B. (1986). *The contagion effect: A study on stress and the provision of support.* Unpublished doctoral dissertation, University of Washington, Seattle.

Adelman, M. B., & Siemon, M. (1986). Communicating the relational shift: Separation among adult twins. *American Journal of Psychotherapy, 60,* 96-109.

Adelson, J. (1980). Adolescence and the generalization gap. In D. Rogers (Ed.), *Issues in life-span human development* (pp. 260-264). Monterey, CA: Brooks/Cole.

Alba, R. D. (1976). Social assimilation among American Catholic national-religion groups. *American Sociological Review, 41,* 1030-1046.

Alba, R. D. (1978). Ethnic networks and tolerant attitudes. *Public Opinion Quarterly, 42,* 1-16.

Alba, R. D. (1982). Taking stock of network analysis: A decade's results. *Research in the Sociology of Organizations, 1,* 39-74.

Alba, R. D., & Chamlin, M. B. (1983). A preliminary examination of ethnic identification among whites. *American Sociological Review, 48,* 240-247.

Albrecht, T. L. (1982). Coping with occupational stress: Relational and individual strategies of nurses in acute health care settings. In M. Burgoon (Ed.), *Communication yearbook 6* (pp. 832-839). Newbury Park, CA: Sage.

Albrecht, T. L. (1984). Managerial communication and work perception. In R. Bostrom (Ed.), *Communication yearbook 8* (pp. 538-557). Newbury Park, CA: Sage.

Albrecht, T. L., & Adelman, M. B. (1984). Social support and life stress: New directions for communication research. *Human Communication Research, 11,* 3-32.

Albrecht, T. L., Adelman, M. B., Brown, M., Christine, J., Oseroff, D., Skans, D., & Underwood, C. (1986, May). *The metaphors of care giving.* Paper presented at the annual meeting of the International Communication Association, Chicago.

Albrecht, T. L., Irey, K. V., & Mundy, A. K. (1982). Integration in a communication network as a mediator of stress. *Social Work, 27,* 229-234.

Albrecht, T. L., & Ropp, V. A. (1982). The study of network structuring in organizations through the use of method triangulation. *Western Journal of Speech Communication, 46,* 162-178.

Albrecht, T. L., & Ropp, V. A. (1984). Communicating about innovation in networks of three U.S. organizations. *Journal of Communication, 34,* 78-91.

Allan, G. (1983). Informal networks of care: Issues raised by Barclay. *British Journal of Social Work, 13,* 417-433.

Allen, C., & Lambert, W. E. (1972). Ethnic identification and personality adjustment of Canadian adolescents of mixed English-French parentage. In J. W. Berry & G.J.S. Wilde (Eds.), *Social psychology: The Canadian context* (pp. 173-192). Toronto: McClelland & Stewart.

Alloy, L. B., & Abramson, L. Y. (1979). Judgment of contingency in depressed and nondepressed students: Sadder but wiser? *Journal of Experimental Psychology: General, 108,* 441-485.

Alloy, L. B., & Abramson, L. Y. (1982). Learned helplessness, depression, and the illusion of control. *Journal of Personality and Social Psychology, 42,* 1114-1126.

Altman, D. (1984). Evaluation of the cancer information service: Implications for health behavior and health services research (Doctoral dissertation, University of California—Irvine, 1984/1985). *Dissertation Abstracts International, 45-09,* 2884-B.

Altman, I. (1975). *The environment and social behavior: Privacy, personal space, territory, crowding.* Monterey, CA: Brooks/Cole.

Altman, I., & Taylor, D. A. (1973). *Social penetration: The development of interpersonal relationships.* New York: Holt, Rinehart & Winston.

Anderson, J. G., & Gray-Toft, P. A. (1982). *Stress, burnout, and turnover among health professionals: A social network approach.* Paper presented at the meeting of the International Sociological Association, Mexico City.

Anderson, R. K., Hart, B. L., & Hart, L. A. (Eds.). (1984). *The pet connection: Its influence on our health and quality of life.* Minneapolis: University of Minnesota, Center to Study Human-Animal Relationships and Environments.

Aneshensel, C. S., & Stone, J. D. (1982). Stress and depression: A test of the buffering model of social support. *Archives of General Psychiatry, 39,* 1392-1396.

Angyal, A. (1965). *Neurosis and treatment: A holistic theory.* New York: John Wiley.

Antonucci, T. C. (1985). Personal characteristics, social support, and social behavior. In R. H. Binstock & E. Shanas (Eds.), *Handbook of aging and the social sciences* (2nd ed., pp. 94-128). New York: Van Nostrand Reinhold.

Antonucci, T. C., & Depner, C. E. (1982). Social support and informal helping relationships. In T. A. Wills (Ed.), *Basic processes in helping relationships* (pp. 233-252). New York: Academic Press.

Antze, P. (1979). Role ideologies in peer psychotherapy groups. In M. A. Lieberman & L. D. Borman (Eds.), *Self help groups for coping with crisis* (pp. 272-304). San Francisco: Jossey-Bass.

Arangio, A. (1975). *Behind the stigma of epilepsy.* Washington, DC: Epilepsy Foundation of America.

Argyle, M., & Furnham, A. (1983). Sources of satisfaction and conflict in long-term relationships. *Journal of Marriage and the Family, 45,* 481-493.

Argyle, M., & Henderson, M. (1985). *The anatomy of relationships.* London: Heinemann.

Arling, G. (1976). The elderly widow and her family, neighbors and friends. *Journal of Marriage and the Family, 38,* 757-768.

Arntson, P. H. (1980, May). *Professional-client communication: The narrative response in self help groups.* Paper presented at the meeting of the International Communication Association, Acapulco, Mexico.

Arntson, P. H., Droge, D., Norton, R., & Murray, E. (1986). The perceived psychosocial consequences of having epilepsy. In S. Whitman & B. P. Hermann (Eds.), *Psychopathology in epilepsy social dimensions* (pp. 143-161). New York: Oxford University Press.

Arntson, P. H., & Montgomery, B. (1980, May). *The antecedent conditions and social consequences of epilepsy.* Paper presented at the meeting of the International Communication Association, Acapulco, Mexico.

Arntson, P. H., & Philipsborn, H. (1982). Pediatrician-parent communication in a continuity of care setting. *Clinical Pediatrics, 21,* 302-307.

Arntson, P. H., Zimmerman, B., Feinsod, P., & Speer, M. (1982). Communication with patients: The perceptions of medical students. In L. Pettegrew (Ed.), *Straight talk: Explorations in provider and patient interaction* (pp. 87-94). Louisville: Humana.

Aronson, E. (1970). Some antecedents of interpersonal attraction. In W. J. Arnold & D. Levine (Eds.), *Nebraska Symposium on Motivation* (pp. 143-173). Lincoln: University of Nebraska Press.

Atkin, C. (1972). Instrumental utilities and information seeking. In P. Clarke (Ed.), *New models for mass communication research* (pp. 205-242). Newbury Park, CA: Sage.

Atwater, E. (1983). *Psychology of adjustment: Personal growth in a changing world.* Englewood Cliffs, NJ: Prentice-Hall.

Badura, B., & Waltz, M. (1982). *Social support and well-being: The measurement of social support.* Paper presented at the meeting of the International Sociological Association, Mexico City.

Bankoff, E. A. (1981). Effects of friendship support on the psychological well-being of widows. In H. Z. Lapota & D. Maines (Eds.), *Research in the interweave of social roles: Friendship* (pp. 109-139). Greenwich, CT: JAI.

Barrera, M., & Ainlay, S. L. (1983). The structure of social support: A conceptual and empirical analysis. *Journal of Community Psychology, 11,* 133-143.

Bart, P. B. (1985). Being a feminist academic: What a nice feminist like me is doing in a place like this. In P. A. Treichler, C. Kramarae, & B. Stafford

278   COMMUNICATING SOCIAL SUPPORT

(Eds.), *For alma mater: Theory and practice in feminist scholarship* (pp. 402-418). Chicago: University of Illinois Press.

Bateson, G. (1972). *Steps to an ecology of mind.* New York: Ballantine.

Beck, A., & Katcher, A. (1983). *Between pets and people: The importance of animal companionship.* New York: G. P. Putnam.

Beehr, T. A. (1985). The role of social support in coping with organizational stress. In T. A. Beehr & R. S. Bhagat (Eds.), *Human stress and cognition in organizations: An integrated perspective* (pp. 375-398). New York: John Wiley.

Bell, R. A. (1985). Conversational involvement and loneliness. *Communication Monographs, 52,* 217-235.

Bell, R. A. (in press). Social involvement and interpersonal communication. In J. C. McCrosky & J. A. Daly (Eds.), *Personality and interpersonal communication.* Newbury Park, CA: Sage.

Bellah, R. N., Madsen, R., Sullivan, W. M., Swidler, A., & Tipton, S. M. (1985). *Habits of the heart: Individualism and commitment in American life.* New York: Harper & Row.

Belle, D. E. (1982a). The impact of poverty on social networks and supports. *Marriage & Family Review, 5,* 89-103.

Belle, D. E. (1982b). The stress of caring: Women as providers of social support. In L. Goldberger & S. Breznitz (Eds.), *Handbook of stress* (pp. 496-505). New York: Free Press.

Bennet, J. W. (1976). *The ecological transition: Cultural anthropology and human adaptation.* New York: Pergamon.

Berger, C. R., & Bradac, J. J. (1982). *Language and social knowledge: Uncertainty in interpersonal relations.* London: Edward Arnold.

Berger, C. R., & Calabrese, R. J. (1975). Some explorations in initial interaction and beyond: Toward a developmental theory of interpersonal communication. *Human Communication Research, 1,* 99-112.

Berger, C. R., & Douglas, W. (1982). Thought and talk: "Excuse me, but have I been talking to myself?" In F.E.X. Dance (Ed.), *Human communication theory* (pp. 42-60). New York: Harper & Row.

Berger, C. R., Gardner, R. R., Parks, M. R., Schulman, L., & Miller, G. R. (1976). Interpersonal epistemology and interpersonal communication. In G. R. Miller (Ed.), *Explorations in interpersonal communication* (pp. 149-171). Newbury Park, CA: Sage.

Berkman, L. F. (1984). Assessing the physical health-effects of social networks and social support. *Annual Review of Public Health, 5,* 413-432.

Berkman, L. F., & Syme, S. L. (1979). Social networks, host resistance, and mortality: A nine-year follow-up study of Alameda county residents. *American Journal of Epidemiology, 109,* 186-204.

Bernstein, B. (1964). Elaborated and restricted codes: Their social origins and some consequences. *American Anthropologist, 66* (2), 55-69.

Berry, J. W. (1980). Acculturation as varieties of adaptation. In A. M. Padilla (Ed.), *Acculturation: Theory, models and some new findings* (pp. 9-25). Washington, DC: Westview.

Berry, J. W., & Kalin, R. (1979). Reciprocity of inter-ethnic attitudes in a multi-cultural society. *International Journal of Intercultural Relations, 3,* 99-112.

Berscheid, E., & Walster, E. (1978). *Interpersonal attraction*. Reading, MA: Addison-Wesley.

Bettinghaus, E. P. (1980). *Persuasive communication*. New York: Holt, Rinehart & Winston.

Bharadwaj, L. K., & Wilkening, E. A. (1980). Life domain satisfactions and personal social integration. *Social Indicators Research, 7,* 337-351.

Biegel, D. E., McCardle, E., & Mendelson, S. (1985). *Social networks and mental health: An annotated bibliography*. Newbury Park, CA: Sage.

Bilge, B., & Kaufman, G. (1983). Children of divorce and one-parent families: Cross-cultural perspectives. *Journal of Applied Family and Child Studies, 32,* 59-71.

Bissonette, R. (1977). The bartender as a mental health service gatekeeper: A role analysis. *Community Mental Health Journal, 13,* 92-99.

Blake, S. (1976). Comforting each other. In P. Chaney (Ed.), *Dealing with death and dying* (pp. 97-105). Jenkintown, PA: Intermed Communications.

Blau, D. M. (1955). *The dynamics of bureaucracy*. Chicago: University of Chicago Press.

Blau, D. M. (1974). Parameters of social structure. *American Sociological Review, 39,* 615-635.

Blau, G. (1981). An empirical investigation of job stress, social support, service length, and job strain. *Organizational Behavior and Human Performance, 27,* 279-302.

Blau, Z. S. (1961). Structural constraints on friendships in old age. *American Sociological Review, 26,* 429-439.

Blau, Z. S. (1973). *Old age in a changing society*. New York: Franklin Watts.

Bloom, J. R. (1982). Social support systems and cancer: A conceptual view. In J. Cohen, J. Cullen, & R. Martin (Eds.), *Research issues in the psychological aspects of cancer* (pp. 129-149). New York: Raven.

Bloom, J. R., & Spiegel, D. (1984). The relationship of two dimensions of social support to the psychological well-being and social functioning of women with advanced breast cancer. *Social Science and Medicine, 19,* 831-837.

Blumberg, B. (1982). NCA's coping with cancer information and education program: Evolution, planning, and implementation. In C. Mettlin & G. P. Murphy (Eds.), *Issues in cancer screening and communications* (pp. 83-90). New York: Alan R. Liss.

Bochner, A. P. (1976). Conceptual frontiers in the study of communication in families: An introduction to the literature. *Human Communication Research, 2,* 381-397.

Bolton, F. G., & Bolton, S. R. (1986). *Working with the violent family: A clinical/legal guide*. Newbury Park, CA: Sage.

Booth, A. (1972). Sex and social participation. *American Sociological Review, 37,* 183-192.

Boss, P. G. (1983). Normative family stress: Family boundary changes across the life-span. In D. H. Olson & B. C. Miller (Eds.), *Family studies review book* (pp. 107-112). Newbury Park, CA: Sage.

Boston Women's Health Book Collective. (1984). *Our bodies, ourselves*. New York: Simon & Schuster.

Bostrom, R. N. (Ed.). (1984). *Competence in communication: A multidisciplinary approach.* Newbury Park, CA: Sage.

Bowlby, J. (1977). The making and breaking of affectional bonds, Part I: Etiology and psychopathology in the light of attachment theory. *British Journal of Psychiatry, 130,* 210.

Bradburn, N. (1969). *The structure of psychological wellbeing.* Chicago: Aldine.

Braiker, H. B., & Kelley, H. H. (1979). Conflict in the development of close relationships. In R. L. Burgess & T. L. Huston (Eds.), *Social exchange in developing relationships* (pp. 135-168). New York: Academic Press.

Bralove, M. (1981). Problems of two-career families start forcing businesses to adapt. *Wall Street Journal* (15 July), sec. 2, p. 29.

Brandt, P. A. (1984). Stress-buffering effects of social support on maternal discipline. *Nursing Research, 33,* 229-234.

Brass, D. J. (1984). Being in the right place: A structural analysis of individual influence in an organization. *Administrative Science Quarterly, 29,* 518-539.

Breton, R. (1964). Institutional completeness of ethnic communities and the personal relations of immigrants. *American Journal of Sociology, 70,* 193-205.

Brickman, P., & Bulman, R. J. (1977). Pleasure and pain in social comparison. In J. M. Suls & R. L. Miller (Eds.), *Social comparison processes* (pp. 149-186). Washington, DC: Hemisphere.

Brickman, P., Rabinowitz, V. C., Karuza, J. Jr., Coates, D., Cohn, E., & Kidder, L. (1982). Models of helping and coping. *American Psychologist, 37,* 368-384.

Brockopp, G. W. (1973). Crisis intervention: Theory, process and practice. In D. Lester & G. W. Brockopp (Eds.), *Crisis intervention and counseling by telephone* (pp. 89-104). Springfield, IL: Charles C Thomas.

Brodsky, C. M. (1968). Clergymen as psychotherapists: Problems in interrole communication. *Community Mental Health Journal, 4,* 482-491.

Brody, E. B. (Ed.). (1970). *Behavior in new environments: Adaptation of migrant populations.* Newbury Park, CA: Sage.

Brody, E. M. (1981). Women in the middle and family help to older people. *Gerontologist, 21,* 471-480.

Broom, L., & Kitsuse, J. (1955). The validation of acculturation. *American Anthropologist, 57,* 44-48.

Brown, B. R. (1968). The effects of need to maintain face on interpersonal bargaining. *Journal of Experimental Social Psychology, 4,* 107-122.

Brown, B. R., & Garland, H. (1971). The effects of incompetency, audience acquaintanceship and anticipated evaluative feedback on face-saving behavior. *Journal of Experimental Social Psychology, 7,* 490-502.

Brown, G. W., Birley, J.L.I., & Wing, J. F. (1972). Influence of family life on the course of schizophrenic disorders: A replication. *British Journal of Psychiatry, 121,* 241-258.

Brown, G. W., & Harris, T. (1978). *Social origins of depression: A study of psychiatric disorders in women.* New York: Free Press.

Brown, M. A. (1986a). Social support during pregnancy: A uni-dimensional or multi-dimensional construct. *Nursing Research, 35,* 4-9.

Brown, M. A. (1986b). Social support, stress, and health: A comparison of expectant mothers and fathers. *Nursing Research, 35,* 72-76.

Brownell, A., & Shumaker, S. A. (1984). Social support: An introduction to a complex phenomenon. *Journal of Social Issues, 40,* 1-9.

Brownell, A., & Shumaker, S. A. (1985). Where do we go from here? The policy implications of social support. *Journal of Social Issues, 41,* 111-121.

Brubaker, T. H. (1985). *Later life families.* Newbury Park, CA: Sage.

Bruhn, J. G., & Philips, B. U. (1984). Measuring social support: A synthesis of current approaches. *Journal of Behavioral Medicine, 7,* 151-169.

Bruner, J. (1986). *Actual minds, possible worlds.* Cambridge, MA: Harvard University Press.

Budner, S. (1962). Intolerance of ambiguity as a personality variable. *Journal of Personality, 30,* 29-50.

Burgess, A., & Holmstrom, L. (1978). Recovery from rape and prior life stress. *Research in Nursing and Health, 1,* 165-174.

Burgess, R. L. (1981). Relationships in marriage and the family. In S. W. Duck & R. Gilmour (Eds.), *Personal relationships, 1: Studying personal relationships* (pp. 179-196). London: Academic Press.

Burgess, R. L., & Huston, T. L. (Eds.). (1979). *Social exchange in developing relationships.* New York: Academic Press.

Burgoon, M., & Ruffner, M. (1978). *Human communication.* New York: Holt, Rinehart & Winston.

Burke, R. J., & Weir, T. (1982). Husband-wife helping relationships as moderators of experienced stress: The "mental hygiene" function in marriage. In H. I. McCubbin, A. E. Cauble, & J. M. Patterson (Eds.), *Family stress, coping, and social support* (pp. 221-238). Springfield, IL: Charles C. Thomas.

Burleson, B. R., & Samter, W. (1985). Consistencies in theoretical and naive evaluations of comforting messages. *Communication Monographs, 52,* 103-123.

Burr, W. (1982). Families under stress. In H. I. McCubbin, A. E. Cauble, & J. M. Patterson (Eds.), *Family stress, coping, and social support* (pp. 5-25). Springfield, IL: Charles C. Thomas.

Butler, M., & Paisley, W. (1977). Communicating cancer control to the public. *Health Education Monograph, 5,* 5-24.

Caldwell, R. A., & Bloom, R. L. (1982). Social support: Its structure and impact on marital disruption. *American Journal of Community Psychology, 10,* 647-667.

Cantor, M. (1980). The informal support system, its relevance in the lives of the elderly. In E. Borgotta & N. McCluskey (Eds.), *Aging and society* (pp. 111-146). Newbury Park, CA: Sage.

Cantor, M., & Little, V. (1985). Aging and social care. In R. H. Binstock & E. Shanas (Eds.), *Handbook of aging and the social sciences* (pp. 745-781). New York: Van Nostrand Reinhold.

Capella, J.N. (1981). Mutual influence in expressive behavior: A review of adult and infant-adult dyadic interaction. *Psychological Bulletin, 89,* 101-132.

Caplan, G. (1964). *Principles of preventive psychiatry.* New York: Basic Books.

Caplan, G. (1972). *Support systems.* Keynote address to conference of Department of Psychiatry, Rutgers Medical School and New Jersey Mental Health Association.

Caplan, G. (1974). *Support systems and community mental health.* New York: Behavioral Publications.

Caplan, G. (1976). The family as a support system. In G. Caplan & M. Killilea (Eds.), *Support systems and mutual help* (pp. 19-36). New York: Grune & Stratton.

Caplan, G. (1981). Mastery of stress: Psychosocial aspects. *American Journal of Psychiatry, 138,* 413-419.

Caplan, R. D. (1979). Social support, person-environment fit, and coping. In L. A. Ferman & J. P. Gordus (Eds.), *Mental health and the economy* (pp. 89-137). Kalamazoo, MI: W.E. Upjohn Institute for Employment Research.

Carey, R. G. (1974). Emotional adjustment in terminal patients: A quantitative approach. *Journal of Counseling Psychology, 21,* 433-439.

Carkhuff, R. R. (1973). *The art of helping.* Amherst, MA: Human Resources Press.

Carothers, J. E., & Inslee, L. J. (1974). Level of empathic understanding offered by volunteer telephone services. *Journal of Counseling Psychology, 21,* 274-276.

Cassel, J. (1976). The contribution of the environment to host resistance. *American Journal of Epidemiology, 104,* 107-123.

Cauce, A. M., Felner, R. D., & Primavera, J. (1982). Social support in high-risk adolescents: Structural components and adaptive impact. *American Journal of Community Psychology, 10,* 417-428.

Chaffee, S. (1972). The interpersonal context of mass communication. In F. G. Kline & P. J. Tichenor (Eds.), *Current perspectives in mass communication research* (pp. 95-120). Newbury Park, CA: Sage.

Chan, Y.N.L. (1978). *Educational needs in intergenerational conflict: A study of immigrant families in N.Y. Chinatown.* Unpublished doctoral dissertation, Cornell University.

Chapman, N. J., & Pancoast, D. (1985). Working with the informal helping networks of the elderly: The experiences of three programs. *Journal of Social Issues, 41,* 47-63.

Cheal, D. J. (1985). Intergenerational family transfers. In B. C. Miller & D. H. Olsen (Eds.), *Family studies review yearbook* (Vol. 3, pp. 494-502). Newbury Park, CA: Sage.

Cherniss, C. (1980). *Staff burnout: Job stress in the social services.* Newbury Park, CA: Sage.

Chesler, M. A., & Barbarin, O. A. (1984). Difficulties of providing help in a crisis: Relationships between parents of children with cancer and their friends. *Journal of Social Issues, 40,* 113-134.

Chiriboga, D. A., Coho, A., Stein, J. A., & Roberts, J. (1979). Divorce, stress and social supports: A study in help seeking behavior. *Journal of Divorce, 3,* 121-125.

Chown, S. M. (1981). Friendship in old age. In S. W. Duck & R. Gilmour (Eds.), *Personal relationships 2: Developing personal relationships* (pp. 231-246). London: Academic Press.

Cicirelli, V. G. (1985). Adult children's attachment and helping behavior to elderly parents: A path model. In B. C. Miller & D. H. Olsen (Eds.), *Family studies review yearbook* (Vol. 3, pp. 413-423). Newbury Park, CA: Sage.

Clark, M. S. (1983). Some implications of close social bonds for help-seeking. In B. M. DePaulo, A. Nadler, & J. D. Fisher (Eds.), *New directions in helping: Vol. 2. Help-seeking* (pp. 205-229). New York: Academic Press.

Coates, D., Renzaglia, G. J., & Embree, M. C. (1983). When helping backfires: Help and helplessness. In J. D. Fisher, A. Nadler, & B. M. DePaulo (Eds.), *New directions in helping: Vol. 1. Recipient reactions to aid* (pp. 251-279). New York: Academic Press.

Coates, D., & Winston, T. (1983). Counteracting the deviance of depression: Peer support groups for victims. *Journal of Social Issues, 39,* 169-194.

Coates, D., Wortman, C. B., & Abbey, A. (1979). Reactions to victims. In I. Frieze, D. Bar-Tel, & J. S. Carroll (Eds.), *New approaches to social problems* (pp. 21-58). San Francisco: Jossey-Bass.

Coates, R. B., Miller, A. D., & Ohlin, L. E. (1978). *Diversity in a youth correctional system: Handling delinquents in Massachusetts.* Cambridge, MA: Ballinger.

Cobb, S. (1976). Social support as a moderator of life stress. *Psychosomatic Medicine, 38,* 300-314.

Cobb, S. (1979). Social support and health through the life course. In M. White Riley (Ed.), *Aging from birth to death: Interdisciplinary perspectives* (pp. 93-105). Boulder, CO: Westview.

Cobb, S. (1982). Social support and health through the life course. In H. I. McCubbin, A. E. Cauble, & J. M. Patterson (Eds.), *Family stress, coping, and social support* (pp. 189-199). Springfield, IL: Charles C. Thomas.

Cobb, S., & Jones, J. M. (1984). Social support, support groups and marital relationships. In S. W. Duck (Ed.), *Personal relationships 5: Repairing personal relationships* (pp. 47-66). London: Academic Press.

Coelho, G. V. (1958). *Changing images of America: A study of Indian students' perceptions.* New York: Free Press.

Cohen, C. I., & Adler, A. (1984). Network interventions: Do they work? *Gerontologist, 24,* 16-22.

Cohen, C. I., & Rajkowski, H. (1982). What's in a friend? Substantive and theoretical issues. *Gerontologist, 22,* 261-266.

Cohen, C. I., & Sokolovsky, J. (1978). Schizophrenia and social networks: Ex-patients in the inner city. *Schizophrenia Bulletin, 4,* 546-560.

Cohen, S., Mermelstein, R., Kamarck, T., & Hoberman, H. M. (1985). Measuring the functional components of social support. In I. G. Sarason & B. R. Sarason (Eds.), *Social support: Theory, research and applications* (pp. 73-94). Dordrecht: Martinus Nijhoff.

Cohen, S., & Syme, S. L. (Eds.). (1985). *Social support and health.* Orlando, FL: Academic Press.

Coke, J. S., Batson, C. D., & McDavis, K. (1978). Empathic mediation of helping: A two-stage model. *Journal of Personality and Social Psychology, 36,* 752-766.

Colletta, N. D., Hadler, S., & Gregg, C. H. (1981). How adolescents cope with the problems of early motherhood. *Adolescence, 16,* 499-512.

Collins, A. H. (1973). Natural delivery systems: Accessible sources of power for mental health. *American Journal of Orthopsychiatry, 43,* 46-52.

Comaroff, J., & Maguire, P. (1981). Ambiguity and the search of meaning: Childhood leukemia in the modern clinical context. *Social Science and Medicine, 15B,* 115-123.

Conner, J. W. (1977). *Tradition and change in three generations of Japanese-Americans.* Chicago: Nelson-Hall.

Cooke, K., & Lawton, D. (1984). Informal support for the carers of disabled children. *Child Care, Health and Development, 10,* 67-79.

Coombs, G. (1978-1979). Opportunities, information networks and the migration-distance relationships. *Social Networks, 1,* 257-276.

Cooper, C. L. (1981). Social support at work and stress management. *Small Group Behavior, 12,* 285-297.

Cooper, C. L., & Payne, R. (1978). *Stress at work.* New York: John Wiley.

Cooper, C. L., & Payne, R. (1980). *Current concerns in occupational stress.* New York: John Wiley.

Coopersmith, S. (1967). *The antecedents of self-esteem.* San Francisco: Freeman.

Costa, P. T., & McCrae, R. R. (1983). Contribution of personality research to an understanding of stress and aging. *Marriage and Family Review, 6,* 157-174.

Cottrell, N. B., & Epley, S. W. (1977). Affiliation, social comparison, and socially mediated stress reduction. In J. M. Suls & R. L. Miller (Eds.), *Social comparison processes* (pp. 43-68). Washington, DC: Hemisphere.

Cowen, E. (1982). Help is where you find it. *American Psychologist, 37,* 385-395.

Cowen, E. L., Gesten, E. L., Boike, M., Norton, P., Wilson, A. B., & DeStefano, M. A. (1979). Hairdressers as caregivers I: A descriptive profile of interpersonal help-giving involvements. *American Journal of Community Psychology, 7,* 633-648.

Cowen, E. L., Gesten, E. L., Davidson, E., & Wilson, A. B. (1981). Hairdressers as caregivers II: Relationships between helper characteristics and helping behaviors and feelings. *Journal of Prevention, 1,* 225-239.

Cowen, E. L., McKim, B. J., & Weissberg, R. P. (1981). Bartenders as informal, interpersonal help-agents. *American Journal of Community Psychology, 9,* 715-729.

Coyne, J. C. (1976). Depression and the response of others. *Journal of Abnormal Psychology, 85,* 186-193.

Craven, P., & Wellman, B. (1973). The network city. *Sociological Inquiry, 43,* 57-88.

Crawford, M. (1977). What is a friend? *New Society, 42,* 116-177.

Crispino, J. A. (1977). *The assimilation of ethnic groups: The Italian case.* Unpublished doctoral dissertation, Columbia University.

Cronen, V. E., Pearce, W. B., & Harris, L. M. (1982). The coordinated management of meaning: A theory of communication. In F.E.X. Dance (Ed.), *Human communication theory* (pp. 61-89). New York: Harper & Row.

Croog, S. H., Lipson, A., & Levine, S. (1972). Help patterns in severe illness: The roles of kin network, non-family resources, and institutions. *Journal of Marriage and the Family, 32,* 32-41.

Cumming, E., & Henry, W. E. (1961). *Growing old: The process of disengagement.* New York: Basic Books.

Cummings, L. L., & Schwab, D. P. (1973). *Performance in organizations.* Glenview, IL: Scott, Foresman.

Cunningham, J. D., & Antill, J. K. (1981). Love in developing romantic relationships. In S. W. Duck & R. Gilmour (Eds.), *Personal relationships 2: Developing personal relationships* (pp. 27-51). London: Academic Press.

Curran, D. (1985). *Stress and the health family.* Atlanta, GA: Active Parenting.

Cutrona, C. E. (1984). Social support and stress in transition to parenthood. *Journal of Abnormal Psychology, 93,* 378-390.

Daft, R., & Wiginton, W. (1979). Language and organization. *Academy of Management Review, 4,* 179-192.

Dance, F.E.X. (1982). *Human communication theory.* New York: Harper & Row.

Danish, S. J., D'Augelli, A. R., & Hauer, A. L. (1980). *Helping skills: A basic training program.* New York: Human Sciences Press.

D'Augelli, A. R., Danish, S. J., & Brock, G. W. (1976). Untrained paraprofessionals' verbal helping behavior: Description and implications for training. *American Journal of Community Psychology, 4,* 275-282.

D'Augelli, A. R., & Levy, M. (1978). The verbal helping skills of trained and untrained human service paraprofessionals. *American Journal of Community Psychology, 6,* 23-32.

Dean, A., & Lin, N. (1977). The stress buffering role of social support: Problems and prospects for systematic investigation. *Journal of Nervous and Mental Disease, 165,* 403-417.

Dean, A., Lin, N., & Ensel, W. M. (1981). The epidemiological significance of social support systems in depression. *Research in Community and Mental Health, 2,* 77-109.

Dean, A., & Tausig, M. (1986). Measuring intimate support: The family and confidant relationships. In N. Lin, A. Dean, & W. Ensel (Eds.), *Social support, life events, and depression* (pp. 117-128). Orlando, FL: Academic Press.

DeCharms, R. (1968). *Personal causation: The internal affective determinants of behavior.* New York: Academic Press.

DeCocq, G. A. (1976). European and North American self-help movements: Some contrasts. In A. H. Katz & E. I. Bender (Eds.), *The strength in us: Self-help groups in the modern world* (pp. 202-208). New York: New Viewpoint.

Decroos, J. F. (1979). *The long journey: Assimilation and ethnicity maintenance among urban Basques in northern California.* Unpublished doctoral dissertation, University of Oregon.

Delia, J. G., O'Keefe, B. J., & O'Keefe, D. J. (1982). The constructivist approach to communication. In F.E.X. Dance (Ed.), *Human communication theory* (pp. 147-191). New York: Harper & Row.

Denoff, M. S. (1982). The differentiation of supportive functions among network members: An empirical inquiry. *Journal of Social Service Research, 5,* 45-59.

286   COMMUNICATING SOCIAL SUPPORT

DePaulo, B. M. (1982). Social-psychological processes in informal help seeking. In T. A. Wills (Ed.), *Basic processes in helping relationships* (pp. 255-279). New York: Academic Press.

Depner, C. E., Wethington, E., & Ingersoll-Dayton, B. (1984). Social support: Methodological issues in design and measurement. *Journal of Social Issues, 40,* 37-54.

Derlega, V. J., & Chaikin, A. L. (1977). Privacy and self-disclosure in social relationships. *Journal of Social Issues, 33,* 102-115.

Derogatis, L., Lipman, R., Rickels, K., Uhlenhuth, E., & Covi, L. (1974). The Hopkins symptom checklist (HSCL): A self-report symptom inventory. *Behavioral Science, 19,* 1-15.

Dervin, B. (1976). Strategies for dealing with human information needs: Information or communication? *Journal of Broadcasting, 20,* 324-333.

Deusen, J.M.V. (1982). Health/mental health studies of Indochinese refugees. *Medical Anthropology, 6,* 231-252.

Deutsch, S. E., & Wong, G.Y.M. (1963). Some factors in the adjustment of foreign nationals in the United States. *Journal of Social Issues, 19,* 115-122.

Devellis, R. F., Devellis, B. M., Wallston, B. S., & Wallston, K. A. (1980). Epilepsy and learned helplessness. *Basic and Applied Social Psychology, 1,* 241-253.

Dickens, W. J., & Perlman, D. (1981). Friendship over the life-cycle. In S. W. Duck & R. Gilmour (Eds.), *Personal relationships 2: Developing personal relationships* (pp. 91-122). London: Academic Press.

Dilks, C. (1984, February). Employers who help with the kids. *Nation's Business,* pp. 59-60.

DiMatteo, M. R., & Hays, R. (1981). Social support and serious illness. In B. H. Gottlieb (Ed.), *Social networks and social support* (pp. 117-148). Newbury Park, CA: Sage.

Diseker, R. A., Michielutte, R., & Morrison, V. (1980). Use and reported effectiveness of Tel-Med: A telephone health information system. *American Journal of Public Health, 70,* 229-234.

Doane, J. A., & Cowen, E. L. (1981). Interpersonal help-giving of family practice lawyers. *American Journal of Community Psychology, 9,* 547-558.

Donahue, T. S. (1982). Toward a broadened context for modern bilingual education. *Journal of Multicultural Development, 3,* 77-87.

Droge, D. A. (1983a). *Epilepsy self help groups, stigma, and social support.* Unpublished Ph.D. dissertation, Northwestern University.

Droge, D. A. (1983b, May). *Talk as social support: Communication in an epilepsy self help group.* Paper presented at the meeting of the International Communication Association, Dallas, TX.

Duck, S. W., & Gilmour, R. (Eds.). (1981). *Personal relationships: Developing personal relationships.* London: Academic Press.

Dweck, C. S. (1975). The role of expectations and attributions in the alleviation of learned helplessness. *Journal of Personality and Social Psychology, 31,* 674-685.

Eckenrode, J. (1983). The mobilization of social supports: Some individual constraints. *American Journal of Community Psychology, 11,* 509-528.

Eckenrode, J., & Gore, S. (1981). Stressful events and social supports: The significance of context. In B. H. Gottlieb (Ed.), *Social networks and social support* (pp. 43-68). Newbury Park, CA: Sage.

Edelman, M. (1977). *Political language.* New York: Free Press.

Egan, G. (1982). *The skilled helper.* Monterey, CA: Brooks/Cole.

Eggert, L. L. (1984). *Adolescents' personal relationships and communication network involvement.* Unpublished Ph.D. dissertation, University of Washington.

Eggert, L. L., & Parks, M. R. (in press). Communication network involvement in adolescents' friendships and romantic relationships. In M. L. McLaughlin (Ed.), *Communication yearbook 10.* Newbury Park, CA: Sage.

Ehrlich, R. P., D'Augelli, A. R., & Conter, K. R. (1981). Evaluation of a community-based system for training natural helpers: I. Effects on verbal helping skills. *American Journal of Community Psychology, 9,* 321-337.

Eiduson, B. T. (1980). Child development in emergent family styles. In D. Rogers (Ed.), *Issues in life-span human development* (pp. 161-171). Monterey, CA: Brooks/Cole.

Eisenberg, E. M. (1984). Ambiguity as strategy in organizational communication. *Communication Monographs, 51,* 227-242.

Emerson, R. W. (1960). Friends. In H. T. Wilson (Ed.), *Strength for living* (p. 44). New York: Abingdon.

Epstein, N. B., Bishop, D. S., & Baldwin, L. M. (1984). McMaster model of family functioning: A view of the normal family. In D. H. Olson & B. C. Miller (Eds.), *Family studies review yearbook* (Vol. 2, pp. 75-102). Newbury Park, CA: Sage.

Erickson, B. (1982). Networks, ideologies, and belief systems. In P. V. Marsden & N. Lin (Eds.), *Social structure and network analysis.* Newbury Park, CA: Sage.

Etzion, D. (1984). Moderating effect of social support on the stress-burnout relationship. *Journal of Applied Psychology, 69,* 615-622.

Etzioni, A. (1980). Youth is not a class. In D. Rogers (Ed.), *Issues in life-span human development* (pp. 258-260). Monterey, CA: Brooks/Cole.

Evans, S.H., & Clarke, P. (1983). When cancer patients fail to get well: Flaws in health communication. In R. N. Bostrom (Ed.), *Communication yearbook 7* (pp. 225-248). Newbury Park, CA: Sage.

Evans, S. H., & Clarke, P. (1986, February). *Using the interactive videodisc to help cancer patients.* Paper presented at the Communicating with Patients Conference, Tampa, FL.

Expectant moms, office dilemma. (1986, March). *U.S. News & World Report,* pp. 52-53.

Eyres, S. J., & MacElveen-Hoehn, P. (1983, April). *Theoretical issues in the study of social support.* Paper presented at the conference on "Social Support: What Is It?" Seattle, WA.

Fairhurst, G. T., Green, S. G., & Snavely, B. K. (1984). Face support in controlling poor performance. *Human Communication Research, 11,* 272-295.

Farace, R. V., Monge, P. R., & Russell, H. (1977). *Communicating and organizing.* Reading, MA: Addison-Wesley.

Farace, R. V., Taylor, J. A., & Stewart, J. (1978). Criteria for evaluation of organizational communication effectiveness: Review and synthesis. In B. Ruben (Ed.), *Communication yearbook 2* (pp. 271-292). New Brunswick, NJ: Transaction.

Farkas, S. (1980). Impact of chronic illness on the patient's spouse. *Health and Social Work, 5,* 39-46.

Feldman, H., & Feldman, M. (1985). *Current controversies in marriage and family.* Newbury Park, CA: Sage.

Fengler, A. P., & Goodrich, N. (1979). Wives of elderly disabled men: The hidden patients. *Gerontologist, 19,* 175-183.

Festinger, L. (1954). A theory of social comparison processes. *Human Relations, 7,* 117-140.

Finkelhor, D., Gelles, R. J., Hotaling, G. T., & Straus, M. A. (1983). *The dark side of families.* Newbury Park, CA: Sage.

Finlayson, A. (1976). Social networks as coping resources: Lay help and consultation patterns used by women in husbands' post-infarction career. *Social Science and Medicine, 10,* 97-103.

Fiore, J., Becker, J., & Coppel, D. B. (1983). Social network interactions: A buffer or a stress. *American Journal of Community Psychology, 11,* 423-439.

Fischer, C. S. (1977). *Networks and places.* New York: Free Press.

Fischer, C. S. (1982). *To dwell among friends: Personal networks in town and city.* Chicago: University of Chicago Press.

Fischer, C. S. (1985). The dispersion of kinship ties in modern society: Contemporary data and historical speculation. In B. C. Miller & D. H. Olsen (Eds.), *Family studies review yearbook* (Vol. 3) (pp. 443-465). Newbury Park, CA: Sage.

Fischer, C. S., & Phillips, S. L. (1982). Who is alone? Social characteristics of people with small networks. In L. A. Peplau & D. Perlman (Eds.), *Loneliness: A sourcebook of current theory, research and therapy* (pp. 21-39). New York: Wiley-Interscience.

Fisher, B. A. (1982). The pragmatic perspective of human communication: A view from system theory. In F.E.X. Dance (Ed.), *Human communication theory: Comparative essays.* New York: Harper & Row.

Fisher, S. (1984). *Stress and the perception of control.* London: Lawrence Erlbaum.

Fiske, D., & Maddi, S. (Eds.). (1961). *Functions of varied experience.* Homewood, IL: Dorsey.

Fiske, S. T., & Taylor, S. E. (1984). *Social cognition.* Reading, MA: Addison-Wesley.

Fitzpatrick, M. A., & Badzinski, D. M. (1985). All in the family: Interpersonal communication in kin relationships. In M. L. Knapp & G. R. Miller (Eds.), *Handbook of interpersonal communication* (pp. 687-736). Newbury Park, CA: Sage.

Flaherty, J. A., Gaviria, F. M., & Pathak, D. S. (1983). The measurement of social support: The social support network inventory. *Comprehensive Psychiatry, 24,* 521-529.

Fogel, D. (1979, November). *Human development and communication competencies.* Paper presented at the annual meeting of the Speech Communication Association, San Antonio, TX.

Fogle, B. (1984). *Pets and their people.* New York: Viking.

Fontaine, G. (in press). Roles of social support systems in overseas relocation: Implications for intercultural training. *International Journal for Intercultural Relations.*

Fox, F. A., & Kotler, P. (1980). The marketing of social causes: The first ten years. *Journal of Marketing, 44,* 24-33.

Freidson, E. (1970). *Profession of medicine.* New York: Dodd, Mead & Co.

Freimuth, V. S., Greenberg, R. H., DeWitt, J., & Romano, R. M. (1984). Covering cancer: Newspapers and the public interest. *Journal of Communication, 34,* 62-73.

French, J.R.P., Jr., Rodgers, W., & Cobb, S. (1974). Adjustment as person-environment fit. In G. V. Coelho, D. A. Hamburg, & J. E. Adams (Eds.), *Coping and adaptation* (pp. 316-333). New York: Basic Books.

Froland, C., Brodsky, G., Olson, M., & Stewart, L. (1979). Social support and social adjustment: Implications for mental health professionals. *Community Mental Health Journal, 15,* 82-93.

Froland, C., Pancoast, D. L., Chapman, N. J., & Kimboko, P. J. (1981). *Helping networks and human services.* Newbury Park, CA: Sage.

Frydman, M. I. (1981). Predictors of psychiatric symptomatology in parents of children with cystic fibrosis and leukemia (Doctoral dissertation, University of New South Wales, 1981). *Dissertation Abstracts International, 41,* 4058B.

Fuchs, V. R. (1983). *How we live.* Cambridge, MA: Harvard University Press.

Gallagher, J. J., Beckman, P., & Cross, A. H. (1983). Families of handicapped children: Sources of stress and its amelioration. *Exceptional Children, 50,* 10-19.

Garber, J., & Seligman, M. (Eds.). (1980). *Human helplessness: Theory and applications.* New York: Academic Press.

Garrison, V. (1978). Support systems of schizophrenic and nonschizophrenic Puerto Rican migrant women in New York City. *Schizophrenia Bulletin, 4,* 561-596.

Garrison, V., & Podell, J. (1981). "Community support systems assessment" for use in clinical interviews. *Schizophrenia Bulletin, 7,* 101-107.

Garrity, T. F. (1973). Vocational adjustment after first myocardial infarction: Comparative assessment of several variables suggested in the literature. *Social Science and Medicine, 7,* 705-717.

Gaudin, J. M., & Pollane, L. (1983). Social networks, stress and child abuse. *Children and Youth Services Review, 5,* 91-102.

Gelles, R. J. (1979). *Family violence.* Newbury Park, CA: Sage.

Gershon, M., & Biller, H. B. (1977). *The other helpers.* Lexington, MA: Lexington Books.

Gerson, A. C., & Perlman, D. (1979). Loneliness and expressive communication. *Journal of Abnormal Psychology, 88,* 258-261.

Geyer, R. F. (1980). *Alienation theories: A general systems approach.* New York: Pergamon.

Gibb, J. R. (1961). Defensive communication. *Journal of Communication, 11,* 141-148.

Gilford, R., & Bengtson, V. (1979). Measuring marital satisfaction in three generations: Positive and negative dimensions. *Journal of Marriage and the Family, 42,* 387-398.

Goering, P., Wasylenki, D., Lancee, W., Freeman, S.J.J. (1983). Social support and post hospital outcome for depressed women. *Canadian Journal of Psychiatry, 28,* 612-618.

Goffman, E. (1959). *The presentation of self in everyday life.* Garden City, NY: Doubleday.

Goffman, E. (1963). *Stigma: Notes on the management of spoiled identity.* Englewood Cliffs, NJ: Prentice-Hall.

Gordon, M. (1964). *Assimilation in American life.* New York: Oxford University Press.

Gottlieb, B. H. (1981). Social networks and social support in community health. In B. H. Gottlieb (Ed.), *Social networks and social support* (pp. 11-42). Newbury Park, CA: Sage.

Gottlieb, B. H. (1983). *Social support strategies: Guidelines for mental health practice.* Newbury Park, CA: Sage.

Gottlieb, B. H. (1985). Social support and the study of personal relationships. *Journal of Social and Personal Relationships, 2,* 351-375.

Gottlieb, B. H., & Todd, D. (1979). Characterizing and promoting social support in natural settings. In R. Munoz, L. Snowden, & J. Kelley (Eds.), *Social and psychological research in community settings.* San Francisco: Jossey-Bass.

Gottman, J. M. (1979). *Marital interaction: Experimental investigations.* New York: Academic Press.

Graen, G. (1976). Role making processes within complex organizations. In M. D. Dunnette (Ed.), *Handbook of industrial and organizational psychology* (pp. 1201-1245). Chicago: Rand McNally.

Granovetter, M. S. (1973). The strength of weak ties. *American Journal of Sociology, 78,* 1360-1380.

Granovetter, M. S. (1982). The strength of weak ties: A network theory revisited. In P. V. Marsden & N. Lin (Eds.), *Social structure and network analysis* (pp. 105-130). Newbury Park, CA: Sage.

Greenberg, M. S. (1980). A theory of indebtedness. In K. J. Gergen, M. S. Greenberg, & R. H. Willis (Eds.), *Social exchange: Advances in theory and research.* New York: Plenum.

Greenberg, M. S., & Shapiro, S. P. (1971). Indebtedness: An adverse aspect of asking for and receiving help. *Sociometry, 34,* 290-301.

Greenberg, R. (1986). *1984 content analysis of newspaper coverage of cancer.* Bethesda, MD: National Cancer Institute.

Gudykunst, W. B., & Kim, Y. Y. (1984). *Communicating with strangers: An approach to intercultural communication.* Reading, MA: Addison-Wesley.

Gupta, N., & Jenkins, G. D., Jr., (1985). Dual career couples: Stress, stressors, strains, and strategies. In T. A. Beehr & R. S. Bhagat (Eds.), *Human stress and cognition in organizations: An integrated perspective* (pp. 141-175). New York: John Wiley.

Gurin, G., Veroff, J., & Feld, S. (1960). *Americans view their mental health.* New York: Basic Books.

Gurin, J. (1985). Exclusive Gallup survey: The us generation. *American Health, 4,* 40-42.

Hakmiller, K. (1966). Need for self-evaluation, perceived similarity and comparison choice. *Journal of Experimental Social Psychology*, Suppl. *1*, 49-54.

Hamburg, B. A., & Killilea, M. (1979). Relation of social support, stress, illness and use of health services. In *Healthy people: The Surgeon General's report on health promotion and disease prevention*. Washington, DC: U.S. Department of Health, Education and Welfare, Public Health Service.

Hammen, C. L., & Peters, S. D. (1978). Interpersonal consequences of depression: Responses to men and women enacting a depressed role. *Journal of Abnormal Psychology*, *87*, 322-332.

Hammer, M. (1963-1964). Influence of small social networks as factors on mental hospital admission. *Human Organization*, *22*, 243-251.

Hammer, M. (1981a). Social support, social networks, and schizophrenia. *Schizophrenia Bulletin*, *7*, 45-57.

Hammer, M. (1981b). Social networks and the long term patient. In S. Budson & M. Barofsky (Eds.), *The chronic psychiatric patient in the community: Principles of treatment*. New York: Spectrum.

Hammer, M. (1983). "Core" and "extended" social networks in relation to health and illness. *Social Science and Medicine*, *17*, 405-414.

Hammer, M., Makiesky-Barrow, S., Gutwirth, L. (1978). Social networks and schizophrenia. *Schizophrenia Bulletin*, *4*, 522-544.

Hansell, S. (1985). Adolescent friendship networks and distress in school. *Social Forces*, *63*, 698-715.

Hanson, S.M.H., & Bozett, F. W. (1985). *Dimensions of fatherhood*. Newbury Park, CA: Sage.

Harris, L. (1975). *The myth and reality of aging in America*. Washington, DC: National Commission on Aging.

Hatfield, E., & Traupmann, J. (1981). Intimate relationships: A perspective from equity theory. In S. W. Duck & R. Gilmour (Eds.), *Personal relationships I: Studying personal relationships* (pp. 165-178). London: Academic Press.

Hatfield, E., Utne, M. K., & Traupmann, J. (1979). Equity theory and intimate relationships. In R. L. Burgess & T. L. Huston (Eds.), *Social exchange in developing relationships* (pp. 99-133). New York: Academic Press.

Hawkins, D. J., & Fraser, M. W. (1983). Social support networks in treating drug abuse. In J. K. Whittaker & J. Garbarino (Eds.), *Social support networks: Informal helping in the human services* (pp. 333-352). New York: Aldine.

Hayes, R. L., & Hayes, B. A. (1986). Remarriage families: Counseling parents, stepparents, and their children. *Counseling and Human Development*, *18*, 1-8.

Hays, R. B. (1984). The development and maintenance of friendship. *Journal of Social and Personal Relationships*, *1*, 75-98.

Heider, F. (1958). *The psychology of interpersonal relations*. New York: John Wiley.

Helfer, R. E. (1970). An objective comparison of the pediatric interviewing skills of freshman and senior medical students. *Pediatrics*, *45*, 623-627.

Henderson, A. S. (1984). Interpreting the evidence on social support. *Social Psychiatry*, *19*, 49-52.

Henderson, S. (1980). Personal networks and the schizophrenias. *Australian & New Zealand Journal of Psychiatry, 14,* 255-259.

Herberg, D. C. (1980). Multicultural workers' network: Taking ethno-culture seriously. In *Symposium on helping networks and the welfare state: Vol. II. Community and state.* Toronto, Canada: University of Toronto.

Hess, B. (1972). Friendship. In M. W. Riley, M. Johnson, & A. Forner (Eds.), *Aging and society: A sociology of age stratification* (Vol. 3, pp. 357-396). New York: Russell Sage.

Hirokawa, R. Y., & Poole, M. S. (Eds.). (1986). *Communication and group decision-making.* Newbury Park, CA: Sage.

Hirsch, B. J. (1979). Psychological dimensions of social networks: A multi-method analysis. *American Journal of Community Psychology, 7,* 263-277.

Hirsch, B. J. (1980). Natural support systems and coping with major life changes. *American Journal of Community Psychology, 8,* 159-172.

Hirsch, B. J. (1981). Coping and adaptation in high-risk population: Toward an integrative model. *Schizophrenia Bulletin, 7,* 164-172.

Hochschild, A. R. (1973). *The unexpected community.* Englewood Cliffs, NJ: Prentice-Hall.

Holahan, C. J. (1983). Interventions to reduce environmental stress: Enhancing social support and personal control. In E. Seidman (Ed.), *Handbook of social intervention* (pp. 542-560). Newbury Park, CA: Sage.

Holman, T. B., & Burr, W. R. (1984). Beyond the beyond: The growth of family theories in the 1970s. In D. H. Olson & B. C. Miller (Eds.), *Family studies review yearbook* (Vol. 2, pp. 33-44). Newbury Park, CA: Sage.

Homans, G. C. (1950). *The human group.* New York: Harcourt Brace & World.

Homans, G. C. (1961). *Social behavior: Its elementary forms.* New York: Harcourt.

Hooper, M. (1982). Explorations in the structure of psychological identifications with social groups and roles. *Multivariate Behavioral Research, 17,* 515-523.

Hopper, R., Knapp, M. L., & Scott, L. (1981). Couples' personal idioms: Exploring intimate talk. *Journal of Communication, 31,* 23-33.

Horowitz, A. (1977). Social networks and pathways to psychiatric treatment. *Social Forces, 56,* 86-105.

House, J. S. (1981). *Work stress and social support.* Reading, MA: Addison-Wesley.

House, J. S. (1984, Autumn). Social support. *ISR Newsletter* (Institute for Social Research, University of Michigan), pp. 5-6.

House, J. S., & Kahn, R. L. (1985). Measures and concepts of social support. In S. Cohen & S. L. Syme (Eds.), *Social support and health* (pp. 83-108). Orlando, FL: Academic Press.

House, J. S., LaRocco, J. M., & French, J.R.P., Jr. (1982). Response to Schaefer. *Journal of Social and Health Behavior, 23,* 98-101.

House, J. S., & Wells, J. A. (1978). Occupational stress, social support, and health. In A. McLean, G. Black, & M. Colligan (Eds.), *Reducing occupational stress: Proceedings of a conference* (pp. 8-29). Washington, DC: DHEW (NIOSH), Publication 78-140.

Hoyt, D. R., & Babchuk, N. (1983). Adult kinship networks: The selective formation of intimate ties with kin. *Social Forces, 62*, 85-101.

Huesmann, L. R., & Levinger, G. (1976). Incremental exchange theory: A formal model for progression in dyadic social interaction. In L. Berkowitz & E. Walster (Eds.), *Advances in experimental social psychology* (Vol. 9, pp. 191-229). New York: Academic Press.

Huston, T. L. (1982). *The topography of marriage: A longitudinal study of changes in husband-wife relationships over the first year.* Paper presented at the International Conference on Personal Relationships, Madison, WI.

Huston, T. L., & Burgess, R. L. (1979). Social exchange in developing relationships: An overview. In R. L. Burgess & T. L. Huston (Eds.), *Social exchange in developing relationships* (pp. 3-28). New York: Academic Press.

Hyman, M. D. (1971). Disability and patients' perceptions of preferential treatment: Some preliminary findings. *Journal of Chronic Diseases, 24*, 329-342.

Inglis, M., & Gudykunst, W. B. (1982). Institutional completeness and communication acculturation: A comparison of Korean immigrants in Chicago and Hartford. *International Journal of Intercultural Relations, 6*, 251-272.

Ivancevich, J. M. (1979). High and low task stimulating jobs: A causal analysis of performance-satisfaction relationships. *Academy of Management Journal, 22*, 55-61.

Ivancevich, J. M., Matteson, M. T., & Richards, E. P., II (1985, March, April). Who's liable for stress on the job? *Harvard Business Review*, pp. 60-72.

Jablin, F. M. (1979). Superior-subordinate communication: The state of the art. *Psychological Bulletin, 86*, 1201-1222.

Jablin, F. M. (1984). Assimilating new members into organizations. In R. N. Bostrom (Ed.), *Communication yearbook 8* (pp. 594-626). Newbury Park, CA: Sage.

Jayaratne, S., & Chess, W. A. (1984). The effects of emotional support on perceived job stress and strain. *Journal of Applied Behavioral Science, 20*, 141-153.

Johnson, J. H., & Sarason, I. G. (1978). Life stress, depression and anxiety: Internal-external control as a moderator variable. *Journal of Psychosomatic Research, 22*, 205-208.

Jones, W. H. (1981). Loneliness and social contact. *Journal of Social Psychology, 113*, 295-296.

Jones, W. H. (1982). Loneliness and social behavior. In L. A. Peplau & D. Perlman (Eds.), *Loneliness: A sourcebook of current theory, research and therapy* (pp. 238-252). New York: Wiley-Interscience.

Jones, W. H. (1985). The psychology of loneliness: Some personality issues in the study of social support. In I. G. Sarason & B. R. Sarason (Eds.), *Social support: Theory, research and applications* (pp. 225-241). Boston: Martinus Nijhoff.

Jones, W. H., & Briggs, S. R. (1983). *Shyness and interpersonal behavior.* Unpublished manuscript, University of Tulsa, OK.

Jones, W. H., Hobbs, S. A., & Hockenbury, D. (1982). Loneliness and social skill deficits. *Journal of Personality and Social Psychology, 42*, 682-689.

Kadushin, C. (1982). Social density and mental health. In P. V. Marsden & N. Lin (Eds.), *Social structure and network analysis* (pp. 147-158). Newbury Park, CA: Sage.

Kagan, J. (1977). The child in the family. *Daedalus, 106*(2), 33-56.

Kahn, R. L. (1981). *Work and health*. New York: John Wiley.

Kahn, R. L., & Antonucci, T. C. (1980). Convoys over the life course: Attachment, roles, and social support. In P. B. Baltes & O. G. Brim (Eds.), *Life span development and behavior* (pp. 253-286). New York: Academic Press.

Kahn, R. L., & Antonucci, T. C. (1983). *Social supports of the elderly: Family/friends/professionals*. Final report to the National Institute on Aging.

Kahn, R. L., Wolfe, D. M., Quinn, R. P., Snoek, J. D., & Rosenthal, R. A. (1964). *Organizational stress: Studies in role conflict and ambiguity*. New York: John Wiley.

Kaiser, L. (Ed.). (1983). *The Chemical People book*. Pittsburg: QED Enterprises.

Kanner, A. D., Kafry, D., & Pines, A. (1978). Conspicuous in its absence: The lack of positive conditions as a source of stress. *Journal of Human Stress, 4,* 33-39.

Kanter, R. M. (1983). *The changemasters*. New York: Simon & Schuster.

Kaplan, H. B., Robbins, C., & Martin, S. S. (1983). Antecedents of psychological distress in young adults: Self-rejection, deprivation of social support, and life events. *Journal of Health & Social Behavior, 24,* 230-244.

Karuza, J., Jr., Zevon, M. A., Rabinowitz, V. C., & Brickman, P. (1982). Attribution of responsibility by helpers and by recipients. In T. A. Wills (Ed.), *Basic processes in helping relationships*. New York: Academic Press.

Katz, D., & Kahn, R. L. (1978). *The social psychology of organizations*. New York: John Wiley.

Katz, R. (1985). Organizational stress and early socialization experiences. In T. A. Beehr & R. S. Bhagat (Eds.), *Human stress and cognition in organizations: An integrated perspective* (pp. 117-134). New York: John Wiley.

Kay, E., Meyer, H., & French, J.R.P. (1965). Effects of threat in a performance appraisal interview. *Journal of Applied Psychology*, pp. 311-317.

Keefe, S. E., Padilla, A. M., & Carlos, M. L. (1978). *Emotional support systems in two cultures: A comparison of Mexican Americans and Anglo Americans*. Santa Barbara: University of California, Spanish Speaking Mental Health Research Center.

Keller, S. (1968). *The urban neighborhood: A sociological perspective*. New York: Random House.

Kelley, H. H. (1972). Attribution in social interaction. In E. E. Jones et al. (Eds.), *Attribution: Perceiving the causes of behavior* (pp. 1-26). Morristown, NJ: General Learning Press.

Kelley, H. H. (1979). *Personal relationships: Their structures and processes*. Hillsdale, NJ: Lawrence Erlbaum.

Kelley, H. H., & Thibaut, J. W. (1978). *Interpersonal relations: A theory of interdependence*. New York: John Wiley.

Kelly, J. G. (1964). The mental health agent in the urban community. In *Urban America and the planning of mental health services*. New York: Group for the Advancement of Psychiatry.

Kerberg, D. C. (1980). Multicultural workers' network: Taking ethno-culture seriously. In *Symposium on helping networks and the welfare state: Vol. II. Community and state.* Toronto, Canada: University of Toronto.

Kerckhoff, A. C., Back, K. W., & Miller, N. (1965). Sociometric patterns in hysterical contagion. *Sociometry, 28,* 2-15.

Kessel, N. (1964). The armour of loneliness. *20th Century, 173,* 134-140.

Kessler, R. C. (1982). Life events, social supports, and mental health. In W. R. Gove (Ed.), *Deviance and mental illness* (pp. 247-271). Newbury Park, CA: Sage.

Kim, J. (1980). Explaining acculturation in a communication framework: An empirical test. *Communication Monographs, 47,* 155-179.

Kim, Y. Y. (1976). *Communication patterns of immigrants in the process of acculturation: A survey among the Korean population in Chicago.* Unpublished doctoral dissertation, Northwestern University, Evanston, IL.

Kim, Y. Y. (1977a). Communication patterns of foreign immigrants in the process of acculturation. *Human Communication Research, 4,* 66-77.

Kim, Y. Y. (1977b). Inter-ethnic and intra-ethnic communication. In N. Jain (Ed.), *International and intercultural communication annual* (Vol. 4). Falls Church, VA: Speech Communication Association.

Kim, Y. Y. (1978a, March). *Communication patterns of Mexican-Americans in the Chicago area.* Paper presented at the meeting of the Third World Conference, Chicago.

Kim, Y. Y. (1978b, Summer). A communication approach to the acculturation process: A study of Korean immigrants in Chicago. *International Journal of Intercultural Relations,* pp. 197-224.

Kim, Y. Y. (1979a). Toward an interactive theory of communication-acculturation. In D. Nimmo (Ed.), *Communication yearbook 3* (pp. 435-453). New Brunswick, NJ: Transaction Books.

Kim, Y. Y. (1979b, November). *Dynamics of intrapersonal and interpersonal communication: A study of Indochinese refugees in the initial phase of acculturation.* Paper presented at the meeting of the Speech Communication Association, San Antonio, TX.

Kim, Y. Y. (1980). *Research project report on Indochinese refugees in the state of Illinois: Vol. IV. Psychological, social, and cultural adjustment of Indochinese refugees.* Chicago: Travelers Aid Society of Metropolitan Chicago.

Kim, Y. Y. (1982). Communication and acculturation. In L. A. Samovar & R. E. Porter (Eds.), *Intercultural communication: A reader* (pp. 359-372). Belmont, CA: Wadsworth.

Kim, Y. Y. (1986a). Communication, information, and adaptation. In B. D. Ruben (Ed.), *Information and behavior, 1.* New Brunswick, NJ: Transaction Books.

Kim, Y. Y. (1986b). Understanding the social context of intergroup communication: A personal network approach. In W. B. Gudykunst (Ed.), *Intergroup communication.* London: Edward Arnold.

King, S. S. (1984). *Natural helping networks among ethnic groups in Hawaii.* Washington, DC: National Institute of Mental Health.

Kitson, G. C., Moir, R. N., & Mason, P. R. (1982). Family social support in crises: The special case of divorce. *American Journal of Orthopsychiatry, 52,* 161-165.

Klein, D. M. (1983). Family problem solving and family stress. *Marriage and Family Review, 6,* 85-112.

Klein, D. M. (1984). Commentary on the linkages between conceptual framework and theory development in sociology. In D. H. Olson & B. C. Miller (Eds.), *Family studies review yearbook* (Vol. 2, pp. 117-128). Newbury Park, CA: Sage.

Knapp, M. L. (1984). *Interpersonal communication and human relationships.* Boston: Allyn & Bacon.

Knapp, M. L., & Struck, D. A. (1983). Index to volumes 1-9. *Human Communication Research, 9,* 367-376.

Knowles, D. (1979). On the tendency for volunteer helpers to give advice. *Journal of Counseling Psychology, 26,* 352-354.

Korsch, B., & Negrete, V. (1972). Doctor-patient communication. *Scientific American, 227,* 66-74.

Kotler, P. (1982). *Marketing for nonprofit organizations* (2nd ed.). Englewood Cliffs, NJ: Prentice-Hall.

Kotler, P., & Levy, S. J. (1969). Broadening the concept of marketing. *Journal of Marketing, 33,* 10-15.

Krant, M. J., & Johnston, L. (1977-1978). Family members' perceptions of communications in late stage cancer. *International Journal of Psychiatry in Medicine, 8,* 203-216.

Krause, C. A. (1978). Urbanization without breakdown: Italian, Jewish, and Slavic immigrant women in Pittsburgh, 1900-1945. *Journal of Urban History, 4,* 291-306.

LaFayette, P., & Wooldridge, J. (1982, May). *Training manual.* Seattle, WA: Fred Hutchinson Cancer Research Center, Washington State Cancer Information Service.

LaGaipa, J. J. (1981). A systems approach to personal relationships. In S. W. Duck & R. Gilmour (Eds.), *Personal relationships, 1: Studying personal relationships* (pp. 67-89). London: Academic Press.

Lakin, M. (1985). *The helping group: Therapeutic principles and issues.* Reading, MA: Addison-Wesley.

Lally, M., Black, E., Thornock, M., & Hawkins, D. (1979). Older women in single room occupant (SRO) hotels: A Seattle profile. *Gerontologist, 19,* 67-73.

Langer, E. J. (1975). The illusion of control. *Journal of Personality and Social Psychology, 32,* 311-328.

Langer, E. J. (1979). The illusion of incompetence. In L. Perlmutter & R. Monty (Eds.), *Choice and perceived control* (pp. 301-313). New York: Lawrence Erlbaum.

Langer, E. J., & Rodin, J. (1976). The effects of choice and enhanced personal responsibility for the aged: A field experiment in an institutional setting. *Journal of Personality and Social Psychology, 34,* 191-198.

LaRocco, J. M. (1983). Theoretical distinctions between causal and interaction effects of social support. *Journal of Health and Social Behavior, 24,* 91-92.

LaRocco, J. M., House, J. S., & French, J.R.P., Jr. (1980). Social support, occupational stress, and health. *Journal of Health and Social Behavior, 21*, 202-218.

LaRocco, J. M., & Jones, A. P. (1978). Coworker and leader support as moderators of stress-strain relationships in work situations. *Journal of Applied Psychology, 63*, 629-634.

Larson, R. W. (1982). *Adolescents' daily experience with family and friends: Contrasting opportunity systems.* Paper presented at the International Conference on Personality Relationships, Madison, WI.

Latane, B., & Nida, S. (1981). Ten years of research on group size and helping. *Psychological Bulletin, 89*, 308-324.

Lazarus, R. (1974). Psychological stress and coping in adaptation and illness. *International Journal of Psychiatry in Medicine, 5*, 321-333.

Lazarus, R. (1975). The self-regulation of emotion. In L. Levi (Ed.), *Emotions, their parameters and measurement* (pp. 47-67). New York: Raven.

Lazarus, R. C., & Launier, R. (1978). Stress related transactions between people and environment. In L. A. Pervin & M. Lewis (Eds.), *Perspectives in interactional psychology* (pp. 287-327). New York: Plenum.

Leavy, R. (1983). Social support and psychological disorder: A review. *Journal of Community Psychology, 11*, 3-21.

Lefcourt, H. M., Martin, R. A., & Saleh, W. E. (1984). Locus of control and social support: Interactive moderators of stress. *Journal of Personality and Social Psychology, 47*, 378-389.

Leigh, G. K. (1985). Kinship interaction over the family life span. In B. C. Miller & D. H. Olson (Eds.), *Family studies review yearbook* (Vol. 3, pp. 477-486). Newbury Park, CA: Sage.

Lester, R. E. (1981, February). *Embedding network analysis constructs in a theoretical framework: A preliminary formulation of a model of intraorganizational communication behavior.* Paper presented at the annual meeting of the Western Speech Communication Association, San Jose, CA.

Leventhal, H., Safer, M. A., & Panagis, D. M. (1983). The impact of communications on the self-regulation of health beliefs, decisions, and behavior. *Health Education Quarterly, 10*, 3-29.

Levinger, G. (1979). A social exchange view on the dissolution of pair relationships. In R. L. Burgess & T. L. Huston (Eds.), *Social exchange in developing relationships* (pp. 169-193). New York: Academic Press.

Levinger, G., & Snoek, J. D. (1972). *Attraction in relationship: A new look at interpersonal attraction.* Morristown, NJ: General Learning Press.

Levy, L. H. (1976). Self help groups: Types and psychological processes. *Journal of Applied Behavioral Sciences, 12*, 310-322.

Levy, L. H. (1979). Processes and activities in groups. In M. A. Lieberman & L. D. Borman (Eds.), *Self help groups for coping with crisis* (pp. 234-271). San Francisco: Jossey-Bass.

Lewis, C. (1966). Factors influencing the return to work of men with congestive heart failure. *Journal of Chronic Diseases, 19*, 1193-1209.

Lewis, R. (1973). Social reaction and the formation of dyads: An interactionist approach to mate selection. *Sociometry, 36*, 409-418.

Lewis, R. A., & Salt, R. E. (Eds.). (1986). *Men in families.* Newbury Park, CA: Sage.

Lieberman, M. A. (1979). Analyzing change mechanisms in groups. In M. A. Lieberman & L. D. Borman (Eds.), *Self help groups for coping with crisis* (pp. 116-149). San Francisco: Jossey-Bass.

Lieberman, M. A., & Borman, L. D. (Eds.). (1979). *Self help groups for coping with crisis.* San Francisco: Jossey-Bass.

Lieberman, M. A., Yalom, I., & Miles, M. (1973). *Encounter groups: First facts.* New York: Basic Books.

Light, D. (1979). Surface data and deep structure: Observing the organization of professional training. *Administrative Science Quarterly, 24,* 551-559.

Likert, R. (1961). *New patterns of management.* New York: McGraw-Hill.

Likert, R. (1967). *The human organization: Its management and value.* New York: McGraw-Hill.

Lin, N. (1986a). Modeling the effect of social support. In N. Lin, A. Dean, & W. Ensel (Eds.), *Social support, life events, and depression* (pp. 173-209). Orlando, FL: Academic Press.

Lin, N. (1986b). Conceptualizing social support. In N. Lin, A. Dean, & W. Ensel (Eds.), *Social support, life events, and depression* (pp. 17-30). Orlando, FL: Academic Press.

Lin, N., Dean, A., & Ensel, W. (1981). Social support scales: A methodological note. *Schizophrenia Bulletin, 7,* 73-89.

Lin, N., Dean, A., & Ensel, W. (Eds.). (1986). *Social support, life events, and depression.* Orlando, FL: Academic Press.

Lin, N., Dumin, M. Y., & Woelfel, M. (1986). Measuring community and network support. In N. Lin, A. Dean, & W. Ensel (Eds.), *Social support, life events, and depression* (pp. 153-170). Orlando, FL: Academic Press.

Lin, N., Woefel, M., & Light, S. C. (1986). Buffering the impact of the most important life event. In N. Lin, A. Dean, & W. Ensel (Eds.), *Social support, life events, and depression* (pp. 307-332). Orlando, FL: Academic Press.

Lipnak, J. (1980, March). The women's health movement. *New Age,* pp. 33-35.

Lipton, F. R., Cohen, C. I., Fischer, E., & Katz, S. E. (1981). Schizophrenia: A network crisis. *Schizophrenia Bulletin, 7,* 144-151.

Litman, T. J. (1966). The family and physical rehabilitation. *Journal of Chronic Diseases, 19,* 211-217.

Litwak, E., & Szelenyi, I. (1969). Primary group structures and their functions: Kin, neighbors and friends. *American Sociological Review, 34,* 465-481.

Long, M. C. (1978, May/June). Television: Help or hindrance to health education? *Health Education,* pp. 32-34.

Louis, M. R. (1980). Surprise and sense making: What newcomers experience in entering unfamiliar organizational settings. *Administrative Science Quarterly, 25,* 226-251.

Lowenthal, M. F., & Haven, C. (1968). Interaction and adaptation: Intimacy as a critical variable. *American Sociological Review, 33,* 20-30.

Lowenthal, M. F., & Robinson, B. (1976). Social networks and isolation. In R. H. Binstock & E. Shanas (Eds.), *Aging and the social sciences* (pp. 432-456). New York: Van Nostrand Reinhold.

Lum, J. (1982). Marginality and multiculturalism. In L. Samovar & R. Porter (Eds.), *Intercultural communication: A reader.* Belmont, CA: Wadsworth.

Malson, M. (1983). The social support systems of black families. *Marriage and Family Review, 5,* 35-57.

Marsden, P. V., & Campbell, K. E. (1983, September). *Measuring tie strength.* Paper presented at the annual meeting of the American Sociological Association, Detroit, MI.

Martin, J. E., & Prue, D. M. (1984). Health marketing in a hospital setting: The behavioral medicine clinic. In L. W. Fredericksen, L. J. Solomon, & K. A. Brehony (Eds.), *Marketing health behavior* (pp. 165-194). New York: Plenum.

McAdoo, H. P. (1982). Levels of stress and family support in black families. In H. I. McCubbin, A. E. Cauble, & J. M. Patterson (Eds.), *Family stress, coping, and social support* (pp. 239-252). Springfield, IL: Charles C. Thomas.

McAuley, J. W., Jacobs, M. D., & Carr, C. S. (1984). Older couples: Patterns of assistance and support. *Journal of Gerontological Social Work, 6,* 35-48.

McCubbin, H. I., Cauble, A. E., & Patterson, J. M. (1982). *Family stress, coping, and social support.* Springfield, IL: Charles C Thomas.

McCubbin, H. I., Joy, C. B., Cauble, A. E., Comeau, J. K., Patterson, J. M., & Needle, R. H. (1980). Family stress and coping: A decade review. *Journal of Marriage and the Family, 42,* 855-871.

McCubbin, H. I., & Patterson, J. M. (1982). Family adaptation to crises. In H. I. McCubbin, A. E. Cauble, & J. M. Patterson (Eds.), *Family stress, coping, and social support* (pp. 26-47). Springfield, IL: Charles C Thomas.

McCubbin, H. I., & Patterson, J. M. (1983a). Family stress and adaptation to crises: A double ABCX model of family behavior. In D. H. Olson & B. C. Miller (Eds.), *Family studies review yearbook* (Vol. 1, pp. 87-106). Newbury Park, CA: Sage.

McCubbin, H. I., & Patterson, J. M. (1983b). The family stress process: The double ABCX model of adjustment and adaptation. In H. I. McCubbin, M. B. Sussman, & J. M. Patterson (Eds.), *Social stress and the family: Advances and developments in family stress theory and research* (pp. 7-37). New York: Haworth.

McCubbin, H. I., Sussman, M. B., & Patterson, J. M. (Eds.). (1983). Social stress and the family: Advances and developments in family stress theory and research (special issue). *Marriage and Family Review, 6*(1/2).

McFarlane, A. H., Norman, G. R., Streiner, D. L., & Roy, R. G. (1983). The process of social stress: Stable, reciprocal and mediating relationships. *Journal of Health and Social Behavior, 24,* 160-173.

McIntosh, J. (1974). Processes of communication, information seeking and control associated with cancer: A selective review of the literature. *Social Science and Medicine, 8,* 167-187.

McKinlay, J. B. (1973). Social networks, lay consultation and help-seeking behavior. *Social Forces, 51,* 275-292.

McKnight, J. (1977). Professionalized service and disabling help. In I. Illich, I. Zola, J. McKnight, J. Caplan, & H. Shaiken (Eds.), *Disabling professions* (pp. 69-92). Boston: Marion Boyars.

McLanahan, S. S., Wedemeyer, N. V., & Adelberg, T. (1981). Network structure, social support, and psychological well-being in the single-parent family. *Journal of Marriage and the Family, 43*, 601-612.

McLean, A. A. (1985). *Work stress.* Reading, MA: Addison-Wesley.

McLeroy, K. R., DeVellis, R., DeVellis, B., Kaplan, B., & Toole, J. (1984). Social support and physical recovery in a stroke population. *Journal of Social and Personal Relationships, 1*, 395-413.

Mechanic, D. (1962). *Students under stress.* New York: Free Press.

Mechanic, D. (1974). Social structure and personal adaptation: Some neglected dimensions. In G. Coelho, D. Hamburg, & J. Adams (Eds.), *Coping and adaptation* (pp. 32-44). New York: Basic Books.

Medea, A., & Thompson, K. (1974). *Against rape.* New York: Farrar, Straus, & Giroux.

Mederer, H., & Hill, R. (1983). Critical transitions over the family life span: Theory and research. *Marriage and Family Review, 6*, 39-60.

Media's muscleman. (1977, September). *Media Decisions, 64-65*, 132-134.

Mehan, H. (1978). Structuring school structure. *Harvard Educational Review, 48*, 32-64.

Menaghan, E. G. (1982). Assessing the impact of family transitions on marital experience. In H. I. McCubbin, A. E. Cauble, & J. M. Patterson (Eds.), *Family stress, coping, and social support* (pp. 90-108). Springfield, IL: Charles C. Thomas.

Menaghan, E. G. (1983). Individual coping efforts and family studies: Conceptual and methodological issues. *Marriage and Family Review, 6*, 113-136.

Meriolis, P. (1979). *Centrality analysis: A methodology for social networks.* Paper presented at the annual meeting of the American Sociological Association, Boston.

Mettee, D. R., & Smith, G. (1977). Social comparison and interpersonal attraction: The case for dissimilarity. In J. M. Suls & R. L. Miller (Eds.), *Social comparison processes: Theoretical and empirical perspectives* (pp. 69-101). New York: John Wiley.

Milardo, R. M. (1982). Friendship networks in developing relationships: Converging and diverging social environments. *Social Psychology Quarterly, 45*, 162-172.

Milardo, R. M. (1984). Social networks and pair relationships: Review of substantive and measurement issues. *Sociology and Social Research, 68*, 1-18.

Miles, M. B. (1979). Qualitative data as an attractive nuisance: The problem of analysis. *Administrative Science Quarterly, 24*, 590-601.

Miles, M. B., & Huberman, A. M. (1984). *Qualitative data analysis: A sourcebook of new methods.* Newbury Park, CA: Sage.

Milgram, S. (1977). *The individual in a social world.* Reading, MA: Addison-Wesley.

Miller, B. C. (1986). *Family research methods.* Newbury Park, CA: Sage.

Miller, B. C., & Olson, D. H. (Eds.). (1985). *Family studies review yearbook* (Vol. 3). Newbury Park, CA: Sage.

Miller, G. R., & Steinberg, M. (1975). *Between people: A new analysis of interpersonal communication.* Chicago: Science Research Associates.

Miller, I. W., & Norman, W. H. (1979). Learned helplessness in humans: A review and attribution-theory model. *Psychological Bulletin, 86*, 93-118.

Miller, K. I., & Monge, P. R. (1985). Social information and employee anxiety about organizational change. *Human Communication Research, 11*, 365-386.

Miller, L. C., Berg, J. H., & Archer, R. L. (1983). Openers: Individuals who elicit intimate self-disclosure. *Journal of Personality and Social Psychology, 44*, 1234-1244.

Miller, M. H. (1973). Seeking advice for cancer symptoms. *American Journal of Public Health, 63*, 955-961.

Minor, M. J. (1983). New directions in multiplexity analysis. In R. S. Burt & M. Minor (Eds.), *Applied network analysis: A methodological introduction* (pp. 223-244). Newbury Park, CA: Sage.

Mishel, M. H. (1984a, August). *Mediators of adjustment in patients with gynecological cancer: Diagnosis to treatment phase.* Paper presented at the meeting of the American Psychological Association, Toronto, Canada.

Mishel, M. H. (1984b). Perceived uncertainty and stress in illness. *Research in Nursing and Health, 7*, 163-171.

Mishel, M. H. (1985). *Uncertainty as a mediator in the relationship between social support and adjustment.* Paper presented at the 18th Annual Communicating Nursing Research Conference, Seattle, WA.

Mishel, M. H., Hostetter, T., King, B., & Graham, V. (1984, August). Predictors of psychosocial adjustment in patients newly diagnosed with gynecological cancer. *Cancer Nursing,* pp. 291-299.

Mitchell, J. C. (1969). The concept and use of social networks. In J. C. Mitchell (Ed.), *Social networks in urban situations* (pp. 1-50). Manchester, England: Manchester University Press.

Mitchell, R. E. (1982). Social networks and psychiatric clients: The personal and environmental context. *American Journal of Community Psychology, 10*, 387-401.

Mitchell, R. E., & Hodson, C. A. (1983). Coping with domestic violence: Social support and psychological health among battered women. *American Journal of Community Psychology, 11*, 629-654.

Mitchell, R. E., & Trickett, E. J. (1980). Task force report: Social networks as mediators of social support. An analysis of the effects and determinants of social networks. *Community Mental Health Journal, 16*, 27-44.

Moos, R. H. (Ed.). (1976). *Human adaptation: Coping with life crises.* Lexington, MA: D. C. Heath.

Moos, R. H. (1979). A social-ecological perspective on health. In G. C. Stone et al. (Eds.), *Health psychology* (pp. 59-79). San Francisco: Jossey-Bass.

Morris, S. C., III, & Rosen, S. (1973). Effects of felt adequacy and opportunity to reciprocate on helpseeking. *Journal of Experimental Social Psychology, 9*, 265-276.

Moss, G. E. (1973). *Illness, immunity and social interaction.* New York: John Wiley.

Mueller, D. P. (1980). Social networks: A promising direction for research on the relationship of social environment to psychiatric disorder. *Social Science and Medicine, 14a*, 147-161.

Nadler, A., Shapira, R., & Ben-Itzhak, S. (1982). Good looks may help: Effects of helper's physical attractiveness and sex of helper on males' and females' help-seeking behavior. *Journal of Personality and Social Psychology, 42,* 90-99.

Naegele, K. D. (1958). An exploration of some social distinctions. *Harvard Educational Review, 28,* 232-252.

Nagata, G. (1969). *A statistical approach to the study of acculturation of an ethnic group based on communication oriented variables: The case of Japanese Americans in Chicago.* Unpublished doctoral dissertation, University of Illinois, Urbana.

Naparstek, A. J., Biegel, D. E., & Spiro, H. R. (1982). *Neighborhood networks for humane mental health care.* New York: Plenum.

National Cancer Institute. (1984, February). *Cancer prevention awareness survey, technical report.* Washington, DC: Department of Health and Human Services. (NIH Publication No. 84-2677).

Nelson, J. I. (1966). Clique contacts and family orientations. *American Sociological Review, 31,* 663-672.

Niehouse, O., & Massoni, K. (1979). Stress: An inevitable part of change. *S.A.M. Advanced Management Journal,* pp. 17-25.

Norbeck, J. S., Lindsey, A. M., & Carrieri, V. L. (1983). Further development of the Norbeck social support questionnaire: Normative data and validity testing. *Nursing Research, 32,* 4-9.

Norton, R. (1978). Foundations of a communicator style construct. *Human Communication Research, 4,* 99-112.

Nouwen, H.J.M. (1975). *Reaching out.* Garden City, NY: Doubleday.

Novelli, W. D. (1984). Developing marketing programs. In L. W. Frederiksen, L. J. Solomon, & K. A. Brehony (Eds.), *Marketing health behavior* (pp. 59-92). New York: Plenum.

O'Connor, P., & Brown, G. W. (1984). Supportive relationships: Fact or fancy? *Journal of Social and Personal Relationships, 1,* 159-175.

Okie, S. (1986, February 5). Art imitates life and death. *Washington Post,* HW, p. 12.

Olson, D. H., & Markoff, R. (Eds.). (1985). *Inventory of marriage and family literature* (Vol. 11). Newbury Park, CA: Sage.

Olson, D. H., McCubbin, H. I., Barnes, H., Larsen, A., Muxen, M., & Wilson, M. (1982). *Family inventories.* St. Paul, MN: Family Social Science.

Olson, D. H., & Miller, B. C. (Eds.). (1983). *Family studies review yearbook* (Vol. 1). Newbury Park, CA: Sage.

Olson, D. H., & Miller, B. C. (Eds.). (1984). *Family studies review yearbook* (Vol. 2). Newbury Park, CA: Sage.

Olson, D. H., Russell, C. S., & Sprenkle, D. H. (1984). Circumplex model of marital and family systems: VI. Theoretical update. In D. H. Olson & B. C. Miller (Eds.), *Family studies review yearbook* (Vol. 2, pp. 59-74). Newbury Park, CA: Sage.

Osgood, C., Tannenbaum, P., & Suci, G. (1957). *The measurement of meaning.* Urbana: University of Illinois Press.

Oshagan, E. P. (1981). *Coorientation as a function of communication: An intercultural test.* Unpublished doctoral dissertation, University of Wisconsin—Madison.

Padilla, A. M. (Ed.). (1980). *Acculturation: Theory, models and some new findings*. Washington, DC: Westview.

Parks, M. R. (1976). *Communication and relational change processes: Conceptualization and findings*. Unpublished Ph.D. dissertation, Department of Communication, Michigan State University.

Parks, M. R. (1977a). Anomia and close friendship communication networks. *Human Communication Research, 4*, 48-57.

Parks, M. R. (1977b). Relational communication: Theory and research. *Human Communication Research, 3*, 372-381.

Parks, M. R. (1982). Ideology in interpersonal communication: Off the couch and into the world. In M. Burgoon (Ed.), *Communication yearbook 5* (pp. 79-107). New Brunswick, NJ: Transaction Books.

Parks, M. R. (1985). Interpersonal communication and the quest for personal competence. In M. L. Knapp & G. R. Miller (Eds.), *Handbook of interpersonal communication* (pp. 171-204). Newbury Park, CA: Sage.

Parks, M. R., & Adelman, M. B. (1983). Communication networks and the development of romantic relationships: An expansion of uncertainty reduction theory. *Human Communication Research, 10*, 55-79.

Parks, M. R., Stan, C. M., & Eggert, L. L. (1983). Romantic involvement and social network involvement. *Social Psychology Quarterly, 46*, 116-131.

Parlee, M. B. (1979). The friendship bond. *Psychology Today, 13*, 43-54.

Parsons, T. (1951). *The social system*. New York: Free Press.

Pattison, E. M., Llamas, R., & Hurd, G. (1979). Social network mediation of anxiety. *Psychiatric Annals, 9*, 56-67.

Pattison, E. M., & Pattison, M. L. (1981). Analysis of a schizophrenic psychosocial network. *Schizophrenia Bulletin, 7*, 135-143.

Pearce, P. L. (1980). Strangers, travelers, and Greyhound terminals: A study of small-scale helping behaviors. *Journal of Personality and Social Psychology, 38*, 935-940.

Pearce, W. B., & Stamm, K. (1973). Coorientational states and interpersonal communication. In P. Clark (Ed.), *New models for communication research* (pp. 177-203). Newbury Park, CA: Sage.

Pearlin, L. I. (1984). Social structure and social support. In S. Cohen & L. Syme (Eds.), *Social support and health*. New York: Academic Press.

Pearlin, L. I., Lieberman, M. S., Menaghan, E. G., & Mullan, J. T. (1981). The stress process. *Journal of Health and Social Behavior, 22*, 337-356.

Pearlin, L. I., & Schooler, C. (1978). The structure of coping. *Journal of Health and Social Behavior, 19*, 2-21.

Pearson, J. E. (1986). The definition and measurement of social support. *Journal of Counseling and Development, 64*, 390-395.

Peck, A. (1972). Emotional reaction to having cancer. *American Journal Roenthology Radium Therapy and Nuclear Medicine, 114*, 591-599.

Penn, J. R. (1980). Intergenerational differences: Scientific fact or scholarly opinion? In D. Rogers (Ed.), *Issues in life-span human development* (pp. 18-23). Monterey, CA: Brooks/Cole.

Peplau, L. A., & Perlman, D. (1979). Blueprint for a social psychological theory of loneliness. In M. Cook & G. Wilson (Eds.), *Love and attraction: An international conference* (pp. 101-110). New York: Pergamon.

Peplau, L. A., & Perlman, D. (1982). Perspectives on loneliness. In L. A. Peplau & D. Perlman (Eds.), *Loneliness: A sourcebook of current theory, research and therapy* (pp. 1-20). New York: Wiley-Interscience.

Perlman, D., & Peplau, L. A. (1981). Toward a social psychology of loneliness. In S. W. Duck & R. Gilmour (Eds.), *Personal relationships 3: Personal relationships in disorder* (pp. 31-56). London: Academic Press.

Peters, T. J., & Waterman, R. H. (1982). *In search of excelence.* New York: Harper & Row.

Peters-Golden, H. (1982). Breast cancer: Varied perceptions of social support in the illness experience. *Social Science and Medicine, 16,* 483-491.

Peterson, W. A., & Quadagno, J. (1985). *Social bonds in later life: Aging and interdependence.* Newbury Park, CA: Sage.

Philblad, C. T., & Adams, D. L. (1972). Widowhood, social participation, and life satisfaction. *Aging and Human Development, 3,* 323-330.

Phillips, S. L. (1981). Network characteristics related to the well-being of normals: A comparative base. *Schizophrenia Bulletin, 7,* 117-124.

Pilisuk, M. (1982). Delivery of social support: The social inoculation. *American Journal of Orthopsychiatry, 52,* 20-31.

Pilisuk, M., & Parks, S. H. (1983). Social support and family stress. *Marriage and Family Review, 6,* 137-156.

Pines, A., & Kafry, D. (1978). Occupational tedium in social services. *Social Work, 23,* 499-507.

Planalp, S., & Honeycutt, J. M. (1985). Events that increase uncertainty in personal relationships. *Human Communication Research, 11,* 593-604.

Pleck, J. H. (1985). *Working wives, working husbands.* Newbury Park, CA: Sage.

Pohl, S. N., & Freimuth, V. S. (1983). Foods for health: Involving organizations in planned change. *Journal of Applied Communication Research, 11,* 17-27.

Politser, P. E. (1980). Network analysis and the logic of social support. In R. H. Price & P. E. Politser (Eds.), *Evaluation and action in the social environment.* New York: Academic Press.

Pollack, L., & Harris, R. (1983). Measurement of social support. *Psychological Reports, 53,* 466.

Pool, I. deS., & Kochen, M. (1978). Contacts and influence. *Social Networks, 1,* 5-51.

Poole, M. S., & McPhee, R. D. (1985). Methodology in interpersonal communication research. In M. L. Knapp & G. R. Miller (Eds.), *Handbook of interpersonal communication* (pp. 100-170). Newbury Park, CA: Sage.

Poresky, R. H., & Atilano, R. B. (1982). Alienation in rural women: A longitudinal cross-lagged analysis of its association with community and family involvement, socioeconomic status, and education. *Home Economics Research Journal, 11,* 183-188.

Porritt, D. (1979). Social support in crisis: Quantity or quality. *Social Science and Medicine, 13A,* 715-721.

Porter, L. W., Lawler, E. E., & Hackman, J. R. (1975). *Behavior in organizations.* New York: McGraw-Hill.

Pratt, L. (1982). Family structure and health work: Coping in the context of social change. In H. I. McCubbin, A. E. Cauble, & J. M. Patterson (Eds.), *Family stress, coping, and social support* (pp. 73-89). Springfield, IL: Charles C Thomas.

President's Commission on Mental Health. (1978). *Task panel reports* (Vols. II-IV). Washington, DC: Government Printing Office.

Procidano, M. E., & Heller, K. (1983). Measures of perceived social support from friends and from family: Three validation studies. *American Journal of Community Psychology, 11*, 1-24.

Quam, J. K. (1983). Older women and informal supports: Impact of prevention. *Prevention in Human Services, 3*, 119-133.

Quisumbing, M. (1982). *Life events, social support and personality: Their impact upon Filipino psychological adjustment.* Unpublished doctoral dissertation, University of Chicago, Chicago, IL.

Rands, M. (1981). Social networks before and after marital separation: A study of recently divorced persons. (Doctoral dissertation, University of Massachusetts, 1981). *Dissertation Abstracts International, 41*, 2828-2829B.

Rapaport, A., & Horvath, W. (1961). A study of a large sociogram. *Behavioral Science, 6*, 279-291.

Rapoport, R., & Rapoport, R. N. (1971). *Dual-career families.* Harmondsworth, U.K.: Penguin.

Raps, C. S., Reinhard, K. E., & Seligman, M. (1980). Reversal of cognitive and affective deficits associated with depression and learned helplessness by mood elevation in patients. *Journal of Abnormal Psychology, 89*, 342-349.

Ray, E. B. (1983). Job burnout from a communication perspective. In R. Bostrom (Ed.), *Communication yearbook 7* (pp. 738-755). Newbury Park, CA: Sage.

Ray, E. B. (1986, November). *Communication network roles as mediators of job stress and burnout: Case studies of two organizations.* Paper presented at the meeting of the Speech Communication Association, Chicago.

Ray, E. B., Waldhart, E. S., & Seibert, J. H. (1985). *Communication networks and job stress among teachers.* Paper presented at the meeting of the Southern Speech Communication Association, Winston-Salem.

Redding, W. C. (1972). *Communication within the organization: An interpretive review of theory and research.* New York: Industrial Communication Council.

Reis, H. T. (1982, July). *Determinants, consequences and characteristics of social relationships.* Paper presented at the International Conference on Personal Relationships, Madison, WI.

Reisman, J. M. (1979). *Anatomy of friendship.* New York: Irvington.

Reisman, J. M. (1981). Adult friendships. In S. W. Duck & R. Gilmour (Eds.), *Personal relationships 2: Developing personal relationships* (pp. 205-230). London: Academic Press.

Reisman, J. M., & Shorr, S. E. (1978). Friendship claims and expectations among children and adults. *Child Development, 49*, 913-916.

Reiss, D., & Oliveri, M. E. (1983a). Family paradigm and family coping: A proposal for linking the family's intrinsic adaptive capacities to its responses to stress. In D. H. Olson & B. C. Miller (Eds.), *Family studies review year-book* (Vol. 1, pp. 113-127). Newbury Park, CA: Sage.

Reiss, D., & Oliveri, M. E. (1983b). Family stress as community frame. *Marriage and Family Review, 6,* 85-112.

Richards, W. D., Jr. (1975). *A manual for network analysis.* Palo Alto, CA: Stanford University, Institute for Communication Research. (Mimeo report)

Richards, W. D., Jr. (1985). Data models and assumptions in network analysis. In R. D. McPhee & P. K. Tompkins (Eds.), *Organizational communication: Traditional themes and new directions* (pp. 109-128). Newbury Park, CA: Sage.

Ridley, C. A., & Avery, A. W. (1979). Social network influence on the dyadic relationship. In R. L. Burgess & T. L. Huston (Eds.), *Social exchange in developing relationships* (pp. 223-246). New York: Academic Press.

Riley, M. W., & Foner, A. (1968). *Aging and society: An inventory of research findings* (Vol. 1). New York: Russell Sage.

Robinson, J., & Shaver, P. (1972). *Measures of social psychological attitudes.* Ann Arbor, MI: Institute for Social Research.

Rodin, J., Rennert, K., & Solomon, S. K. (1980). Intrinsic motivation for control: Fact or fiction. In A. Baum & J. E. Singer (Eds.), *Advances in environmental psychology* (Vol. 2, pp. 131-148). Hillsdale, NJ: Lawrence Erlbaum.

Rogers, D. (1980). *Issues in life-span human development.* Monterey, CA: Brooks/Cole.

Rogers, E. M. (1983). *Diffusion of innovations* (3rd ed.). New York: Free Press.

Rogers, E. M., & Adhikarya, R. (1979). Diffusion of innovations: An up-to-date review and commentary. In D. Nimmo (Ed.), *Communication yearbook 3* (pp. 67-82). New Brunswick, NJ: Transaction Books.

Rogers, E. M., & Kincaid, D. L. (1981). *Communication networks: Toward a new paradigm for research.* New York: Free Press.

Rook, K. S. (1984). The negative side of social interaction: Impact on psychological well-being. *Journal of Personality and Social Psychology, 46,* 1097-1108.

Rook, K. S. (1985). The functions of social bonds: Perspectives from research on social support, loneliness and social isolation. In I. G. Sarason & B. R. Sarason (Eds.), *Social support: Theory, research and applications* (pp. 243-267). Dordrecht: Martinus Nijhoff.

Rook, K. S., & Dooley, D. (1985). Applying social support research: Theoretical problems and future directions. *Journal of Social Issues, 41,* 5-28.

Rosenbaum, A., & Calhoun, J. F. (1977). The use of the telephone hotline in crisis intervention: A review. *Journal of Community Psychology, 5,* 325-339.

Rosow, I. (1970). Old people: Their friends and neighbors. *American Behavioral Scientist, 14,* 56-69.

Rozenblatt, P. C., Johnson, P. A., & Anderson, R. M. (1985). When out-of-town relatives visit. In B. C. Miller & D. H. Olsen (Eds.), *Family studies review yearbook* (Vol. 3, pp. 487-493). Newbury Park, CA: Sage.

Rubin, A. M., Perse, E. M., & Powell, R. A. (1985). Loneliness, parasocial interaction, and local television news viewing. *Human Communication Research, 12,* 155-180.

Rubin, Z. (1975). Disclosing oneself to a stranger: Reciprocity and its limits. *Journal of Experimental Social Psychology, 11,* 233-260.

Ruesch, J. (1968). Communication and mental illness: A psychiatric approach. In J. Ruesch & G. Bateson (Eds.), *Communication: The social matrix of psychiatry* (pp. 50-93). New York: W. W. Norton. (Original work published 1951)

Ruesch, J. (1968). Values, communication, and culture: An introduction. In J. Ruesch & G. Bateson (Eds.), *Communication: The social matrix of psychiatry* (pp. 3-20). New York: W. W. Norton.

Rueveni, U. (1979). *Networking families in crisis.* New York: Human Services Press.

Russell, D. W. (1982). The measurement of loneliness. In L. A. Peplau & D. Perlman (Eds.), *Loneliness: A sourcebook of current theory, research and therapy* (pp. 81-104). New York: Wiley-Interscience.

Ruzek, B. (1978). *The women's health movement: Feminist alternatives to medical control.* New York: Praeger.

Ryan, B., & Gross, N. C. (1943). The diffusion of hybrid seed corn in two Iowa communities. *Rural Sociology, 8,* 15-25.

Salinger, L. L. (1982). The ties that bind: The effect of clustering on dyadic relationships. *Social Networks, 4,* 117-145.

Salzinger, S., Kaplan, S., & Artemyeff, C. (1983). Mothers' personal social networks and child maltreatment. *Journal of Abnormal Psychology, 92,* 68-76.

Samter, W., & Burleson, B. R. (1984). Cognitive and motivational influences on spontaneous comforting behavior. *Human Communication Research, 11,* 231-260.

Sandler, I. N., & Lakey, B. (1982). Locus of control as a stress moderator: The role of control perceptions and social support. *American Journal of Community Psychology, 10,* 65-80.

Sarason, I. G., Levine, H. M., Basham, R. B., & Sarason, B. R. (1983). Assessing social support: The social support questionnaire. *Journal of Personality and Social Psychology, 44,* 127-139.

Scanzoni, J. (1979). Social exchange and behavioral interdependence. In R. L. Burgess & R. L. Huston (Eds.), *Social exchange in developing relationships* (pp. 61-98). New York: Academic Press.

Schaefer, C. (1982). Shoring up the "buffer" of social support. *Journal of Health and Social Behavior, 23,* 96-98.

Schaefer, C., Coyne, J. D., & Lazarus, R. S. (1981). The health-related functions of social support. *Journal of Behavioral Medicine, 4,* 381-406.

Scheidel, T. M., & Crowell, L. L. (1979). *Discussing and deciding.* New York: Macmillan.

Schein, E. H. (1968). Organizational socialization and the profession of management. *Industrial Management Review, 9,* 1-16.

Schlenker, B. R. (1984). Identities, identifications, and relationships. In V. J. Derlega (Ed.), *Communication, intimacy and close relationships* (pp. 71-104). New York: Academic Press.

Schoenfeld, P. (1984). Network therapy: Clinical theory and practice with disturbed adolescents. *Psychotherapy: Theory, research and practice, 21,* 92-100.

Schoenfeld, P., Halevy-Martini, J., Hemley-Van Der Velden, E., & Ruhf, L. (1985). Network therapy: An outcome study of twelve social networks. *Journal of Community Psychology, 13*, 281-287.

Schuetz, A. (1944/1963). The stranger. *American Journal of Sociology, 49*, 499-507. Reprinted in M. Stein & A. Vidich (Eds.), *Identity and anxiety.* Glencoe, IL: Free Press.

Schulz, R. (1980). Aging and control. In J. Garber & J.E.P. Seligman (Eds.), *Human helplessness* (pp. 261-278). New York: Academic Press.

Schwartz, M., & Baden, M. A. (1973). Female adolescent self concept: An examination of the relative influence of peers and adults. *Youth and Society, 5*, 115-128.

Scott, R. (1964). *The making of blind men.* Newbury Park, CA: Sage.

Scott, W. G., & Hart, D. K. (1979). *Organizational America.* Boston: Houghton Mifflin.

Seeman, M., & Seeman, T. E. (1983). Health behavior and personal autonomy: A longitudinal study of the sense of control in illness. *Journal of Health and Social Behavior, 24*, 144-160.

Seers, A., McGee, G. W., Serey, T. T., & Graen, G. B. (1983). The interaction of job stress and social support: A strong inference investigation. *Academy of Management Journal, 26*, 273-284.

Seligman, M. (1975). *Helplessness: On depression, development, and death.* San Francisco: W. H. Freeman.

Sennett, R. (1977). *The fall of public man.* New York: Vintage.

Shapiro, E. G. (1980). Is seeking help from a friend like seeking help from a stranger? *Social Psychology Quarterly, 43*, 259-263.

Shapiro, E. G. (1983). Embarrassment and help-seeking. In B. M. DePaulo, A. Nadler, & J. D. Fisher (Eds.), *New directions in helping: Vol. 2. Help-seeking* (pp. 143-163). New York: Academic Press.

Shaver, P., Furman, W., & Buhrmester, D. (1985). Transition to college: Network changes, social skills, and loneliness. In S. W. Duck & D. Perlman (Eds.), *Understanding personal relationships: An interdisciplinary approach* (pp. 193-219). Newbury Park, CA: Sage.

Shepard, L. A. (1983). Researching family stress. *Marriage and Family Review, 6*, 227-231.

Sherman, B. (1979). Emergence of ideology in a bereaved parents group. In M. A. Lieberman & L. D. Borman (Eds.), *Self help groups for coping with crisis* (pp. 305-322). San Francisco: Jossey-Bass.

Shibutani, T., & Kwan, M. (1965). *Ethnic stratification.* New York: Macmillan.

Shumaker, S. A., & Brownell, A. (1984). Toward a theory of social support: Closing conceptual gaps. *Journal of Social Issues, 40*, 11-36.

Shuval, J. T. (1982). Migration and stress. In L. Goldberg & S. Breznitz (Eds.), *Handbook of stress* (pp. 677-691). New York: Free Press.

Silver, R., & Wortman, C. (1980). Coping with undesirable life events. In J. Garber & M. Seligman (Eds.), *Human helplessness: Theory and applications* (pp. 279-340). New York: Academic Press.

Silverman, M. L. (1979, October). *Vietnamese in Denver: Cultural conflicts in health care.* Paper presented at the Conference on Indochinese Refugees, George Mason University, Fairfax, VA.

Simmel, G. (1950). *The sociology of Georg Simmel* (K. H. Wolff, Trans.). New York: Free Press.

Skinner, D. A. (1982). The stressor and coping patterns of dual-career families. In H. I. McCubbin, A. E. Cauble, & J. M. Patterson (Eds.), *Family stress, coping, and social support* (pp. 136-150). Springfield, IL: Charles C Thomas.

Skipper, J. K., Jr., & Leonard, R. C. (Eds.). (1965). *Social interaction and patient care.* Philadelphia, Lippincott.

Slater, J., & Depue, R. A. (1981). The contribution of environmental events and social support to serious suicide attempts in primary depressive disorder. *Journal of Abnormal Psychology, 90,* 275-285.

Slaughter, E. P., Napolitano, C. S., & Freimuth, V. S. (1985, July). *The influence of social interaction on the diffusion of health information.* Paper presented at the Health Communication Summer Conference, Chicago.

Smith, M. E. (1976). Networks and migration resettlement: Cherchez la femme. *Anthropology Quarterly, 49,* 20-27.

Snyder, P.A. (1976). Neighborhood gatekeepers in the process of urban adaptation: Cross-ethnic commonalities. *Urban Anthropology, 5,* 35-52.

Sokolovsky, J., & Cohen, C. I. (1981). Toward a resolution of methodological dilemmas in network mapping. *Schizophrenia Bulletin, 7,* 109-116.

Sokolovsky, J., Cohen, C., Berger, D., & Geiger, J. (1978). Personal networks of ex-mental patients in a Manhattan SRO hotel. *Human Organization, 37,* 5-15.

Sommer, R. (1974). *Tight spaces: Hard architecture and how to humanize it.* Englewood Cliffs, NJ: Prentice-Hall.

Sontag, S. (1977). *Illness as metaphor.* New York: Vintage.

Spears, M. K. (1963). *The poetry of W. H. Auden: The disenchanted island.* New York: Oxford University Press.

Speck, R., & Attneave, C. (1973). *Family networks.* New York: Pantheon.

Spitzberg, B. H., & Cupach, W. R. (1984). Interpersonal communication competence. Newbury Park, CA: Sage.

Stokes, J. P. (1983). Predicting satisfaction with social support from social network structure. *American Journal of Community Psychology, 11,* 141-152.

Stokes, J. P. (1985). The relation of social network and individual difference variables to loneliness. *Journal of Personality and Social Psychology, 48,* 981-990.

Stokes, J. P. (in press). The relation of loneliness and self-disclosure. In V. J. Derlega & J. Berg (Eds.), *Self-disclosure: Theory, research, and therapy.* New York: Plenum.

Stoller, E. P., & Earl, L. L. (1983). Help with activities of everyday life: Sources of support for the noninstitutionalized elderly. *Gerontologist, 23,* 64-70.

Street, R. L., & Cappella, J. N. (Eds.). (1985). *Sequence and pattern in communication behavior.* London: Edward Arnold.

Stroebe, M. S., & Stroebe, W. (1985). Social support and the alleviation of loss. In I. G. Sarason & B. R. Sarason (Eds.), *Social support: Theory, research and applications* (pp. 439-462). Dordrecht: Martinus Nijhoff.

Stueve, A. (1982). The elderly as network members. *Marriage and Family Review, 5,* 59-87.

Suedfeld, P. (1982). Aloneness as a healing experience. In L. A. Peplau & D. Perlman (Eds.), *Loneliness: A sourcebook of current theory, research and therapy* (pp. 54-67). New York: Wiley-Interscience.

Suelzle, M., & Keenan, V. (1981). Changes in family support networks over the life cycle of mentally retarded persons. *American Journal of Mental Deficiency, 86,* 267-274.

Sullivan, C. F., & Reardon, K. K. (1986). Social support satisfaction and health locus of control: Discriminators of breast cancer patients' styles of coping. In M. McLaughlin (Ed.), *Communication yearbook 9* (pp. 707-722). Newbury Park, CA: Sage.

Sussman, M. (1980). The family today: Is it an endangered species? In D. Rogers (Ed.), *Issues in life-span human development* (pp. 154-160). Monterey, CA: Brooks/Cole.

Sypher, B. D., & Ray, E. B. (1984). Communication as a mediator of job stress in a health organization. In R. Bostrom (Ed.), *Communication yearbook 8* (pp. 779-789). Newbury Park, CA: Sage.

Szilagyi, A. D., & Holland, W. E. (1980). Changes in social density: Relationships with functional interaction and perceptions of job characteristics, role stress and work satisfaction. *Journal of Applied Psychology, 65,* 28-33.

Tardy, C. H. (1985). Social support measurement. *American Journal of Community Psychology, 13,* 187-202.

Taylor, D., & Harrison, R. (1976). On being categorized in the speech of others: Medical and psychiatric diagnosis. In R. Harre (Ed.), *Life sentences: Aspects of the social role of language* (pp. 21-30). London: John Wiley.

Taylor, S. E. (1982). Social cognition and health. *Personality and Social Psychology Bulletin, 8,* 549-562.

Terborg, J. R. (1985). Working women and stress. In T. A. Beehr & R. S. Bhagat (Eds.), *Human stress and cognition in organizations: An integrated perspective* (pp. 245-286). New York: John Wiley.

Thoits, P. A. (1982). Conceptual, methodological, and theoretical problems in studying social support as a buffer against life stress. *Journal of Health and Social Behavior, 23,* 145-159.

Thoits, P. A. (1983). Main and interactive effects of social support: Response to LaRocco. *Journal of Health and Social Behavior, 24,* 92-95.

Thoits, P. A. (1984). Explaining distributions of psychological vulnerability: Lack of social support in the face of life stress. *Social Forces, 63,* 453-481.

Thoits, P. A. (1985). Social support and psychological well being: Theoretical possibilities. In I. G. Sarason & B. R. Sarason (Eds.), *Social support: Theory, research and applications* (pp. 51-72). Dordrecht: Martinus Nijhoff.

Thompson, S. C. (1981). Will it hurt less if I can control it? A complex answer to a simple question. *Psychological Bulletin, 90,* 89-101.

Thurman, B. (1979/1980). In the office: Networks and coalitions. *Social Networks, 2,* 47-63.

Thurnher, M., Spence, D., & Lowenthal, M. F. (1974). Value confluence and behavioral conflict in intergenerational relations. *Journal of Marriage and the Family, 36,* 308-319.

Tichy, N. M., Tushman, M., & Fombrun, C. (1979). Social network analysis for organizations. *Academy of Management Review, 4,* 507-519.

Ting-Toomey, S. (1983). An analysis of verbal communication patterns in high and low marital adjustment groups. *Human Communication Research, 9,* 306-319.

Tolsdorf, C. C. (1976). Social networks, support, and coping: Exploratory study. *Family Process, 15,* 407-417.

Turner, J. G. (1980). Patterns of intergenerational exchange: A developmental approach. In D. Rogers (Ed.), *Issues in life-span human development* (pp. 23-27). Monterey, CA: Brooks/Cole.

Turner, R. J. (1981). Social support as a contingency in psychological well-being. *Journal of Health and Social Behavior, 22,* 357-367.

Turner, R. J., & Noh, S. (1983). Class and psychological vulnerability among women: The significance of social support and personal control. *Journal of Health and Social Behavior, 24,* 2-15.

Turow, J., & Coe, L. (1985). Curing television's ills: The portrayal of health care. *Journal of Communication, 35,* 36-51.

Unger, D. G., & Wandersman, A. (1985). The importance of neighbors: The social, cognitive, and affective components of neighboring. *American Journal of Community Psychology, 13,* 139-169.

University of Toronto. (1980, May). *Symposium on helping networks and the welfare state.* Toronto, Canada: Author.

Valdez, A. (1979). *The social and occupational integration among Mexican and Puerto Rican ethnics in an urban industrial society.* Unpublished doctoral dissertation, University of California, Los Angeles.

Van Maanen, J. (1981, March). *Fieldwork on the beat: An informal introduction to organizational ethnography.* Paper presented at the Innovations in Methodology Conference, American Psychological Association, Greensboro, NC.

Verbrugge, L. M. (1977). The structure of adult friendship choices. *Social Forces, 56,* 576-597.

Veroff, J., Douvan, E., & Kulka, R. (1981). *The inner American: A self-portrait from 1957-1976.* New York: Basic Books.

Vredenburgh, D. J., & Trinkaus, R. J. (1981). *Job stress among hospital nurses.* Paper presented at the meeting of the Academy of Management, San Diego, CA.

Waitzkin, H. (1985). Information giving in medical care. *Journal of Health and Social Behavior, 26,* 81-101.

Waitzkin, H., & Stoeckle, J. D. (1976). Information control and the micropolitics of health care: Summary of an ongoing research project. *Social Science and Medicine, 10,* 263-276.

Waller, W., & Hill, R. (1951). *The family: A dynamic interpretation.* New York: Holt, Rinehart & Winston.

Wallston, K. A., Wallston, B. S., & Devellis, R. (1978). Development of the multidimensional health locus of control (MHLC) scales. *Health Education Monographs, 6,* 160-170.

Walster, E., Walster, G. W., & Berscheid, E. (1978). *Equity: Theory and research.* Boston: Allyn & Bacon.

Ward, R. A., Sherman, S. R., & LaGory, M. (1984). Subjective network assessments and subjective well-being. *Journal of Gerontology, 39,* 93-101.

Wark, V. (1982). A look at the work of the telephone counseling center. *Personnel and Guidance Journal, 61,* 110-112.

Warren, D. I. (1977). Neighborhoods in urban areas. In J. B. Turner (Ed.), *Encyclopedia of social work* (Vol. 2, pp. 993-1005). Washington, DC: National Association of Social Workers.

Warren, D. I. (1982). Using helping networks: A key social bond of urbanites. In D. Biegel & A. J. Naparstek (Eds.), *Community support systems and mental health* (pp. 5-20). New York: Springer.

Warren, R. (1963). *The community in America*. Chicago: Rand McNally.

Watson, D., & Clark, L. A. (1984). Negative affectivity: The disposition to experience aversive emotional states. *Psychological Bulletin, 3*, 465-490.

Watzlawick, P., Beavin, J. H., & Jackson, D. D. (1967). *Pragmatics of human communication*. New York: Norton.

Weber, G. H., & Cohen, L. M. (Eds.). (1982). *Beliefs and self-help: Cross-cultural perspectives and approaches*. New York: Human Sciences Press.

Weick, K. E. (1976). Educational organizations as loosely coupled systems. *Administrative Science Quarterly, 21*, 1-19.

Weick, K. E. (1979). *The social psychology of organizing*. Reading, MA: Addison-Wesley.

Weisman, A. D., & Worden, J. W. (1975). Psychosocial analysis of cancer death. *Omega, 6*, 61-75.

Weiss, R. S. (1974). The provisions of social relationships. In Z. Rubin (Ed.), *Doing unto others* (pp. 17-26). Englewood Cliffs, NJ: Prentice-Hall.

Wellman, B. (1979). The community question: The intimate networks of East Yonkers. *American Sociological Review, 84*, 1201-1231.

Wellman, B. (1981). Applying network analysis to the study of support. In B. H. Gottlieb (Ed.), *Social networks and social support* (pp. 171-200). Newbury Park, CA: Sage.

Wentowski, G. J. (1981). Reciprocity and the coping strategies of older people: Cultural dimensions of network building. *Gerontologist, 21*, 600-609.

West, J. D., Zarski, J. J., & Harvill, R. (1986). Influence of family triangle on intimacy. *American Mental Health Counselor Association Journal, 8*, 166-174.

White, S. W., & Mika, K. (1983). Family divorce and separation: Theory and research. *Marriage and Family Review, 6*, 175-192.

Whittaker, J. K., & Garbarino, S. (1983). *Social support networks: Informal helping in the human services*. New York: Aldine.

Wiesenfeld, A. R., & Weis, H. M. (1979). Hairdressers and helping: Influencing the behavior of informal caregivers. *Professional Psychology, 10*, 786-792.

Wilcox, B. L. (1981). Social support, life stress, and psychological adjustment: A test of the buffering hypothesis. *American Journal of Community Psychology, 9*, 371-386.

Williams, K. B., & Williams, K. D. (1983). Social inhibition and asking for help: The effects of number, strength, and immediacy of potential help givers. *Journal of Personality and Social Psychology, 44*, 67-77.

Williams, T., & Douds, J. (1973). The unique contribution of telephone therapy. In D. Lester & G. W. Brockopp (Eds.), *Crisis intervention and counseling by telephone* (pp. 80-88). Springfield, IL: Charles C Thomas.

Wills, T. A. (1983). Social comparison in coping and help-seeking. In B. M. DePaulo, A. Nadler, & J. D. Fisher (Eds.), *New directions in helping: Vol. 2. Help-seeking* (pp. 109-141). New York: Academic Press.

Wilson, C. E. (1986). *The influence of communication network involvement on socialization in organizations.* Unpublished doctoral dissertation, University of Washington, Seattle.

Wilson, E. O. (1975). *Sociobiology: The new synthesis.* Cambridge, MA: Belknap.

Wilson, H. T. (1960). *Strength for living.* New York: Abingdon Press.

Wittenberg, M. T., & Reis, H. T. (1986). Loneliness, social skills, and social perception. *Personality and Social Psychology Bulletin, 12,* 121-130.

Wittgenstein, L. (1958). *Philosophical investigations* (G.E.M. Anscombe, Trans.). Oxford, England: Blackwell.

Wollert, R. W., Levy, L. H., & Knight, B. (1982). Help-giving in behavioral control and stress coping self-help groups. *Small Group Behavior, 13,* 204-218.

Wood, V., & Robertson, J. F. (1978). Friendship and kinship interaction: Differential effect on the morale of the elderly. *Journal of Marriage and the Family, 40,* 367-375.

Working around motherhood. (1982, May). *Business Week,* p. 188.

Wortman, C. B. (1976). Causal attributions and personal control. In J. H. Harvey, W. J. Ickes, & R. F. Kidd (Eds.), *New directions in attribution research* (Vol. 1, pp. 23-52). Hillsdale, NJ: Lawrence Erlbaum.

Wortman, C. B. (1984). Social support and the cancer patient: Conceptual and methodological issues. *Cancer, 53,* 2339-2360.

Wortman, C. B., & Dunkel-Schetter, C. (1979). Interpersonal relationships and cancer. *Journal of Social Issues, 35,* 120-155.

Wortman, C. B., & Lehman, D. R. (1985). Reactions to victims of life crises: Support attempts that fail. In I. G. Sarason & B. R. Sarason (Eds.), *Social support: Theory, research and applications* (pp. 463-489). Dordrecht: Martinus Nijhoff.

Yahil, L. (1969). *The rescue of Danish Jewry.* Philadelphia: Jewish Publication Society of America.

Yalom, I. (1975). *The theory and practice of group psychotherapy.* New York: Basic Books.

Young, C. E., Giles, D. E., & Plantz, M. C. (1982). Natural networks: Help-giving and help-seeking in two rural communities. *American Journal of Community Psychology, 10,* 457-469.

Yum, J. O. (1982). Communication patterns and information acquisition among Korean immigrants in Hawaii. *Human Communication Research, 8,* 154-169.

Yum, J. O. (1983). Social network patterns of five ethnic groups in Hawaii. In R. Bostrom (Ed.), *Communication yearbook 7* (pp. 574-591). Newbury Park, CA: Sage.

Yum, J. O. (1984). Network analysis. In W. B. Gudykunst & Y. Y. Kim (Eds.), *Methods for intercultural communication* (pp. 95-116). Newbury Park, CA: Sage.

Zarit, S., Reever, K., & Bach-Peterson, J. (1980). Relatives of the impaired elderly: Correlates of feelings of burden. *Gerontologist, 20,* 649-655.

Zwingmann, C., & Pfister-Ammende, M. (1973). *Uprooting and after.* New York: Springer-Verlag.

About the Authors

Terrance L. Albrecht is currently an Associate Professor of Speech Communication at the University of Washington, Seattle. She holds Ph.D. and master's degrees in communication and a second master's degree in labor and industrial relations from Michigan State University. Her research interests include the role of communication processes and networks in occupational stress and organizational innovation. Her articles have appeared in *Human Communication Research, Journal of Communication, Communication Yearbooks 3, 4, 6, 8, 11, Western Journal of Speech Communication, Social Work,* and *Nursing Administration Quarterly.*

Mara B. Adelman (Ph.D., University of Washington, 1986) is currently Assistant Professor of Communication Studies at Northwestern University. Her research interests include social support networks in organizational and intercultural contexts with a special emphasis on coping with life-threatening illness and adjustment to new environments. As a volunteer for a cancer support hotline during the last four years she has engaged in extensive client support, training, and data analysis. Her work has appeared in *Human Communication Research, American Journal of Psychotherapy,* and *International Journal of Intercultural Relations.*

Associates

Paul Arntson is an Associate Professor of Communication Studies and a Faculty Associate at the Center of Urban Affairs and Policy Research at Northwestern University. He received his Ph.D. from the University of Wisconsin in communication arts and educational psychology. His current research focuses on how communication in health care activities can engender health competence for the participants. He is currently Chairperson of the Health Communication Division of the International Communication Association.

David Droge is an Associate Professor of Communication and Theater Arts at the University of Puget Sound. He received his Ph.D. from Northwestern University in communication studies. He is currently investigating the relationships among rhetoric, medicine, and myth in both ancient Greek and contemporary society as well as continuing his work with self-help groups.

Leona L. Eggert is an Assistant Professor of Psychosocial Nursing at the University of Washington. She received her M.A. in nursing and cultural anthropology in 1970 and her Ph.D. from the University of Washington in speech communication in 1984. Her research interests are in the dynamics of relationship development and maintenance within personal communication networks, therapeutic communication in nurse/client relationships, and intervention programs for adolescent drug users/abusers. She has published several articles on individual and group work with adolescents and their families, on the psychosocial development of adolescents, on therapeutic communication, and most recently on adolescents' personal relationships and family/peer network involvement in *Communication Yearbook 10* (Sage, 1987).

Vicki S. Freimuth (Ph.D., Florida State University, 1974) is Director of Health Communication and Associate Professor in the Department of Communication Arts & Theatre at the University of Maryland, College Park. She teaches courses in health communication, diffusion of innovations, and research methods. Her research focuses on the dissemination of health information in this country and in developing countries. Her publications have appeared in *Human Communication Research, Journal of Communication, Public Health Reports, Health Education,* and *Journal of International Health Education.* She consults regularly for the National Cancer Institute, the National Heart, Lung, and Blood Institute, the National Institute on Alcohol Abuse and Alcoholism, and the Agency for International Development. She is a Vice-Chairperson Elect of the Health Communication Division of the International Communication Association.

Young Yun Kim is Professor of Communication at Governors State University, University Park, Illinois. She received her M.A. degree from the University of Hawaii and Ph.D. from Northwestern University. Her teaching areas include communication theory, research methods, intercultural communication, nonverbal communication, and communication training. The main area of her research and writing has been the communication phenomena in the context of cross-cultural adaptation of immigrants. She is the coauthor of *Communicating with Strangers: An Approach to Intercultural Communication* (with William B. Gudykunst) and has edited *Methods for Intercultural Communication Research* (with William B. Gudykunst) and *Interethnic Communication* (in press).

Malcolm R. Parks (Ph.D., Human Communication, Michigan State University, 1976) is currently Associate Professor of Speech Communication at the University of Washington. His research has focused on the development and dissolution of friendships, premarital romantic relationships, and marital relationships, with a special concern for the dynamics of communication networks. He has also conducted research on related topics such as communicative competence, shyness, alienation, marital interaction, matchmaking, and privacy/disclosure dialectics. His work has appeared in *Human Communication Research, Communication Monographs, Communication Yearbook,* and *Social Psychology Quarterly,* as well as numerous edited volumes.

Eileen Berlin Ray (Ph.D., University of Washington, 1981) is an Assistant Professor in the Department of Communication at the University of Kentucky. Her research interests are in the areas of organizational and health communication, most recently focusing on the role of communication in the job stress of human service workers. She has published in outlets such as *Communication Yearbook 7* and *8* and the *Journal of Applied Communication Research.*

NOTES